A Global History of Indigenous Peoples

Also by Ken S. Coates

JAPAN AND THE INTERNET REVOLUTION *(with Carin Holroyd)*

A GLOBAL HISTORY OF INDIGENOUS PEOPLES

STRUGGLE AND SURVIVAL

KEN S. COATES

First published 2004 by
PALGRAVE MACMILLAN
Houndmills, Basingstoke, Hampshire RG21 6XS and
175 Fifth Avenue, New York, N.Y. 10010
Companies and representatives throughout the world

PALGRAVE MACMILLAN is the global academic imprint of the Palgrave Macmillan division of St. Martin's Press, LLC and of Palgrave Macmillan Ltd. Macmillan® is a registered trademark in the United States, United Kingdom and other countries. Palgrave is a registered trademark in the European Union and other countries.

ISBN 0–333–92150–x hardback

This book is printed on paper suitable for recycling and made from fully managed and sustained forest sources.

A catalogue record for this book is available from the British Library.

Library of Congress Cataloging-in-Publication Data

Coates, Kenneth, 1956–
    A global history of indigenous peoples struggle and survival / Ken Coates.
        p. cm.
    Includes bibliographical references and index.
    ISBN 0–333–92150–x (cloth) – ISBN 1–4039–3929–2 (pbk.)
        1. Indigenous peoples – History. 2. Indigenous peoples – Social conditions. 3. Indigenous peoples – Government relations. I. Title.

GN380.C63 2004
305.8—dc22   2004049118

10 9 8 7 6 5 4 3
13 12 11 10 09 08 07 06 05

Printed and bound in Great Britain by
Antony Rowe Ltd, Chippenham and Eastbourne

CONTENTS

ACKNOWLEDGEMENTS

Each work of scholarship draws, directly and indirectly, on the contributions of numerous academics, commentators, and friends. This book is no different. I have benefited enormously from the opportunity to work at the University of Saskatchewan from 2001 to 2004. My colleagues in the History Department, particularly Keith Carlson, J. R. Miller, and Bill Waiser, have made the university a center for the study of native–newcomer encounter. That my friend and colleague, Dave de Brou, died shortly before this book was published is a matter of particular sadness and loss. Trish Monture and Rodolpho Pino have provided unique insights, support and encouragement. I have gained a great deal from countless debates with Trish about all manner of issues relating to indigenous issues. I have benefited from the endless support and encouragement of President Peter Mackinnon, Provost Michael Atkinson, and Vice-Provost Mark Evered. I hope that they know how much they have meant to me over the past few years. The assistance provided by Jennifer Simpson and Amber McQuaig in the Provost's Office and Sharon Ford in the Dean of Arts and Science Office has been invaluable. I acknowledge, with gratitude, the financial assistance provided by the President's Publications Fund.

The web of support extends much further afield. I have benefited greatly from the writing and insights of hundreds of academics around the world, only a handful of whom I have ever met in person. Their work has been essential to the preparation of this preliminary exploration of the history of indigenous–newcomer relations. I must extend particular thanks to a group of scholars whose work has been inspirational, both in terms of the quality of their scholarship and their engagement with contemporary issues. The work of Peter Jull, Henry Reynolds, James Belich, Kerry Howe, Robin Fisher, Julie Cruikshank, Peter Iverson, Richard White, and James Axtell has been particularly instructive. Greg Poelzer, with whom I have debated issues relating to global indigenous issues for over a decade, has been supportive and challenging; this book is much better for his comments. My good friend and regular co-author, Bill Morrison, has been a constant source of encouragement and advice for over twenty years. On this, as with everything I have written, Bill has been an invaluable colleague.

I have been assisted in my work by several superb research assistants. Erin Millions helped me with several projects in the field. Dara Hrytsak provided excellent help with aspects of contemporary indigenous political activity. For the past year, Darren Friesen and Jennifer Hamel provided timely, reliable and very professional assistance with the final stages of the project. The good folks at Palgrave Macmillan have been extraordinarily patient and supportive. Their understanding about the repeated delays in producing the final manuscript made it possible for me to complete the work. Special thanks to Luciana O'Flaherty, who managed the project, and Janey Fisher, my supportive and gracious copy-editor. The editors and my academic colleagues bear no responsibilities for the shortcomings of this book, but they are accountable for whatever contributions it may make to this important field.

My family, as always, has been a great source of encouragement. The continued achievements of my brother, Colin Coates, have been inspirational. Having Colin and his wife, Megan Davies, back in Canada and teaching history at York University is delightful. Janice is the kind of person who gives enormously to her community and demonstrates the importance of giving back to society. And knowing that Mom will be anxious to receive the first copy of the book off the presses is a delight. My oldest children, Bradley, Mark, and Laura, have gone from passive, sometimes bewildered, observers of the academic enterprise to knowledgeable and insightful participants in the scholarly world. Their passion for learning and for life is their father's greatest joy. During the time that this book was being written, three new members have joined the family. Mark's marriage added Wendy to our growing clan, and what a welcome addition she is. Hana and Marlon, my two youngest children, arrived in the last four years. Their enthusiasm and their energy have been challenging for an ageing historian, but they have reinvigorated me and reaffirmed my commitment to the broader world.

But this book – and so very much more – belongs to Carin. And all who know our family understand why. As the manuscript was coming together, Carin was stricken with cancer. In less than two years, she has endured numerous surgeries, chemotherapy and radiation treatments.

And she has kept her smile, her determination and her commitment to the world of ideas. She insisted that I keep working on this book, at a time when my mind was properly fixated on her. Carin truly believes that ideas change the world and that active engagement with contemporary issues is the essence of scholarship. She is my love, my inspiration. Dedicating this book to her seems like such a small thing to do. But she knows, I hope, how much she means to me, and how much my words and ideas carry her passion for life and her commitment to positive social change.

Ken Coates
Department of History
University of Saskatchewan
Saskatoon, Saskatchewan

PREFACE

Writing a comparative history of indigenous peoples is a challenging and humbling experience. There is a great deal of first-rate scholarship on indigenous–newcomer relations and indigenous history around the world. There are major gaps in the literature as well, and the writing, understandably, is typically in the language of the country under investigation. Add to this the very complexity of the task – covering many centuries, dozens of countries, and thousand of contact situations – and the assignment become even more daunting. *A Global History of Indigenous Peoples* came out of a desire to search for patterns and processes in the history of indigenous–newcomer encounter and to make connections across continents and centuries. The book offers a general overview, and hopes to stimulate debate and further investigations of the comparative dimension of the indigenous experiences and, in particular, to highlight the value of broadening the discussion beyond the European empires and to incorporate indigenous contact with other colonial and national powers. Comparative history is a humbling corner of the discipline, for one ventures forth in full recognition that one's thoughts and interpretations are tentative, seeking to draw lines between disparate spots on chronological and geographical templates. This work, then, is a speculation on a broad, globally significant issue; I welcome the opportunity to expand, enhance, and rethink the conclusions as debate about indigenous–newcomer experiences around the world continue.

Introduction: Indigenous Peoples in the Age of Globalization

Definitions

Among the many challenging aspects of understanding indigenous peoples is the fundamental difficulty of defining just who is an indigenous person. The concept has been widely used and there is no consensus as to the precise meaning of the term. The United Nations Working Group on the Rights of Indigenous Peoples, for example, could not agree on a formal definition. They opted (or opted out) to leave the issue unresolved; each group could, they decided, self-identify as indigenous. The attempt at inclusiveness left the central question unresolved, particularly when groups as diverse at Orkney Islanders (Scotland), Boers (South Africans of European ancestry), and Welshmen asserted their indigeniety. There is almost uniform agreement about certain cultural groups – First Nations/Native Americans of North America, the residents of the Amazon jungles, Inuit from the far North, and the indigenous peoples of Papua New Guinea. Scholars, activists and politicians disagree about many others. Are the small societies of the mountainous regions of India, Thailand, the Philippines, and Vietnam indigenous? While the reindeer herders of Siberia seemingly qualify in the minds of most, there is less unanimity about the island societies of the South Pacific and Micronesia. Is the size, as in smallness of population, the main criteria for indigeneity, or is it some other factor, such as attachment to the land, longevity in place, or commitment to traditional non-industrial lifeways? Or is it perhaps the product of more recent historical processes? Is being indigenous simply to have been the victim of colonization?

1

To complicate matters further, there are difficulties identifying the unique identities of specific cultural groups. Some identified as indigenous are, others argue, really subsets of another culture. And the difficulty of identifying and describing small hunting-gathering societies has resulted, on occasions such as that involving the alleged Tasaday culture of the Philippines, in debates about the inclusion of a specific people as indigenous.

The debate over definition is, at one level, one of those arcane discussions which preoccupy lawyers, excite academics, and bore most observers. At one level, the issue generates tremendous passions. To be defined as aboriginal in Canada carries special legal, harvesting, and political rights. To fall outside the definition in Australia has considerable individual and community implications. The creation of a global movement of indigenous peoples has had profound effects on long-ignored and marginalized peoples, who have found common cause and political voice with comparable societies around the world. Many non-aboriginal people shake their heads in astonishment, and often dismay, with the expanding definitions of indigenous and the growing assertiveness of indigenous groups. The debate rages within indigenous populations as well. Many indigenous peoples recoil at the increasing reliance on legal definitions, established under national laws or court interpretations of treaties, and argue that mindset, spiritual orientation, and attachment to traditional values matter more than bloodlines and fit with externally imposed legal descriptions.

But the question is, at many levels, important. There are several major international organizations of indigenous peoples. Their membership defines, for that organization, the meaning of indigenous. There are numerous international groups with the self-appointed task of supporting indigenous communities in their political, legal, and other struggles. But here again the definitions vary widely. Survival International focuses on groups following what they define as a traditional lifestyle. The International Work Group on Indigenous Affairs adopts a much broader model, including societies in transition and many groups that are defined elsewhere as ethnic minorities.

Consider some practical examples. Every definition of indigenous would include the Yanomami of the Amazon River basin. They live in a traditional way and face enormous challenges based on major resource developments on their lands. But what about the Ainu? The original inhabitants of Japan's Hokkaido Island live, for the most part, amongst the Japanese people of the region and are indistinguishable to most outsiders. The Mayan and Inca peoples of Central and South America are the ancestors of large and complex societies that, at the time of European contact, dominated the region. Subsequent depopulation and Spanish conquest transformed these peoples into impoverished and colonized societies, sharing many economic and political characteristics with the so-called traditional indigenous cultures. Africa presents comparable problems of definition, particularly in the postcolonial era. In Africa, is indigenous status a function of population size, land use systems, or access to political power? The Hutu and Tutsi of Rwanda are large, complex, and mutually antagonistic peoples. Are they indigenous? They are rarely seen as such, by dint of their role within modern political structures in the region. In contrast, the !Kung of Botswana, a small, mobile population who live in the Kalahari desert, are typically seen as indigenous and attract a great deal of international attention. And what about China, a modern state that denies the existence of indigenous peoples within its borders? In the case of Mongolia, the dominant population is rooted in a mobile, pastoral lifestyle. Can an entire country be considered indigenous? And, in a similar vein, are the now (largely) independent island nations of the South Pacific indigenous peoples?

One of the most intriguing groups, often active participants in international indigenous activities, are the Mapuche people of southern Chile. The Mapuche had a large, agricultural society for generations before the arrival of the Spaniards. While their communities did not have the dramatic cities and architecture of the Inca and Aztec, they had a complex social and administration system which, in fact, helped them keep the colonial authorities at bay for quite some time. After the Spaniards arrived in 1541, they moved aggressively against the Mapuche, attacking the people and often engaging in brutal raids. But the Mapuche retained their independence and, in fact, maintained an independent state. A comprehensive "War of the Pacification of Araucanía" saw the government, enriched by mineral discoveries and much better armed, move against the Mapuche settlements and culture and, by 1883, force them off their lands and onto a government reservation. The size of the population – over one million in the 1990s – protected the people against the government's actions, which escalated through a series of land dispossessions, the use of *colonias* or *reducciones* to replace collective landholdings with individual property rights, restrictions on their rights, and various assimilationist efforts. The Mapuche faced even greater dislocations under the Allende regime and organized domestically and internationally for greater recognition of their rights and needs, declaring:

> We have a heavy responsibility before our people, a responsibility which cannot only be turned into solidarity support from exiles. We should consider that our Chilean brothers are providing new examples of daily combat against Fascism. The tyrannical regime is already showing signs of exhaustion and weakness as the present economic and political crisis shows us. The conditions for its destruction are presenting themselves. Let us support our brothers in order to finish once and for all with the murderer of our people. The alliance and unity with the working class ought to manifest itself in all its forms. Only unity offers a guaranteed success in our struggle. With all our strength we shall overcome ten times over![1]

While very few dispute the intensity and seriousness of the Mapuche struggle, the question remains: are they an indigenous people? Because of their large population, largely sedentary existence, and state of agricultural and political development in the years before the expansion of Europe, it would seem doubtful – although the Mapuche clearly have found common cause with indigenous peoples facing attacks on their culture, land, and political rights.

Guatemala presents similar questions. The Mayan people, who have endured shocking oppression throughout a period of military rule and civil conflict, often attend political gatherings of indigenous peoples. They are not a mobile population, but rather live as peasants in a society dominated by a small elite of landowners. The issue for the Mayan, much like the Mapuche, is that they had developed an extensive agriculture society before being overrun by the Spaniards. Subsequent to the invasion by newcomers, they have been stripped of their lands, subject to missionization, and forced to endure generations of marginalization, brutal attacks, and genocide. Beginning with the interventionist measures of the Barrios regime in the 1870s, the Mayans were forced to serve as laborers for rich landowners and had few social, cultural, or political rights. Poverty became endemic, and throughout the twentieth century, the state routinely used its military authority and police powers to overwhelm Mayan aspirations. There is no doubt but that the Guatemalan peasants have had a difficult and often painful history; it is debatable whether they fit into the various definitions of indigenous, save for those that focus almost exclusively on the relationship of colonized to colonizer.

In India, indigenous populations have been described under a variety of titles: Adivasis (original inhabitants), Aborigines, Adim Jati (ancient

tribes) or Vanavasi (forest dwellers). The government of India refers to
them as "Scheduled Tribes" and their territories as "Scheduled Areas."
India offered no official definition of how a group became indigenous,
but an official suggested that such peoples had "'primitive' traits,
distinctive culture, geographical isolation, shyness of contact with the
community at large and backwardness." Under this definition, the
groups ranged in size from the Gondas and Bhils, with millions of people, to the Great Andamanese, with less than two dozen, and according
to government records counted for over 51 million people in 1981. As
one observer wrote of the peoples:

> The indigenous tribal peoples of India have lost most of their tranquil habi-
> tats; they have also lost some of their confidence and identity. Forces of
> oppression and exploitation have encroached upon tribal life and have
> reduced many of them to sub-human conditions. The laws meant for their
> protection have remained largely ineffective. However, efforts made for the
> spread of education and development of tribal areas have made some impact
> in raising their standard of living. Social activists have contributed to mobi-
> lizing them for the protection of their rights. The picture is rather gloomy
> and unclear but there are rays of hope on the horizon.[2]

Viewed through the lens of colonial victimization, interesting definitions
of otherness have emerged in recent decades. Fijians, for example, are
rarely considered to be indigenous peoples, because they control their
country. Other, larger populations such as Mayans in Central America,
which had a substantial and complex agrarian society before the age of
European expansion, are deemed to be indigenous because of their
political powerlessness and exploitation by government and military
elites. Over time, the concepts of indigenous and aboriginal have
become increasingly synonymous with powerlessness, marginality,
and social distress – approaches which are Eurocentric in origin and
crisis-based.
    Julian Berger, a long-time United Nations official and international
political advocate, determined that:

> The notion of belonging to a separate culture with all its various elements –
> language, religion, social and political systems, moral values, scientific and
> philosophical knowledge, beliefs, legends, laws, economic systems, technology,
> art, clothing, music, dance, architecture, and so on – is central to indigenous
> peoples' own definition.[3]

The same definition, of course, could apply to being "ethnic," a much more inclusive category than indigenous. He then continued to argue that

> An indigenous people may contain all of the following elements or just some. Indigenous peoples:
>   i) are the descendants of the original inhabitants of a territory which has been overcome by conquest;
> ii) are nomadic and semi-nomadic peoples, such as shifting cultivators, herders and hunters and gatherers, and practice a labour-intensive form of agriculture which produces little surplus and has low energy needs;
> iii) do not have centralized political institutions and organize at the level of the community and make decisions on a consensus basis;
> iv) have all the characteristics of a national minority: they share a common language, religion, culture, and other identifying characteristics and a relationship to a particular territory but are subjugated by a dominant culture and society;
>   v) have a different world view, consisting of a custodial and non-materialist attitude to land and natural resources, and want to pursue a separate development to that proffered by the dominant society;
> vi) consist of individuals who subjectively consider themselves to be indigenous, and are accepted by the group as such.

Perhaps the most widely cited definition is that of José Martinez Cobo, an Ecuadorian diplomat, written when he was working for a United Nations subcommittee on the rights of indigenous peoples in the early 1970s.

> Indigenous communities, peoples and nations are those which, having a historical continuity with pre-invasion and pre-colonial societies that developed on their territories, consider themselves distinct from other sectors of the societies now prevailing in those territories, or parts of them. They form at present non-dominant sectors of society and are determined to preserve, develop and transmit to future generations their ancestral territories, and their ethnic identity, as the basis of their continued existence as peoples, in accordance with their own cultural patterns, social institutions and legal systems.[4]

In expanding on this basic definition, Martinez Cobo highlighted the importance of the continued occupation of traditional lands, a direct link with the original inhabitants of these lands, and a unique and identifiable culture and language. He also emphasized the importance of the definition of indigenous resting with the group and the self-identification by the individuals involved:

> On an individual basis, an indigenous person is one who belongs to these indigenous peoples through self-identification as indigenous (group consciousness) and is recognized and accepted by the group as one of its members (acceptance by the group). This preserves for these communities the sovereign right and power to decide who belongs to them, without external interference.

Another important definition of indigenous comes from the Commission on Human Rights, United Nations Economic and Social Council. They have stated it thus:

> Indigenous Populations are composed of the existing descendants of the peoples who inhabited the present territory of a country wholly or partially at the time when persons of a different culture or ethnic origin arrived there from other parts of the world, overcame them and, by conquest, settlement or other means, reduced them to a non-dominant or colonial situation; who today live more in conformity with their particular social, economic and cultural customs and traditions than the institutions of the country of which they now form a part, under a state structure that incorporates mainly the national, social and cultural characteristics of other segments of the population that are predominant.
>
> Although they have not suffered conquest or colonization, isolated or marginal groups existing in the country should be regarded as covered by the notion of "Indigenous Populations" for the following reasons:
>
> a) they are descendants of groups which were in the territory of the country at the time when other groups of different cultures or ethnic origins arrived there;
>
> b) precisely because of their isolation from other segments of the country's population they have preserved almost intact the customs and traditions of their ancestors which are similar to those characterized as indigenous;
>
> c) they are, even if only formally, placed under a state structure which incorporates national, social and cultural characteristics alien to theirs.

As one observer wrote of this attempt.

> This complex and somewhat legalistic definition has been adopted by the United Nations, and is now generally accepted worldwide. In its simplest sense, it serves to identify pre-existing societies that have been overrun by global capitalism, and who have previously had a long identification with a land they considered their source of life and their birthright.[5]

Despite its obvious strengths and comprehensive nature, this definition was not picked up by other UN agencies, and has not formed the basis of the work of the most important UN initiative in this area, the Draft Declaration on the Rights of Indigenous Peoples.

The draft Universal Declaration on the Rights of the Indigenous Peoples prepared by the Working Group does not include a definition of indigenous peoples or populations. In an effort designed to ensure that no groups were excluded, by way of technical definitions, from participating in the discussions of the Working Group, they opted to rely on self-definition. The refusal to codify questions of membership has had the effect of weakening the efforts of the Working Group and has muddied the waters in the international political community about the very nature of the indigenous population and hence their claims to international attention. Despite these shortcomings, and because of the complexity of the indigenous experience around the world, there has been little urgency attached to creating a working and sustainable definition of indigenous peoples.

The problem with definitions rooted in contemporary political circumstances is that they ignore the ebb and flow of human history. That is to say, while being sensitive to political realities they fail to account for historical context and developments. Much of the political agitation has focused on the activities of European colonial powers and on the small, indigenous societies displaced by intrusions associated with the transplanting of European settlements. This emphasis ignores equally disruptive and authoritarian invasions of indigenous territories by Asian, African, and other societies and skips over the experience of indigenous societies separate from their contact with and conquest by outsiders. The standard definition, seeking to capitalize on public support and motivated by political movements on a national, regional, and global scale, highlights weaknesses and freezes indigenous cultures in a specific time, space, and relationship to other peoples. It is, ironically, a strikingly eurocentric approach, in that it times and orients indigenous cultures to the actions of outsiders. Put another way, such definitions tend to be driven by non-indigenous, liberal agendas that set indigenous peoples up as foils for the excesses and shortcomings of western industrial society.

As Tapan Bose, a leading activist on indigenous rights, observes,

> Among other things, this approach also fails to explain the phenomena of survival of the "indigenous" identity in the face of adversity. Moreover, ethnic identities have also survived. But not all ethnic communities have lived in

isolation. Many ethnic communities have completely lost control over their "homeland" or the terrain which was the cradle of their culture. Yet their identities have survived. What then are the differences between the ethnic groups and the indigenous peoples?

This does raise a rather ticklish issue. The white Afrikaners from South Africa, after the abolition of apartheid, went to the Working Group as an indigenous people. Likewise, the Kashmiri Pundits community of India has been attending the sessions of the Working Group with the blessings of the Indian Government. Both these ethnic communities did not suffer from isolation or discrimination. On the contrary, until recently they were in power and were practising discrimination against others.

Historical context is clearly important. At different points in time, indigenous peoples have warred with and displaced other indigenous peoples, such as the Iroquois moves on the Huron, the Blackfoot intrusions into Cree territory and Kwakuitl incursions into Coast Salish lands. To put it more simply, indigenous peoples have not all been marginalized, discriminated against, or conquered. Indigenous peoples have exploited, defeated, ruled over, and dislocated other indigenous societies. Indigenous cultures flourished in most parts of the world, before and after the age of European expansionism, and the struggle for survival in the contemporary world continues in Africa, Asia, South America, South East Asia, the Pacific Islands, and many other regions of the world. Definitions of indigenous in most common usage arise out of the European colonial experience, originated in western industrial nations, and reflect the historical and contemporary realities of these social relationships.

Even a brief consideration of the complexity of the indigenous situation reveals the difficulty of finding a precise and uniformly acceptable definition. Who, for example, qualifies as indigenous in Africa, the Middle East, or South Asia? If the hill tribes of India and Southeast Asia are included in the definition, in recognition of their relative powerlessness within contemporary nation-states, does the concept of indigenous invariably relate to weaknesses and inability to control one's territory, resources, and economic independence? For many observers, indigenous peoples are invariably mobile, hunter-gatherer societies; are agricultural cultures automatically excluded from inclusion? Colonialism, seen as the defining characteristic of many indigenous peoples in North America and Australasia and other districts, cannot be a central determinant without including the peoples of India/South Asia, Indonesia, and other such locations. How, under these confusing situations, does one differentiate between ethnic minorities and indigenous peoples? This line has been difficult to draw at the political level within the United Nations, where indigenous societies are viewed as a sub-group of minorities. In Canada, to be indigenous is to qualify for aboriginal rights as an Indian, Inuit, or Métis person under the constitution and British common law. Indigenous, in this context, equates to being a descendant from original occupants. By this definition and by the application of the law, this means that aboriginal people from Australia are not indigenous if they take up residence in Canada.

The issue of definition is of crucial political importance in the contemporary world, and has shaped both government policy and public reaction. Since the 1970s, supporters of "indigenous" societies in crisis have generally been better able to attract attention than ethnic minorities facing discrimination and hostility within a nation-state. Western governments, capitalizing on the flexibility provided by national wealth, have taken comparatively generous approaches to indigenous peoples, tackling long-festering legal issues and seeking to provide a greater measure of social justice. Poorer nations in Asia and Africa, in contrast, have paid much less attention to the "special" status of indigenous societies and have been loath to slow development, land reclamation or other policies deemed in the interest of the broader population. When supporters of indigenous peoples have been able to link the indigenous label with contemporary struggles – as they have done in Sarawak, the hills of Bangladesh, and Papua New Guinea – they have enjoyed considerable success in drawing media attention. Language, labels and definitions do matter.[6]

The complexity of the situation is outlined in a key statement by Survival International, one of the most active global support groups in this field. Declaring itself to be devoted to the support of "indigenous peoples," Survival International provides the following definition:

> Tribal peoples are those who have lived in tribal societies for many generations; they are usually the original inhabitants of the places they live in, or have at least lived there for hundreds if not thousands of years. They usually provide for themselves, living off the land by hunting, fishing, gathering or growing vegetables or keeping their own animals. They usually also have an extremely strong cultural, emotional and spiritual attachment to their land.

Indigenous peoples tend to be "minorities": fewer in number than the other (non-indigenous) peoples who are often their neighbours. Their societies are distinct from those of non-indigenous peoples – they often have a different language, customs and culture inherited from their ancestors, and think of themselves as being different from neighbouring peoples.
Tribal peoples are not necessarily the same as indigenous peoples. "Indigenous peoples" are all the original inhabitants of a country, but "indigenous peoples" are only those who live in distinct indigenous societies. For instance, all Aborigines in Australia are "indigenous", but only some still live in indigenous societies and see themselves as indigenous people.[7]

Survival International, therefore, defines indigenous in terms of current lifestyle; an indigenous person living in a city and pursuing a professional career would not conform to the organization's concept of indigenous.
The International Work Group on Indigenous Affairs, adopting a broader, more comprehensive approach, defines indigenous as follows:

Indigenous peoples are the disadvantaged descendants of those peoples that inhabited a territory prior to the formation of a state. The term indigenous may be defined as a characteristic relating the identity of a particular people to a particular area and distinguishing them culturally from other people or peoples. When, for example, immigrants from Europe settled in the Americas and Oceania, or when new states were created after colonialism was abolished in Africa and Asia, certain peoples became marginalised and discriminated against, because their language, their religion, their culture and their whole way of life were different and perceived by the dominant society as being inferior. Insisting on their right to self-determination is indigenous peoples' way of overcoming these obstacles.
Today many indigenous peoples are still excluded from society and often even deprived of their rights as equal citizens of a state. Nevertheless they are determined to preserve, develop and transmit to future generations their ancestral territories and their ethnic identity. Self-identification as an indigenous individual and acceptance as such by the group is an essential component of indigenous peoples' sense of identity. Their continued existence as peoples is closely connected to their possibility to influence their own fate and to live in accordance with their own cultural patterns, social institutions and legal systems.
Indigenous peoples face other serious difficulties such as the constant threat of territorial invasion and murder, the plundering of their resources, cultural and legal discrimination, as well as a lack of recognition suffered by indigenous institutions.

At least 350 million people worldwide are considered to be indigenous. Most of them live in remote areas in the world. Indigenous peoples are divided into at least 5000 peoples ranging from the forest peoples of the Amazon to the indigenous peoples of India and from the Inuit of the Arctic to the Aborigines in Australia. Very often they inhabit land which is rich in minerals and natural resources.

Indigenous peoples have prior rights to their territories, lands and resources, but often these have been taken from them or are threatened. They have distinct cultures and economies compared to those of the dominant society. The importance of indigenous peoples' self-identification is crucial and a part of their identity.

Indigenous peoples face serious difficulties such as the constant threat of territorial invasion and murder, the plundering of their resources, cultural and legal discrimination, as well as a lack of recognition of their own institutions.[8]

The IWGIA definition retains the now-standard emphasis on marginalization, loss of autonomy and control over resources, and the prospect and reality of cultural decline. It highlights, in a variety of ways, the idea of indigenous peoples as being victims of broader processes, buffeted by the forces of development and rendered largely powerless within the nation state.

The issue at hand is clearly a complicated one. Depending on the approach taken, the concepts of indigenous, tribal and ethnic minority could be interchangeable or, at the minimum, substantially overlapping. The challenge is to find a definition that works historically. It cannot or should not be framed entirely within contemporary terms, like that of Survival International, for to do so would obscure important historical transitions. Ideally, it would not be Eurocentric and would not define an entire category of people solely on the basis of their relationship to a external group/force. It would incorporate the experiences of small societies in Asia, Africa and other regions and would not be influenced by the contemporary efforts of Asian governments to exclude their indigenous and small societies from inclusion within the indigenous political world. To be meaningful, a workable definition needs to focus on historical processes and relationships while remaining sensitive to the circumstances of local indigenous societies. At the same time, efforts to be comprehensive and inclusion in terms of definition, as with various United Nations' efforts, can strip the concept of its meaning. Equally, defining indigenous peoples in oppositional terms, principally in conflict with western, industrial societies, has its attractions.

The standard definitions of indigenous peoples suggest that colonization – the unwelcome domination of a people by an external political, economic and military power – is the key factor in determining the historical evolution of the society. In many definitions, the colonial relationship is typically highlighted as the most important determination of indigeniety. This approach is not advocated here, although colonial status is clearly a central element in the history of most indigenous peoples. For the purposes of this book, indigenous peoples have been defined as having the following characteristics:

1. Indigenous peoples, in the contemporary world, lack political power and autonomy and exist under the control of an immigrant or ethnic group-dominated state. It is the argument of this book that indigeneity does not spring from the lack of political power but, instead and crucially, that the absence of political power springs from their indigeneity. Adherence to indigenous values and traditions, it will be argued, ensured that the indigenous peoples remained outside evolving economic, social and political systems and, in fact, were generally seen as posing a threat to the evolving or imposed order.

2. They live in small scale societies, and have comparatively small populations. There should be no precise population cut-off.

3. Indigenous societies derive a profound sense of identity from place, and are strongly connected to their traditional territories and resources. As such, the alienation of their land or the lack of control over resources is often viewed as a critical element in ongoing definitions of the collective identity. Indigenous peoples have strong, multi-generational attachments to the land.

4. Historically, and in some instances at present, they are mobile peoples, ranging fairly widely over ancestral territories in a complex seasonal cycle tied to the rhythms of the year. Indigenous peoples tend to relocate throughout the year to take advantage of seasonal resources. Often they retain a major settlement where critical cultural and social activities are anchored.

5. Indigenous peoples are not socially static or unchanging, but they have tended to be conservative, in the sense that they did not respond quickly to social trends and cultural influences.

6. Indigenous societies did not adhere to western/industrial notions of individual wealth and generally approached the concept of a surplus economy with caution. The older definitions emphasized, implicitly

and formerly explicitly, the primitive/modern, subsistence/industrial dichotomy, and suggest, often incorrectly, that these societies lacked material wealth. The long-standing notion of indigenous societies as poor and marginal is not useful. Many indigenous populations were stable, well-fed and comfortable, often more so than many of the non-elite members of European societies until the twentieth century.

7. Adaptations away from traditional land use patterns, lifestyles and material culture do not, by definition, signal the abandonment of ancestral affiliations or values, and therefore do not cause these people to cease being indigenous.

8. Indigenous peoples are historical societies with a strong understanding of the past, often passed on through oral testimony, ceremonies and cultural activities. They view their experience from a very long perspective, celebrating their ancient attachment to specific territories and devoting a great deal of community time to the remembrance of ancestors and important events and processes. The sense of rootedness in the past is highlighted by the attachment of stories and legends to traditional lands and to the richness and texture of indigenous languages, both of which play a vital role in preserving the indigenous understanding of history.

9. Most indigenous societies are engaged in the decolonization and re-indigenousization processes. They are participating in protests organized against colonial powers, global influences, environmental degradation and the like. They are seeking to maintain and protect their cultural independence in the face of formidable economic and political pressures to adapt to the national or global mainstream.

This is a lengthy and cumbersome definition. It draws heavily on Julian Berger's interpretation, but avoids relying on contemporary political power or powerlessness as the prime determinant of inclusion. It is important that indigenous peoples be defined by who they are, not who they are not. The role of outsiders/colonizing powers is obviously critical, but it is not the prime determinant of indigeneity. Indigenous peoples share some central characteristics: small size, attachment to the land, value system and culture rooted in the environment, commitment to a sustainable lifestyle, mobility, and cultural conservatism. With the inevitable regional and historical variations, they also share several key historical circumstances: economic and political domination by outsiders, selected integration/participation with non-indigenous societies, limited or non-existent power within the nation state, emerging involvement in a local or international process of decolonization. The definition, appropriately, reflects the pre-expansion realities of indigenous peoples, conditions which defined these societies for numerous generations. It also acknowledges the shared experience of the post-expansion and contemporary world, where indigenous peoples seek unity and collective action in the face of powerful forces for change.

The Contemporary Situation

The contemporary situation of indigenous peoples around the world is complex, to say the least. In the outback of Australia, young Aborigines wear "Air Jordan" t-shirts. Inuit in northern Canada watch "Sex in the City" on televisions connected to the 100-channel universe. Maori in New Zealand attend the best business schools in the country and, buttressed with professional credentials, find work with aggressive finance companies. The Ainu of Japan, struggling to hold onto the vestiges of language and culture in the face of an officially monocultural state, are at ease with the technology of the mobile internet. Aboriginal people in Brazil, although typically trapped at the bottom end of a poor society, ride to work on articulated buses and occasionally eat at McDonald's. American Indians across the United States work in luxurious casinos, drawing in millions of dollars from free-spending non-aboriginal patrons. Sami in Scandinavia drive Volvos to homes in modern northern cities. In an age of rampant globalization, as corporate influences and the dominance of free market forces link peoples around the world, indigenous societies find themselves torn between the localizing power of their cultures and the unifying forces of the contemporary world.

Outsiders have simple notions about indigenous peoples. Those who maintain clear aboriginal traditions – living off the land, speaking their language, adhering to ancient customs and rituals, following the dictates of established social and political structures – are clearly defined as aboriginal. Those who have shifted off the land, even if not by choice, who live amongst non-aboriginals, and who speak the language of the newcomer society and participate in the lifestyle of the majority, are viewed as peoples in crisis, or without identity, or as assimilated into the social mainstream. In most countries, so long as they do not cost taxpayers money or get in the way of development, indigenous peoples tend to be regarded as quaint, if anachronistic, reminders of an earlier time. To the extent that they are seen as impeding development or chronically drawing on government resources, indigenous peoples are seen as a problem or, at best, as societies with problems. Reduced in the minds of most to caricatures, stereotypes, and museum exhibits, indigenous peoples find themselves fighting for acceptance and survival in a rapidly changing world that shows little respect for their rights or unique histories.

For non-aboriginal peoples the situation was easier a century ago. Nineteenth-century analysts of indigenous peoples knew who they were studying. The European world was awash in simplistic descriptions of indigenous peoples. Words like primitive, savage, pre-industrial, and heathen stood opposite Eurocentric self-descriptions of their cultures as modern, civilized, industrial, and Christian. This was a simple world, of nations destined by God to win and dominate, and of cultures doomed by history to wither and die. Notions of cultural supremacy characterized the entire colonial enterprise, and determined the manner in which generations of readers, students, and scholars understood the lifeways and cultures of indigenous peoples.

It is important to remember how much western understanding of indigenous societies has changed over the past centuries. Well into the eighteenth and nineteenth centuries, many intellectuals, politicians, government officials, and religious leaders held to a very simple concept of civilization. There was, under this longstanding construct, a single definition of civilization into which all cultures were supposed to fit. The British, French, Germans, and Italians – the ones who, in the main, wrote and defended the concept – held that they were "civilized" people, having separated themselves through their industry, innovation, and God's blessings from "lesser" societies. At the opposite end of the civilized–uncivilized continuum, a simple way of presenting the relative merits of different peoples, rested Native Americans, Africans, and others. This paradigm held sway for a very long time, and fueled and justified much of the aggressiveness of the age of European expansion. Intellectually, these ideas were expressed in studies by scholars like Louis Henry Morgan and Edward Tylor. They and others argued that societies evolved from the lower stages of the ladder of civilization, moving steadily toward the better cultures of northern Europe and its settler colonies.

In the late nineteenth and early twentieth century, new assumptions came into play. Led by the work of German anthropologist Franz Boas, a greater appreciation for cultural diversity and uniqueness found a strong academic following. Boas's approach rejected the idea that all societies followed a common evolutionary path and instead focused on the manner in which each culture reflected its historical and geographical context. Boas rejected the idea of one society being superior to another in intellectual or evolutionary terms, and emphasized that each culture had to be respected and understood on its own. Under this paradigm, cultures were unique, sharing some common influences and characteristics but reflecting a complex combination of economic, historical, geographic and social factors. The academic interpretations advanced by Boas and his contemporaries took many generations to filter into the public consciousness, and indeed assumptions about the primitiveness and backwardness of indigenous peoples continue to enjoy considerable currency in many countries.

Boas provided descriptions of indigenous societies which clearly differentiated them from western industrial societies. He wrote of the

> general lack of differentiation of mental activities. In primitive life, religion and science; music, poetry and dance; myth and history; fashion and ethics, – appear to us inextricably interwoven. We may express this general observation also by saying that primitive man views each action not only as adapted to its main object, each thought as related to its main end, as we should perceive them, but that he associates them with other ideas, often of a religious or at least of a symbolic nature.

Boas described inherently conservative peoples, "so among primitive tribes, the resistance to a deviation from firmly established customs is due to an emotional reaction, not to conscious reasoning." He highlighted the importance of ritual and ceremony, the deep spirituality of indigenous peoples, and the fundamental importance of relationships to land and animals.[9] By describing indigenous peoples in a positive, if distinctive, manner, Boas provided a foundation for a more comprehensive search for understanding of the diverse and very different original peoples of the world.

For very good reasons, then, simplistic evolutionary descriptions no longer hold. There is much greater appreciation of the cultural richness and social integrity of the small indigenous populations that have emerged around the world. Sparked by the assertion of cultural autonomy and political self-determination by and for the indigenous peoples, the new interpretation has found considerable favor around the world. But words on pages make for fine rhetoric and do not necessarily translate into a restructuring of relationships between indigenous societies and expansionist newcomers. And so, although holding their own, and sometimes even winning the battle over language, description, and characterization, many indigenous peoples are losing the struggles over land, resources, political autonomy, and environmental security.

Struggle and Survival

Perhaps unwittingly, advocates of indigenous rights have strengthened the impression that indigenous societies are powerless in the face of the unrelenting force of non-indigenous expansion. The adoption of the rhetoric of anti-colonialism and postmodernism has emphasized the various means that dominant societies, almost always European, used to dominate and destroy the indigenous world. The postcolonial struggle, one of the last half century's most critical political movements, has become the central feature of the analysis of indigenous cultures in transition. Not without justification, analysts from India to the American West, from New Zealand to Scandinavia, have highlighted the manner in which the actions, values, assumptions, and biases of the western capitalist and industrialist world undermined indigenous cultures. The sentiment is vividly expressed in the title of John Bodley's important work on indigenous societies in transition: *Victims of Progress*. These three words carry a succinct message: indigenous peoples were and are victims, the implication being that they were powerless in the face of European expansion. Progress, of course, represents European material and industrial values and ideology, with Bodley implying that the Europeans would not let indigenous peoples stand in the way of the pursuit of land, wealth, and strategic opportunity.

There is obviously a great deal of merit in this approach. Indigenous peoples have been pushed, prodded, administered, and otherwise dominated by external powers (as, it should be noted, have many European societies, from the Celts onward). The disruptions, on occasion, resulted in annihilation or decimation, intentional or otherwise. The mechanisms of non-indigenous control were many, and were often cruelly effective. It would be absurd and disingenuous to suggest that the advance of industrial, materialist, and politically expansionist states did not cause enormous pain and hardship for indigenous peoples around the world. But there is something simplistic in a mono-casual explanation, in which complex human relationships are attributed entirely to the influences of colonialism. If nothing else, this approach strips indigenous societies of agency and, ironically, builds an explanatory framework which is dramatically Eurocentric in nature. Moreover, and more importantly, it fails to account for the survival of indigenous people and societies. If anything, indigenous people have found new and innovative ways to remain distinctive despite the power of global economies, western ideologies, and colonial militaries, as is fairly common in Third World and decolonization situations. Europe is blamed for the historical and contemporary problems of former colonies, a process which is emotionally appealing and politically safe. It does not, however, necessarily help explain as much about the indigenous–expansionist contact experience as many writers and advocates believe.

The fault, in part, lies with the very nature of scholarship. Academics, historians most notably among them, are preoccupied with identifying and explaining change. Researchers are drawn to conflicts and to the assessment of the impact and implications of social, economic, cultural, and political tensions. While scholars are very good at explaining these elements, they are significantly less successful at explaining continuity. The absence of change is, however, often as critical to understanding the past as are a series of specific transformations. This is nowhere more true than with the study of indigenous peoples. Because of the array of forces marshaled against them, the mere fact of cultural and social survival by indigenous peoples is a critical part of the story. Visit an *iwi* (meeting) among the Tainui people of New Zealand and convince yourself that indigenous cultures are dead and dying. Spend time in the Kalahari desert among the San, long believed to have been a dying culture, and convince yourself that the traditional ways are gone. Talk to a Mohawk matriarch and then argue that traditional social structures have been destroyed among First Nations who have lived closely with the newcomers. Follow an Inuit elder out onto the ice and try to sustain the idea that indigenous environmental knowledge is little more than superstition. Observe Aboriginal indigenous rituals in Australia's Northern Territory and assert that western culture dominates and obliterates all in its path. And so it goes around the globe, with Sami reindeer herders in Norway, Yanomami hunters in Brazil, Ilongots in the Philippines, the hill tribes of northern Thailand. These societies may be struggling, but they are also surviving and indeed many continue to thrive. Yet, surprisingly, this crucial element in the story is typically ignored or accorded very little attention.

The contemporary media and many scholars appear attracted by the prospect of cultural demise – a phenomena which has been around since the nineteenth century. Indigenous languages are a good case in point. The death, dispossession, and suffering of indigenous peoples generate only occasional media coverage. Major construction projects, the expansion of logging activity or military occupations generate short-term sympathy for a displaced people, but focus quickly shifts to other world crises. This is particularly the case when indigenous interests parallel environmentalists' concerns; at such a time, indigenous values can be presented as a foil against western power structures and material excesses. The indigenous protesters and survivors fade to the back pages and eventually out of the public's view. But people react to the death of a language, a distressingly common occurrence in the post-World War II era.

The scene unfolds in a standard way. The media latch onto the fact that only one or a small handful of speakers of an indigenous language remain alive. In a manner that James Fenimore Cooper captured in his long-famous and still influential novel, *The Last of the Mohicans*, journalists sense that there is public interest in a death watch. For a few years, the stories are presented in a partially optimistic light: the elder is struggling to preserve what he or she can of the language, often working with linguists, anthropologists, and educators to record place-names, grammar, and vocabulary and thereby provide an oral archive for later generations. But there is an inevitability about it all. The elder is aging, no other indigenous members have come forward to learn and preserve the language, and death will signal the end of a centuries-old tradition. The stories are poignant and truly significant, and so a death watch ensues, as the "last of the [fill in the blank]" speakers disappears from the face of the earth. In such scenarios, it is not clear that the interest derives from a sincere concern about the indigenous culture. Instead, part of the attraction lies in the fact that such dramas reveal the excesses and shortcomings of western societies.

There is, among the non-indigenous observers, acquiescence to the inevitability of cultural death. After all, government officials, missionaries, teachers, and others have been forecasting the disappearance of indigenous cultures for almost two centuries. The strength and persistence of the industrial, commercial world, they have accepted, is such that the small, isolated indigenous societies have little chance. That they were generally wrong in the 1850s, typically misguided in the 1920s, and overly pessimistic in the 1950s, does not seem to deter the newest generation of pessimists from sounding the death knell of societies which have functioned and flourished in place for hundreds of years. Language, for many, seems to be the ultimate symbol of cultural death, even though the experience of the Irish – dominated by the British, largely stripped of their language, and yet major contributors to the literary and cultural world – suggests that the loss of language does not inevitably result in a loss of identity. And so, the evidence that a staggering percentage of the world's languages have died out in the past 100 years or are in imminent danger of disappearing is taken as a sign that indigenous peoples are – this time – truly about to disappear. Scholars debate passionately the importance of language in cultural survival. Many point to the manner in which indigenous languages are imbedded in land, lifeways and cultural ritual to support their argument that, without the language, indigenous cultures simply cannot survive. Speaking English, Chinese, Hindi, Spanish, Portuguese, or some other imposed language, the assumption goes, overwhelms traditional values and cultures and renders the indigenous society a pathetic shell of its former self. Indigenous leaders often echo these sentiments (often in the boarding-school or university language of the dominant society) and demand educational programs to sustain language fluency. In the process, their arguments lend credence to the sentiment that social systems will disappear without a strong and widely spoken language. And yet, even after the tragedy of having lost their language, indigenous societies persist. They find new ways to retain their uniqueness.

Consequently, in the first decade of the twenty-first century, a generations-old debate continues. Language issues form only part of the discussion. Other observers point to the decline of traditional harvesting, intermarriage with other cultures, social and economic crises, government intervention, and many other forces as representing both cause and symbol of the ongoing destruction of indigenous cultures. Across the continents, in political, cultural, and social meetings, the arguments continue. Will indigenous societies survive, in the face of all manner of human, biological, economic, and cultural domination? Can the remaining small, isolated, indigenous peoples, often inhabitants of the most remote and difficult terrain in the world but now found in densely populated urban environments, flourish in an age of globalization, resource development, and ecological change? Are the forces and influences of colonization so powerful that the remaining vestiges of indigenous societies will be undermined by the wealth, power, and determination of domineering industrial peoples? What possible resources can the small, politically isolated indigenous societies marshal in their efforts to survive, other than the liberal guilt of western societies? Are these cultures on their death-beds, sure to disappear in the crush of the modern world?

This attempt to write a global history of indigenous peoples seeks to balance two critical elements. The impact of the newcomers is crucial to understanding the transformation and, at times, the destruction, of indigenous cultures. Parts of this story are well-known, although European activity has typically been emphasized and the colonizing activities of Asian and African states and societies have received little notice. The second element – the manner in which indigenous peoples survived in the face of massive pressures of change – has to be given expanded emphasis. This point is not trivial. Peoples as diverse as the Inuit and Maori, Chittagong Hill Tribes and Navajo, Sami and Mohawk, have faced and survived the multiple forces of colonization. They changed, adapted, resisted, protested, accommodated, and otherwise responded to a series of efforts to undercut, undermine, and disrupt their societies. Yet, to a degree that the contemporary rhetoric about colonization does not fully explain, these indigenous peoples remember their central stories and customs, retain centuries-old value systems, and continue to respect and understand the land and resources of their people. To a much greater degree than most outsiders recognize, long-standing family and community relationships remain pivotal in their lives. Even in highly developed western industrial countries, indigenous societies are not dead – and in most instances are not even dying – despite the efforts of newcomers and analysts to signal their impending doom.

To the surprise of several generations of observers, indigenous peoples have emerged as a potent political force in the late twentieth and early twenty-first century. Cynics attribute much of this rise in prominence to rampant liberalism, tied to guilt over the errors of paternalism and ecological destruction, but they do so in error. Indigenous societies have been struggling for survival for centuries, in some instances, and decades in others. Tactics have changed, as have the intrusions of outsiders, but the level of determination remains much as before. Indigenous peoples are organized on local, regional, national, and international levels. They have learned the tactics of political struggle and are mastering the techniques of the information age to generate support for their causes. They are at the forefront of struggles around the world, over control of traditional lands, the protection of the environment, economic and social rights, and against the intrusions of colonialism and the neo-colonialism of economic and cultural globalization and racism. Their battles hit the front pages, typically, when the struggle is over land and economic development but rarely on more social issues. The indigenous societies themselves tend to devote their greatest attention to matters of cultural sustainability and continuity or, at a minimum, to managing change within certain cultural parameters. The specific struggles have changed. The European colonial powers of the eighteenth and nineteenth century have, in many places, been displaced by the domination of local social and economic elites. The reach of modern technology and contemporary economics affects indigenous peoples in profound ways, and in areas markedly different than earlier intrusions. But the indigenous will to survive lives on. Indigenous peoples have not yet surrendered to the power of external forces. It is important to remember, in order to place the centuries-long struggle in context, that most of the colonial empires which first colonized indigenous societies around the globe have disappeared or declined dramatically. The indigenous societies they colonized have persisted.

What follows, then, is an interweaving of two closely related threads in the lives of indigenous peoples around the world – the processes of externally driven change and the force of internally motivated cultural continuity. The book begins by exploring the manner in which human society divided – and the division was never precise – into surplus-based and needs-based cultures. It documents the manner in which the ideological, spiritual, and economic imperatives of expansion, largely but not exclusively European, resulted in the occupation of indigenous lands and the dislocations of indigenous peoples. It considers the manner in which indigenous peoples responded to the many changes and influences which threatened to overwhelm their lives. By taking the account through to the present, where the politics of assertive and demanding indigenous peoples has re-emerged as a significant influence in world affairs, this study seeks to remind readers about the vital connections between the past and present, history and contemporary grievances, social change and cultural continuity.

Non-indigenous peoples will continue their death watch. They will look for signs – wealthy Native Americans, Maori marrying Pakeha New Zealanders, Aborigines completing university degrees, Inuit children playing video games, Sami moving into cities, alcohol abuse among the Small Peoples of the Russia North – that traditional values are being undermined and that cultural globalization is overcoming the last vestiges of traditional ways. They will be right, in part, just as they are partially accurate when they observe with shallow sorrow the demise of yet another indigenous language and the loss of the cultural knowledge embedded therein. But a greater awareness of history and of the resilience, determination, and creativity of indigenous societies around the world will alert the newcomers to a different pattern, one that they see all too seldom. The continuity of indigenous peoples, the manner in which they have lived, adapted, and responded to powerful, often devastating influences from outside their communities, is a critical element in world history. This, then, is a two-part story, of a difficult and often unsuccessful struggle to overcome the external forces of occupation, colonization, and destruction and of the internal and cultural determination to survive in the face of daunting pressures to change and disappear.

1

PEOPLING THE EARTH: THE GREATEST MIGRATION

The initial peopling of the earth is one of the most remarkable of human experiences, and yet we know very little about this expansion. Over many centuries, and in ways as yet not clearly understood, human beings found their way into virtually all of the habitable areas of the world. Indigenous peoples have clear and consistent explanations for their emergence in their homelands, ideas and explanations which often conflict with the arguments advanced by western science. Archeologists, now joined by biologists, linguists, geneticists, and others, have been painstakingly attempting to reconstruct one of the world's great mysteries. How, when, and why did human beings spread out across the globe? This great migration played a crucial role in shaping human history, and is obviously at the foundation of any attempt to understand the emergence of aboriginal societies.

Aboriginal Accounts of the Origins of the Earth and Human Life

All societies have ways of explaining the origins of the earth and the emergence of humanity. In industrial nations, the scientific ethos is so profound that (even though scientists themselves indicate their theories are, at best, works in progress) all non-scientific explanations for the development of humankind are dismissed as myth and legend. Accounts of creation, however, are a crucial part of the indigenous world view and reflect the deep and profound understanding Aboriginal peoples have of their relationship with the natural environment. These accounts of human origins vary widely across cultures around the world; there is no simple way of capturing the richness and diversity of these spiritual beliefs and cultural traditions.[1]

Consider, for example, the Aborigines Dreamtime story, their account of creation. At the point of creation, the earth lacked distinctive features. There was no night or daytime. All that marked the earth were small hollows, or waterholes. The earth contained all things – the stars, sky, sun, moon, and all forms of life – but everything was asleep. Then, at the Dreamtime, time divided into sleeping and waking time. Life erupted from the earth. The sun burst forth and warmed the earth, bringing more life to the waterholes. Under the waterholes, the Ancestors gave birth to their children, which made up all living things, from plants to animals. As the Ancestors arose from the earth, mud fell from their eyes and they saw what each had created.

They celebrated their creations. One yelled "I am kangaroo." Another proclaimed, "I am cockatoo." Still another announced "I am lizard." They walked as they proudly introduced their creations to the world, calling all living things into being, and through their song and their walking, wove their creation into memory. The Ancestors walked and sang the earth, giving shape to the land and bring life to all of its corners. They left, as well, the songs to mark their passing. The work tired them out, for they had brought all things into creation. Exhausted, they returned to the earth to sleep. The Aborigines of Australia remember their Ancestors and the stories of Dreamtime. When they go walkabout, they are honouring the memory of their Ancestors and retracing the creation experiences of their land.

The Ainu of Japan have provided a variety of creation stories accounting for the emergence of human beings on the earth. In one Ainu account, the creator completed the work of forming the islands, leaving the land without animals or humans. A goddess came to the islands in a divine boat, meeting the shore at a place called Shizunai, where she wrecked upon the rocks. The goddess sought shelter, but struggled to find food and a way to survive. A dog miraculously appeared and saved the goddess by pulling her to a supply of water. The goddess subsequently gave birth to a boy and a girl, being the first inhabitants of the islands. Another Ainu creation story focused on the role of the sun god, Kando Koro Kamui, who was the father of all humans.[2] These stories, which varied quite widely when told to early ethnographers, reveal the fairly standard belief of emerging as peoples on their traditional lands and of owing their existence to the interventions of spiritual powers. According to an early observer, John Norton, the Iroquois creation story began as follows:

> [I]n the beginning before the formation of the earth; the country above the sky was inhabited by Superior Beings over whom the Great Spirit presided. His daughter having become pregnant by an illicit connection, he pulled up a great tree by the roots, and threw her through the cavity thereby formed; but, to prevent her utter destruction, he previously ordered the Great Turtle, to get from the bottom of the waters, some slime on its back, and to wait on the surface of the water to receive her on it. When she had fallen on the back of the Turtle, with the mud she found there, she began to form the earth, and by the time of her delivery had increased it to the extent of a little island. Her child was a daughter, and as she grew up the earth extended under their hands. When the young woman had arrived at the age of discretion, the Spirits who roved about, in human forms, made proposals of marriage for the young woman: the mother rejected their offers, until a middle aged man, of a dignified appearance, his bow in his hand, and his quiver on his back, paid his addresses. On being accepted, he entered the house, and seated himself on the berth of his intended spouse; the mother was in a berth on the other side of the fire. She observed that her son-in-law did not lie down all night; but taking two arrows out of his quiver, he put them by the side of his bride: at the dawn he took them up, and having replaced them in his quiver, he went out.[3]

The remainder of the account describes the disappearance of the husband, the birth of twin boys, Tawiskaron and Teharonghyawago, the death of their mother, and the boys' subsequent conflicts and efforts to populate the Iroquois territories.

There are hundreds of comparable accounts, each rooted in the geographic location of the specific indigenous group and each reflecting the strong relationship between the creative force, the local environment, and the indigenous culture. Among the Hopi, for example, creation originated in caves deep under the earth and was instigated by two brothers who brought humans to the surface. Indigenous groups attribute the creation of the world to the Raven, Eagle, Turtle, the Wind, the Creator, or other mysterious spiritual forces. The creation stories are typically rich in detail, tying critical events in the evolution of the physical and natural world to specific aspects of the local eco-system. Operating without written sacred texts (like the Bible or the Koran), indigenous peoples had a rich understanding of creation and history, available to them through a reading and awareness of their natural setting.

Western Science and Explanations of the First Peoples

Western societies operated, for centuries, on the basis of comparable explanations. Those cultures dominated by the Christian church adhered to very simple chronology, one described in a few short chapters of Genesis, the first book in the Bible. God created the earth, filled it with plant and animal life, added human beings through the bodies of Adam and Eve, and then rested. Biblical literalists dated the creation story to approximately 6,000 years ago, arguing that all of the developments of humankind can be explained within this time frame. The Christian explanation, now referred to as fundamentalist or literalist by critics, held sway for centuries, underpinning European conceptions of human history. Oddly, many of the same Christians who ridiculed indigenous explanations for the origin of the earth and of their societies ignored the contradiction of holding to a biblically based interpretation.

The application of the tools and perspectives of western science to the questions of the origins of humankind and the peopling of the earth began in earnest in the nineteenth century. Archeologists began to scour the globe for evidence of ancient cultures, and speculated on the manner in which the various peoples came into existence. Piece by piece, they gradually created a partially completed puzzle. Early accounts emphasized the importance of the Middle East in the expansion of human settlement, research not coincidentally focused on the region that also spawned Christianity. Most of the gaps were filled with conjecture. While it was easy to figure out how peoples came to live in the northern districts of Siberia or the hills of South East Asia, areas part of the same land mass as Africa and the Middle East, it was much harder to account for the arrival of human beings in North and South America, to say nothing of Australia and the islands of the South Pacific. Two major questions drove the research: how far into the distant past could human or humanoid peoples be identified and, in a different direction, how did the people spread themselves across the world?

The struggle to explain in scientific terms the evolution of human societies faced formidable opposition. This research pointed to an evolutionary path which saw human beings (*homo sapiens*) emerge from their distance ancestors, the apes. Advocates of evolution, like Charles Darwin, attracted the wrath of Christian preachers and politicians. Most people gave little thought to the connections or lack thereof between the societies of Western Europe and the tribal peoples they continued to meet in the wilderness areas of the world. Christianity explained the parts that needed to be known in detail; the rest was a less than compelling story of how societies the world over fell from favour with God. The scientists plugged away, even in the face of vilification by Christian critics. Little by little, in fields as diverse as human evolution and the story of the dinosaurs, scientists began to overwhelm Christian theologians with a preponderance of evidence. European and western governments gradually backed away from an insistence on the literal teaching of the Bible. The solidification of public support behind the scientific method, itself reflecting the excitement of an industrial age fueled by countless discoveries and material improvements, gave greater credence to the work of archeologists and others seeking to explain the origins and movements of humankind.

Through the twentieth century, additional research refined and embellished the early scientific understanding of early human life. Much of the work involved searching for evidence in hitherto little-known districts. Archeologists scoured the Australian outback, river banks in northern Canada and Alaska, unique sites in California and Brazil, underwater locations along the North American coast line and dozens of Pacific islands. Each new discovery provided either more precision, supporting early discoveries, or pushed the date of initial habitation back a few thousand more years.

Refinements have continued into the present. Linguists have identified ties of language and culture which follow the patterns of migration noted by the archeologists. Biologists and geneticists have likewise used new DNA tests to match indigenous societies across vast expanses of time and space. The continued application of carbon dating has provided ever-greater specificity to the discoveries, providing a higher level of confidence in the collective results. But the preponderance of the evidence has not silenced the critics. There has been a resurgent Christian critique of these discoveries. Based largely in the United States, the attempts of the Christian Right to insist upon the teaching of the biblical creation story have forced public debates over these issues. The scientists have prevailed in these discussions (although many Christians have responded by pulling their children from public schools and sending them to Christian institutions).

Archeologists and their allies have rejected the idea of polygenesis (the suggestion that human beings emerged in more than one place on earth) and argued for monogenesis (which held that all human beings emerged from a single location). Research focused increasingly on Africa, capped by the discoveries of Richard Leakey, whose 1975 uncovering of the skeleton of "*Homo erectus*" appeared to provide convincing evidence that the cradle of human existence lay in the center of this vast continent. Other discoveries of early human existence in Asia, North America, and South America added complexity and accuracy to the puzzle. It appeared as though a map of the greatest migration was finally coming together.

The insistence on monogenesis angered many indigenous peoples, who saw centuries-old explanations rejected as little more than fairy tales. The scientists seemingly rigid adherence to the proof afforded by a handful of archaeological sites and a small amount of evidence further frustrated tribal societies, whose oral evidence for their interpretation of the history of their peoples seemed abundant in comparison. The rejection of indigenous explanations, and the refusal of most scientists to assign much credence to aboriginal knowledge, drove a wedge between indigenous peoples and those who sought to explain human evolution in scientific terms. Aboriginal communities rose up in protest against the very practice of archaeology, which involved the disinterring of ancestors for the purposes of science. The uncategorical tossing aside of indigenous beliefs and the rummaging around in indigenous burial sites combined to create a forceful tribal critique of the scientific enterprise.

Struggles with archeologists erupted around the world. A highly publicized case at the beginning of the twentieth century involved Minik, a Inuit boy from Greenland. Minik had been brought to the United States by the famed and controversial explorer Robert Peary. His troubled life in that country was capped by the discovery of his father's skeleton in the American Museum of Natural History and by his spirited battle to regain control of his father's remains. Native Americans battled with scientists across the United States and insisted upon having ancient remains returned to their people for reburial.[4] While cooperative arrangements were often worked out, allowing research to be completed before the internment in undisclosed locations, several bitter controversies broke out. The most noteworthy involved Kennewick Man, a body discovered in 1996 on the banks of the Columbia River in the Pacific Northwest and dated between 8,000 and 9,300 years old. Early examination of the remains suggested the existence of a society not connected genetically to the current tribal inhabitants of the region. In other words, the people long considered to have been indigenous to the area may have been preceded, perhaps by centuries, by other cultures. Native Americans protested and insisted through the courts that the human remains be returned to them. Scientists fought back, arguing that the current Native American population were not their ancestors and therefore had no claims on the bones. Further, they argued, the needs of science outweighed the political demands of the local Native Americans. Bitter conflict ensured, resulting in a hotly contested decision to honour the Native American Graves Protection and Repatriation Act and return the remains to the Native Americans, an act that has been postponed in appeals. (In an unexpected twist, the Kennewick debate also resulted in a claim by a Samoan, Joseph Siofele, who argued that the skeleton was from Samoa and he therefore had rights of ownership.)

The contest was not restricted to the United States, although the most widely publicized debates occurred in that country. Australia had perhaps the most vigorous conflict, sparked in large measure by the scale and rapaciousness of the collection of Aboriginal remains in the late nineteenth and early twentieth centuries. High-level political and legal battles managed to embarrass museums, universities, and other collectors into recognizing the difficulty of retaining the materials. On a broader scale, Aboriginal peoples approached museums and galleries around the world, seeking to repatriate human remains and artefacts, a significant number of which were claimed to have been stolen from indigenous grave sites. By the end of the twentieth century, numerous museums had agreed to repatriation processes, much to the delight of the indigenous communities.

The cultural and political battles over indigenous remains have had a direct effect on the scientific search for further evidence of the Great Migrations. Archeologists found indigenous peoples more reluctant to provide access to tribal sites. New protocols in western nations restricted the scientists' freedom and required the negotiation of suitable arrangements well in advance of the field work. Further, the politicization of the battle over the interpretation of the evidence was seen by some scientists as limiting academic freedom. The possibility looms that the contemporary struggles will discourage new scholars from entering the field and will convince governments and funding agencies to refrain from funding such research. There are other problems as well. In Japan, fevered interest in the early dating of human occupation of the Japanese archipelago created a situation where an amateur archeologist fraudulently seeded a number of critical sites, temporarily sparking a nationalist frenzy about the longevity of the Japanese occupation of the islands. This said, major discoveries continue to be made. Within the last decade, explorations in Australia have solidified the understanding that Aborigines have been on the continent for at least 40,000 and possibly 60,000 years. These numbers proved particularly potent during Australia's bicentenary celebrations in 1988. Aboriginal politicians, pointing to the 40,000 years of their habitation, referred to their bicentenary of a bicentenary. Continued explorations in Africa have enriched the scientific understanding of human habitation on that continent. In one of the most hotly contested developments, researchers active along Canada's west coast have provided evidence challenging the longstanding interpretation of how indigenous peoples settled western North America. More recent work, focusing on the nineteenth and twentieth centuries, has provided additional documentation about the impact of disease and, through newly introduced scientific methods, nutrition, health, life expectancy, and the like among indigenous populations. Archeology is far from moribund as a scientific discipline, and work on indigenous societies continues, often with the active participation of aboriginal communities, and increased training of aboriginal researchers.

The Scientific Explanation for the Great Migration

Assuming that the scientific approach has merit, if not the final word, it is useful to summarize the collective account of the movement of human beings into the far corners of the world. The description offered here is, of necessity, brief. Moreover, in the comparative absence of evidence, it rests on a vast and complex array of data points, conjecture and educated supposition. It remains a work in progress, with scientific work continuing and with the interpreting of the dates of key movements continuing to generate enormous debate. One of the most useful books on this complex and highly politicized debate, Kerry Howe's study of the settlement of New Zealand, *The Quest for Origins*, documents how positions on Maori migration reflect changing assumptions about contemporary New Zealand, widely speculative conceptions of human movements, the application of the hard science of genetics and DNA research to what have been historical and archaeological questions, and the complex world of contemporary indigenous politics.

The best evidence suggests that the first humans evolved in central Africa. From an initially tenuous base, and over tens of thousands of years, the populations inhabited the resource-rich territories in this area. Population pressures and, no doubt, curiosity resulted in people gradually expanding into temperate zones to the south and north. It is likely, given the abundance of land rich in animal, fish, bird, and plant life, that they moved around and through resource-poor regions. Deserts, tundra lands, dense jungles, and the like may have attracted short-term inhabitants, but they likely moved on to contiguous areas which offered easier harvesting opportunities. But this assumption, like so many related to the movement of humankind, may reflect contemporary sensibilities and may not actually explain the patterns and direction of migration.

Archeological sites in what is now known as the Middle East, Europe, South Asia, China, Japan, and elsewhere chart the gradual expansion of human populations. The movements were extremely slow, taking hundreds if not thousands of years to cover relatively small distances. It is assumed – assumption being a critical element in the analysis of early populations and cultures – that population surplus, wars, or other conflicts, or severe declines in resources related to climate change, volcanic eruptions, or other natural phenomena, convinced fragment groups to leave the main society and head into previously unknown territory. Curiosity played a role as well, as tribal explorers, adventurers, and warriors pressed on in search of new lands, new opportunities for leadership, and new resources. And so, slowly and inexorably, the landscape of Eurasia came under human occupation. In each ecological niche, a new culture gradually evolved, reflecting the unique characteristics of the people, resources, and geography. And so it was, over a very long time, that the cultural map of Africa, Asia, and Europe unfolded.

If, as the science suggests, human societies headed first for ecologically rich areas, vast expanses of Eurasia remained substantially empty. Across the deserts of the Middle East and Africa, in the high mountain areas of South Asia, and across the vast tundra lands of the far north, the quality of resources and the nature of the climate served as a deterrent to, not an incentive for, expansion. Over time, neighboring and often surrounding territories were fully occupied, at a level consistent with subsistence societies. Pressure mounted, again, for population to expand into new zones. Over hundreds of years, people moved into the cold lands of Siberia and northern Scandinavia (particularly the inland districts), found secure places in the jungles of central Africa and in desert

territories across that continent and through Asia, and moved successfully into the high mountain regions, particularly in South Asia.
The expansion also continued to the south. Debate continues about
how the first inhabitants crossed the Straits of Malacca and reached the
Australian continent. There is also a great deal of controversy about
when this migration occured. The widely accepted date is approximately
40,000 years ago; some discoveries have suggested that the first habitation could be dated some 20,000 years earlier. Scientists have speculated
that the Aborigines either crossed over to Australia by boat or, depending on the timing of the migration, could have walked south at a time
when an ice age lowered the ocean levels sufficiently to make such
passage possible.

New social groups formed in what had initially been seen as harsh and
unfriendly areas. These societies, the ancestors of the tribal peoples of
the nineteenth and twentieth centuries, adapted their harvesting activities, seasonal movements and lifeways to the realities of cold/hot,
dry/wet, rocky/sandy environments. They soon differed in values, customs, and activities from those peoples inhabiting richer ecological
niches, where experiments in agriculture eventually produced subsistence and later surplus agriculture. Such options were generally not
available in the more harsh lands inhabited by tribal peoples, although
rich fishing, hunting, or gathering grounds often provided these societies with a steady and reliable food supply and with the resources
necessary to build complex societies.

The settlement of Eurasia left almost half the world's land surface
uninhabited. From the early days of European exploration, western
thinkers puzzled about the origins of the peoples in North and South
America and across the islands of the Pacific. Some attributed these societies, biblically, to the lost tribe of Israel. Others assumed that they were
not fully human and therefore need not to be accounted for in terms of
relationships to other populations. But the question remained: how did
human beings end up in the western hemisphere? Did lengthy boat
journeys, perhaps from Africa, bring the first peoples across the
Atlantic? Later, when the idea of continental drift established the
likelihood that South America and Africa had once been joined
geographically, it was proposed that human beings had been left on
either side of dividing continents, even though the geological movement
easily predated the emergence of *homo sapiens*.

Evidence drawn from the animal kingdom provided the first compelling pieces of the puzzle. The realization, based on mastodon bones

and other ancient animal remains found in Alaska, that there had once been a land bridge across what is now the Bering Strait, created a new possibility. Human beings could, during the final stages of the last great ice age, have followed animal populations across the Bering land bridge and into what is now Alaska. The northwest corner of North America was not covered by sheet ice, like the center of the continent, and there appear to have been abundant harvestable resources in this region. Subsequent archeological discoveries demonstrated that tribal peoples had been in the area for thousands of years – at least 12,000 and possibly as many as 25,000. These dates rocked the scientific world and generated extensive debate several decades ago, for the evidence established that indigenous peoples had been in North America for a very long time indeed.

Linguistic evidence subsequently made it clear to scientists that the indigenous peoples of Alaska were related to the tribal societies of the American Southwest. The simple matter of getting from Alaska to the middle part of the continent, however, was complicated by a basic problem – a large ice sheet stretched across the mid-West and much of what is now the Rocky Mountains. How did the people migrate southward in the face of this forbidding and formidable barrier? Geologists and glaciologists identified a late ice-age shift which created a corridor between the Rockies and the slowly retreating ice-sheets. This corridor, archeologists and others argued, was the passage that the early inhabitants needed to make their way from the far north to the center of the continent. There was little detailed evidence to back this supposition, but it retained considerable currency over the following decades. Sceptics pointed out that the retreating ice sheets left a land barren of plant and animal life, and that it would have taken centuries for the corridor to have provided sufficient nutrients to sustain migrating peoples. In the absence of competing evidence and interpretations, however, the Bering Strait and ice corridor argument held sway.

At the end of the twentieth century, a new idea found favor. Scientists realized that the water level was much lower along the coast during the last ice age. Evidence of early southward migrations, they reasoned, would likely be found at ancient sites now lying dozens of feet underwater. Preliminary excavations and further analysis provided additional support for the argument that the early inhabitants of North America made their way south along the coast. Having reached an area south of the ice sheet, the argument goes, they then headed further south and east, eventually peopling the entire continent. The leading scholar of this development, K. R. Fladmark, concluded:

> Given the presence of inhabitable refugia, available resources, and a culture able to reach and exploit them, we can hypothesize that people moved southwards and eastwards around the North Pacific. They used watercraft to cross larger water gaps in the summer, while sea ice may have aided travel in other seasons ... . Here, eventual movement inland along major rivers such as the Columbia once again prompted a split between coastal and interior cultural variants, leading ultimately on the one hand to the hunting and gathering cultures of the interior intermountain regions, and on the other hand providing the in situ basis for later coastal and riverine cultures.[5]

Other competing interpretations emerged. A suggestive, but not conclusive, discovery in South America appeared to predate the earliest scientific discoveries in the far north. Was it possible that humans had migrated westward from Africa, populated the southern continent and then moved northward? A few went so far as to argue that the migration might have been the opposite of what had long been held: namely, that the first peoples emerged in the western hemisphere and then moved westward to Eurasia. Speculation vied with assertion in the attempt to provide a scientific foundation for the explanation of indigenous habitation of North America.

Few archeologists argue against the prevailing wisdom, which holds that the first peoples of North America crossed the Bering Strait and, over hundreds of years, moved southward and then eastward. The dating of sites from Alaska to the Canadian Maritimes and from the American Southwest to Florida appeared to support this argument. The northeast appeared to have had its first migrants about 7000–8000 BCE, becoming the last of the temperate areas to be occupied. The migration, scientists argue, pushed steadily to the south, until the entire continent from the northern sub-Arctic to Patagonia (southern Argentina and Chile) was occupied. The process took several millennia. In the process, groups separated one from the other, creating unique cultures tied closely to their specific environment and reflecting the unique combination of human characteristics and natural ecosystem which is indicative of the tribal world.

Continued archaeological research has made the picture of early habitation more complicated and, on occasion, less clear. Discoveries at Monte Verde in southern Chile

> revealed evidence preserved in a peat bog for about twelve and a half millennia: a twenty foot-long, wood-built, hide-covered dwelling with a big mastodon

butchery and tool manufactory nearby ... This discovery stood the early history of the Americas on its head: the received story unfolded from north and south, but now the most impressive early culture – judged by material standards – had emerged in the far south, deep inside the South American cone.[6]

How this discovery fits into broader continental patterns remains to be seen. The high Arctic regions, among the least hospitable environments on the globe, had not attracted human inhabitants as late as 6000 BCE. A warming trend around this time made the area more attractive. Late migrants from western Siberia, searching for new fields to explore and settle, pushed into the Alaskan district. Finding the sub-Arctic regions occupied, they moved north- and eastward, gradually spreading along the coastline and eventually up to the Arctic islands and across to Greenland. During this Thule period, they occupied territory as far north as Ellesmere Island, capitalizing on the surprisingly rich food resources to be found on the land and in the waters of the region. Subsequent cooling forced the initial inhabitants, ancestors of today's Inuit, further south. Many capitalized on the huge caribou herds of the eastern Arctic; others built their lives around fish, whales, seals, and other resources. By 4000 BCE even the vast Arctic regions had been occupied.

The Great Migration was not yet complete. The vast Pacific basin, millions of square miles of ocean dotted by hundreds of small island archipelagos and coral reefs, remained unoccupied. The development of ocean-going boats, fitted with sails, and navigation techniques made it possible for people to venture out into the Pacific. And venture out they did, in a serious of daring and heroic expeditions well-documented in indigenous oral tradition. The migrations occurred in two separate strands. The first involved a Melanesian expansion originate in South East Asia and involved the gradual migration through Micronesia, the Solomon Islands, Papua New Guinea, and Vanuatu. Uniquely Melanesian cultures developed in these areas, reflecting a certain level of cultural continuity and regional difference. These migrations were comparatively straightforward, involving the movement from one island system to another and a gradual filling in of the western portion of the Pacific.

But consider the remaining challenge – peopling the disparate islands of the Pacific. A navigator with modern maps and navigation equipment would find this a daunting task. Tackling this same assignment with ancient vessels and no knowledge of the outlying islands and oceans is one of the most formidable challenges in human history. One scholar,

Geoffrey Irwin, argues that the Polynesians ventured forth with care and planning. He argued that they waited until weather systems turned in unusual directions, counting on the standard prevailing winds to return them to the point of departure (if need be). This explanation, which challenges the standard explanation that the immigrants faced serious dangers and suffered substantial losses, fits logically with the unusual pattern of settlement, which started in the west and moved steadily east.

However they managed it – either through a carefully developed strategy or a hit-and-miss approach – the Polynesians completed a remarkable migration. The expansion is generally believed to have originated in China/Taiwan, spreading in 1600–1200 BCE from New Guinea (Melanesia) and spreading east to Fiji, Samoa, and Tonga. Navigators pushed further afield. Somewhere around 3000 BCE, Samoans and Tongas reached the Cook Islands, Tahiti and the Marquesas Islands. Hundreds of years later, around 300 CE, migrants reached Easter Island and, about 100 years later, expanded northward to Hawaii. The expansion then doubled back on itself, reaching Aotearoa (New Zealand) somewhere around 900–1250 CE. Each expedition resulted in the establishment of a new society in the recently discovered islands, most of which were rich with fish and plant resources and which could easily hold substantial populations. The migrations themselves were of crucial importance to the newly established societies. Maori populations in New Zealand – there is a debate as to whether or not they were the first or second significant population to reach the islands – traced their origins to one of the canoes which made the voyage to New Zealand.

The completion of this ethnographic puzzle has taken scientists decades, and the work is far from finished. Oral testimony has played an important role in the investigation, as tribal traditions provided significant evidence of the timing and origins of specific explorations. (Maori oral testimony, for example, spoke of the departure of canoes from Hawaiki, and the consistency of this reference made the location of Hawaiki a matter for intense speculation among scholars.) Archeologists have relied on the traditional techniques of excavation to document population movements and to better understand their cultures. In more recent years, genetics and linguistics research have further clarified complex historic relationships and provided greater confidence as to the precise nature of migrations and societal contacts across the Pacific. Ethno-botanical research on the distribution of plants has proven of particular value in this region as it documents the carriage of food sources – taro, sugar cane, bamboo, yam, banana, coconut, and sweet potato, among others – by the migrants and offers compelling evidence of the movement of peoples throughout the Pacific.

There is little documentation about the wonder and glory of new discoveries that greeted the first peoples to walk or float into new lands. History books are filled with accounts of Europeans' first reaction to newly discovered lands. These descriptions speak to their wonderment at seeing vast herds of bison, kangaroos, the magnificent Foz de Igazu (the massive waterfalls on the Brazil/Paraguay border), the intricate jungles of Africa and other stunning sights and sounds of the new worlds. The first humans similarly stumbled upon countless new discoveries. What, we can only imagine, was the reaction of Polynesians making the first sighting of land after weeks on small craft, of peoples crossing the Bering Strait and seeing the vast expanse of the Yukon River basin, of Aborigines making their way onto the Australian continent, of people witnessing for the first time the massive schools of salmon along the west coast, and the thousands of other encounters between the migrants and their newly found homelands? They saw more than land and water; they also encountered new plants, new animals, and identified the opportunity and the need to adapt to the new surroundings.

The adaptations of the first inhabitants often carried significant costs. Animal, plant, and bird life in the new lands lived for generations without the most creative and systematic of all predators, human beings. Large birds, like the moa in New Zealand, had little chance against the Maori. Large, slow-moving animals in North America appear to have disappeared following the arrival of the first peoples. These changes, and many like them, are hardly surprising, for all human societies have encountered difficulties responding to new eco-systems. In subsequent generations, non-indigenous newcomers wrecked havoc on newly inhabited biospheres, planting the wrong crops, diverting water to disastrous effect, overhunting valued species, and undermining the local ecosystem by introducing alien species. The participants in the Great Migration had nothing like the massive impact of subsequent wealth-driven economic and social movements, but they did not walk as gently on the land as the Ancestors soon learned to do.

Conclusion

The Great Migration, as described through the insights of western science, overlapped with the more widely known and discussed expansion of Europe. The process began tens of thousands of years ago, and involved an incredible series of expeditions, adaptations. As early as 1000 CE, Viking explorers and migrants headed west from Iceland in search of new territories, discovering Greenland, already occupied, and the east coast of North America, also already occupied. At roughly the same time, the final stage in the Great Migration was taking place in the southwest corner of the Pacific Islands, as the ancestors of the Maori moved to Aotearoa, thus completing the remarkable habitation of the Pacific Islands. Throughout the long history of humankind, whether marked by oral tradition or documented through western science, people moved, expanded, adapted, and responded. They reacted to human forces – competition for resources, territorial rivalries, and a desire to explore new territories – and to natural influences – volcanic eruptions, periods of warming, ice ages and mini-ice ages, and the climatic cycles and changes in the animal, plant, and fish populations.

Historians have typically divided the history of the world into pre- and post-contact periods. The expansion of Europe has long been viewed as the pivotal process in human history, bringing the complex, technological societies of the northern hemisphere into contact with hundreds of different tribal and settlement populations. This division of human evolution still resonates in our understanding of societal relationships, for the residue of the colonial era is often cited as being the cause of the disruption and dislocation of indigenous cultures. While this approach makes considerable sense in the context of contemporary political debates, it does not explain the broader, global pattern of the nature of the tribal experience. Nor does it properly account for the fact that many people, from the early *homo sapiens* in central Africa to the Polynesians, from tribespeople in South Asia to the first inhabitants of Alaska, went through similar processes of expansion. And, like the Europeans who set out to explore the world, they went in search of resources, room for excess population, and to satisfy an innate curiosity about the earth.

Until the twentieth century – and even now in some quarters – non-indigenous views of tribal societies suggested that these peoples were "savage," "uncivilized," and "barbarian." The next chapter explores the nuances and characteristics of several of the hundreds of diverse and complex societies that made up the tribal world. They were (and are) responsive to their environments, their values and cultures reflecting a deep sensitivity to their surroundings. The peopling of the earth is one of the remarkable and little-known stages in the history of humankind.

It is subject to countless interpretations and to a fierce although often unspoken tension between the analysis of western science and indigenous interpretations of the origins of the world and human settlement. These stories, in any of the many versions, share common elements: the length of time involved, the deep ties between indigenous peoples and their surroundings, and the creativity and determination of the first inhabitants of each of the world's unique ecological zones.

2

PEOPLES OF THE LAND: SPIRITUAL AND CULTURAL ROOTS OF INDIGENOUS SOCIETIES

At no time in history have human populations been static. From the earliest centuries, societies expanded, contracted, fought, cooperated, merged, conquered, collapsed, struggled, adapted, and innovated. Peoples of a variety of cultural backgrounds undertook lengthy explorations and sought to impose their will on neighbors or distant societies, often with little success. The indigenous societies of historic times (that is, typically and inaccurately tied to the point of European expansion) have not been fixed for all time, any more than have other human populations. Some had retreated into isolated corners in the face of the advance of other cultures, seeking to maintain a way of life. Others had been forced off traditional lands and pushed into less desirable territories, where they faced little competition for resources. For all peoples, the passage of time was marked by change, choice, and a struggle to determine their destiny.

For most of human history – and among many societies to the present day – subsistence living was the norm. These peoples lived off the fruits of hunting, fishing, and gathering, supplemented by minimal agricultural activity. These societies lived very close to the land, their prosperity resting on the ability to understand and adjust to the seasons, the movements of animals and fish, and the uncertainties of climate. They suffered at times and feasted on other occasions. They developed social structures, rules and codes, interpreted the spiritual world, and purposefully created a human infrastructure around their physical setting.

Tribal peoples once inhabited the forests of France and Spain; the famed cave paintings of Lascaux and Chauvet Pont D'Arc came from these societies. The ancestors of contemporary Han and Cantonese (Chinese) and Japanese cultures migrated into new lands in ways strikingly similar to those of the Apache, Maori, and Sami. Historians used to portray the human experience as a contest between primitivism and progress, and slotted societies into several key blocks: those locked in tribal barbarism, those which responded to the possibilities of agriculture and, at the top of the racial hierarchy these writers constructed, those whose commitment to "progress" resulted in greater social complexity, the development of surplus-based economies, and the early stages of industrialization and innovation. This simplistic evolutionary structure became the foundation of the European story, and was a potent element in the narrative of other expansive cultures, including several on the Indian subcontinent, China's ruling dynasties and the aggressive societies of Japan. While this culturally insensitive division of the peoples of the world into simple categories is no longer accepted uncritically, the reality holds that societies did not follow a common path throughout history.

Over centuries, major developments occurred in the economic and social structures of many peoples around the world. Societies living on rich soils and in temperate climates discovered the potential of agriculture and livestock raising. The adaptive process was often slow, and involved a great deal of experimentation and failure, but new social structures slowly emerged. Agriculture fostered a sedentary lifestyle, provided that the farmers learned how to replenish the nutrients in the soil. The production of agricultural surpluses permitted other social changes, including specialization in work, more complex social hierarchies, and greater emphasis on leisure time. These societies spent a great deal of time interpreting the spiritual world, thus developing the theological and organizational foundations of complex religions. Innovations in government, military structures, and economic relationships and procedures likewise built off the reliability of agricultural production and the certainty of sustainable surpluses.

For hundreds of years, the standard assumption was that this evolutionary path was unique to the European sphere. From beginnings in the Middle East, and gradually moving northward through Greece and Rome to Western Europe and the British Isles, western civilizations changed in response to the complex interplay of human invention, military conquest, and economic adaptation. Societies that had once battled for supremacy in the Mediterranean, like those led by Alexander the Great and Julius Caesar, sought to extend empires into distant lands. They were, in time, superseded by the aggressive Mongols and later by the increasingly technologically rich and economically expansive societies of Northern Europe. These struggles for control of portions of what is now Europe and contiguous territories eventually led the kingdoms of Portugal, Spain, France, Holland, and England to extend the European empire to distant territories. The urge to expand, in turn, was driven in substantial measure by shortages of land and resources at home, and by the increasing demands of a growing and sedentary society for food, luxury goods, and raw materials.

Other societies made similar, and in some areas, more dramatic transitions from subsistence lifestyles to surplus economies. The dynasties of China, for example, were more complex, technologically advanced, literate, and theologically enriched than those of Western Europe at the time of European expansion. For a variety of reasons, however, Chinese leaders chose after the fifteenth century not to launch expansionary activities or to impose themselves on other societies. These peoples did not believe that their future lay in the conquest of foreign lands and peoples. Similarly, the major dynasties of South Asia produced remarkable works of architecture, rich literatures, and strongly differentiated societies. They used their control of government and the military to impose their will on vast peasant populations. And it was much the same in Japan, where ancient societies had tight hierarchies, complex social values and customs, and extensive agricultural development. The Mayan, Tawantinsuyu (or Four Directions, the proper name for the group generally called the Inca) and Aztec societies, plus lesser-known cultural complexes like the peoples who lived in the Mississippi and Pueblo cultures in the southwest, built large-scale settlements and were among the most densely populated and architecturally gifted in the world. The settlement at Cahokia, in the Mississippi, was, in the thirteenth century, home to some 10,000 people. Communities in Mexico and Peru were easily as large. Large settlements, long dismissed as the imaginings of the earliest European explorers, were also found in the Amazon basin, hosting complex societies with considerable artistic and productive capacity. It is easy to forget that these societies had complicated hierarchical political systems, intensive agriculture, and detailed religious formulations. Much less well-known but equally impressive empires flourished in central Africa, where dominant rulers created elaborate kingdoms and controlled large populations. In almost all instances, extensive agriculture produced large food surpluses which, in turn, fueled trade and economic diversification. Likewise, the production of surpluses resulted in other adaptations, including complex social structures, religious institutions, urban environments, and occupational change.

The process of social differentiation had been underway for centuries, forcing societies to make critical choices, both personal and collective, about how they intended to organize their affairs. Societies did not all follow the subsistence–agriculture–pre-industrial–industrial pathway which was long assumed to be the only logical progression, and which ultimately drove the process of exploration and expansion. The urban societies of the Mississippi, for example, did not evolve into a long-term stable and expansive order. The Aztec and Mayan societies did not develop industrial processes and commit themselves to overseas navigation. The Chinese, as noted, held back from imposing themselves on other societies. The Japanese developed a strong agricultural base and formidable armies but sought the protection of separation, not the opportunities of expansion. In point of fact, relatively few societies sought to reach far beyond their boundaries. Those that did were propelled by dreams of wealth and spiritual conviction, by the imperatives of discovery and the technologies of navigation and warfare.

Indigenous peoples generally stayed even further removed from the subsistence-to-industrial transition. They did so in part because their traditional territories lacked the environmental basis for stable agriculture. By sticking with mobile harvesting pursuits, they simply made the most efficient pre-industrial use of available resources. Peoples like those in the African and Australian deserts, in dense jungles, and in the sub-Arctic and Arctic followed this approach. Others, like the peoples of the Pacific Islands, the Maori of Aotearoa (New Zealand), societies along the salmon-rich west coast of North America and in selected other locations had abundant food, rich ceremonial life, and a comfortable, reliable existence. Agriculture was either not required or was not suitable. In many other areas – the vast temperate expanse of North and South America – agriculture was possible and was practised to a reasonable extent. Even here, however, the unreliability of cultivated crops and the consistent availability of other food stuffs (fish, large game, and wild plants) removed the pressure to develop more complex agricultural systems.

Indigenous peoples were famously described by anthropologist Marshall Sahlins as the "original affluent society." Sahlins contended that affluence is a cultural construct. People are affluent when they feel that they have achieved the material and personal well-being expected within their society. In contemporary western industrial society, true affluence has been pegged at nearly unreachable heights, available only to rock stars, professional athletes and a handful of extremely rich entrepreneurs. Indigenous peoples, in contrast, placed little value on material wealth – what possessions they owned had to be carried about when camps moved, making them something of a liability – and empha- sized leisure time, travel, story-telling, and cultural opportunities. Sahlins argued that these peoples did not, as the stereotype had it, spend every hour of their lives searching for food. Rather, he suggested that they met their food and material needs with comparatively little effort – much less time and work, for example, than required by an early industrial factory worker or the long-suffering agrarian yeoman. Their world was not, it bears repeating, without hardship; indigenous and non-indigenous life in the pre-industrial age was fraught with uncer- tainty. But it is equally crucial to note that indigenous peoples were not living a life of perpetual hardship, a condition from which they were desperate to escape.

Why, the question remains, did some people remain in tribal settings long after the first encounters with technologically enriched, colonial, or industrial societies? In the harshest construction of societal change, tribal peoples have been characterized as the societies progress left behind. Many expansionists simply could not believe that the indige- nous societies would not be awestruck by the new order and would not leap to emulate it. The simple fact of cultural survival was evidence of inherent primitivism. More liberal scholars, like John Bodley, have described tribal peoples as "victims of progress." In this formulation, the proponents of western "civilization" and modernization ran amok over tribal cultures, seeing little of more than curiosity value in them and assuming that change toward European or industrial norms was pre- ferred. Indigenous political leaders, in contrast, emphasize two key ele- ments in the adaptive process: a preference for determining the pace of change away from a harvesting, mobile lifestyle and the lack of effective control over social trajectories under colonial regimes. They argue, con- vincingly, that indigenous peoples opposed forced change, not change itself. They point to numerous examples of indigenous societies volun- tarily adopting and adapting many aspects of colonial cultures and to an even greater number of examples of aboriginal peoples denied the opportunity to participate fully in newly established economic and social regimes.

Seen on a broader scale, it is clear that indigenous peoples, occupying well-defined ecological niches and comfortable with their way of life, were not desperate to adjust to a new social, economic, or political order. These societies survived, and survive, because of the inherent momentum of cultures, because they adapted and resisted as required, and because the people saw much that was valuable in their traditional ways. In many places around the world, the indigenous way made sense, and people maintained cultural traditions over hundreds, if not thousands of years. These societies varied enormously, from salmon-based societies in the Pacific Northwest to desert cultures in the Kalahari Desert. They bore little resemblance to each other; the cultural difference between a Sami reindeer herder and a Yanomami hunter was as great as that between a sixteenth-century British laborer and a Chinese rice farmer. What the indigenous societies shared in common was a deep and complex relationship within their natural world, one which presumed no fundamental superiority over the land, the plants, and the animals.

A connection to the land suffuses the tribal world. Indigenous peoples find their medicines in the plants and their sustenance in the rivers and streams. The mountains, stars, and trees define their spiritual worlds. Many such societies have elaborate rituals of thanks and prayers associated with the taking of animals for food, for they believe themselves to share spiritual space with the very beings which sustain their lives. Knowledge of the land became deeply embedded in the language and vocabulary. Landmarks are used both to record historical events or processes and to mark significant cultural and sacred sites. To speak an indigenous language is to gain access to the history, cultural, values, and understandings of a centuries-old people. Indigenous peoples are oral peoples, who emphasize the skills of story-telling and the rituals of dance and ceremony as a primary means of maintaining values, collective knowledge, and shared understandings.

The tribal societies themselves varied enormously in structure and function. In the harshest lands on earth – the high Arctic and in certain desert areas – a concentration of population could quickly overwhelm local resources and create hardship and starvation. Under such conditions, the people generally traveled in extended family groups, gathering as seasons and resources dictated for collective ceremonial, economic, and other activities. These societies remained flexible, mobile, and highly responsive. Other populations which see themselves, in the early twenty-first century, as indigenous historically had much more complex structures. The Maori, for example, lived a largely sedentary life and had a great deal of formality to their social hierarchy, cultural activities, and political structures. Their social order was not dissimilar to that of other Pacific island peoples and those on Pacific Northwest coast, but was radically different from that of the tribal peoples in the Chittagong Hills or in Siberia. Social structure reflected, in many ways, ecological conditions and opportunities. Stable and massive salmon runs on the Pacific coast provided an equally sure foundation for social organization as the herds of bison on the Great Plains of North America, but the required harvesting systems differed greatly. One required mobility and the other favored occupancy of key fishing spots.

As suggested in the introduction, the definition of indigenous societies owes a great deal to contemporary circumstances. The Japanese, Germans, Thais, and many others shifted away from subsistence lifestyles toward, over centuries, lifeways based on a sedentary existence, specialization of work, the creation and marketing of economic surpluses, and ultimately to pre-industrial and industrial production and social organization. One rarely looks upon these nations and societies as indigenous (even though Japan and Thailand have indigenous minorities in their midst). Other cultures, typically preserved by distance, isolation, and the limited agricultural potential of their homelands, remained outside the commercial/industrial world until the nineteenth and twentieth centuries. In these areas, the subsistence or mobile existence is either a strong memory or a continuing element in indigenous life. Although indigenous societies, both over the centuries and in contemporary times, vary widely in social, economic, and cultural profile, certain key elements can be seen as integral to all of them.

Indigenous societies have traditionally been built around a symbiotic relationship with their homelands. Harvesting patterns and land-use cycles reflected the movements of animals and fish, the changing of the seasons, and the specific characteristics of local or regional eco-systems. Several of the most culturally diverse areas in the world – the Top End of Australia, the Amazon basin and Papau New Guinea – each hosted dozens of distinct indigenous societies, each one well-adapted to the specific resources and harvesting opportunities of a relatively small eco-system. In arid and less ecologically rich areas, such as Siberia, the Canadian North or the Australian outback, small numbers of indigenous peoples inhabited vast tracts of territories, roaming widely over the land in a well-rehearsed and knowledge-rich pursuit of limited sources of food and water. The indigenous societies identified closely with their specific setting and developed cultural forms, habits, movements, and harvesting activities which permitted them to sustain life in a particular ecological niche. Life in these societies revolved around rich and complex belief systems. Christian missionaries who later moved among indigenous populations in a search for souls often decried the absence of codified and highly ceremonial religions. But many of these missionaries identified deeply held and widely shared spiritual beliefs. The spiritual worlds appeared, on the surface, to vary enormously. They shared many characteristics, however, including a general confidence in the afterlife, a belief in a powerful god or gods and, most critically, the assumption that the natural world was suffused with spiritual authority, opportunity, and danger. In the indigenous world, animals, fish, plants, and the elements all had and exercised power. The close identification with the physical surroundings, therefore, blended with the indigenous belief that they lived in a highly spiritualized environment, one that demanded interpretation and interaction by spiritual leaders.

Indigenous societies were not, in the main, extensively organized; in fact, one of the most commonly used definitions of indigenous populations is that they functioned as small-scale societies, with little hierarchical or organizational complexity. The dictates of natural settings and the social imperatives attached to near-constant mobility militated against the establishment of permanent settlements or highly coordinated political structures. While many non-European groups – the Aztec, Incas, Chinese, Indians, and others – developed complex social and political systems that rivaled European nations in scale and authority, indigenous societies (by definition) lacked the formality and organizational rigidity of these other populations. These peoples did have strong social structures and observable political organization and activities, and strong social mores and convictions. The Mohawk of the North American Great Lakes, the Maori of New Zealand, other Pacific Islanders, and many other peoples had hierarchical social and political systems, with identifiable power structures, clear leadership authority, and considerable permanence. Small-scale societies, particularly those living in the resource-poor regions which dictated extensive seasonal movements, had less formalized systems, typically working through extended families/ clans and loose affiliations between peoples sharing a common language.

In the nineteenth and twentieth centuries, pivotal political and legal debates erupted around the globe focusing on a single critical question: did the indigenous peoples have a system of land ownership and tenure? European and derivative societies, operating with highly codified land tenure systems, looked for evidence of property holding, clear land titles, and a clearly identified system for determining resource ownership. Seeing none, they declared the land to be open for development and settlement. In Australia, famously, the High Court declared that the continent had been *terra nullius* (or empty land) at the time of European discovery. This interpretation, a variation of which has been asserted in many countries around the world, ignored centuries-old indigenous occupations of the land and declared it open for non-indigenous use. Without land title documents and, equally important, without being able to demonstrate that the land had been placed into economically productive use, the indigenous peoples were unable to demonstrate to colonial or European fragment governments that they "owned" the land in accordance with European standards.

Tribal land use was typically understood in terms of stewardship and responsibility, rather than ownership. Land was to be used, but not destroyed. Resources could and should be taken from the land, but logic and spiritual necessity dictated that the land had to be left in a sustainable and natural state. In the post-World War II era, romanticized notions of aboriginal land tenure led many non-European observers to contend that indigenous peoples lived in perfect harmony with the land. While the impact of indigenous use differed greatly from the soil-exhausting habits of commercial farmers, the land-destroying activities of miners, and the ecology-altering pressures of sedentary populations, it is both logical to assume and clear from the evidence that indigenous societies occasionally had deleterious effects on local resources and the surrounding eco-system.

Tribal populations differed greatly in how they conceptualized and managed the question of land tenure and resource use. Societies able to draw on large, reliable sources of food – bison hunters of the Great Plains in North America, fishers of the Pacific Northwest coast, reindeer herders of Scandinavia – developed complex means of exploiting the resource and granting key people, families, or clans control over specific pieces of territory or preferred access to resources. Other populations apportioned large harvesting territories to extended families, which maintained the right to use the resources as they saw fit and which developed strong cultural and spiritual ties to specific pieces of territories. The pattern of Australian Aborigines developing *songlines* which demonstrated their knowledge and ownership, in an Aboriginal sense, of a specific piece or stretch of land had variants in many other cultures. Land ownership and tenure was not as fixed or unalterable as in surplus-based societies, where control over prime real estate or resources could bring enormous personal wealth, prestige, and authority. In resource-poor regions, harvesting territories often overlapped considerably (with indigenous names of landmarks providing some of the most important evidence of the extent and nature of land-holding). Neighboring groups, in this situation, often moved across the others' land and, when necessary, harvested food from that territory. Most indigenous societies had a strong sense of belonging to the land, the opposite of the situation in commercially based cultures. This sense of attachment, which has been documented in many different parts of the world, illustrates the degree to which indigenous peoples were connected with their land, exercised control over resources, maintained tenure over generations if not centuries, and thereby demonstrated ownership over traditional territories.

Tribal societies of the age before expansion and incorporation varied enormously in complexity, social structure, subsistence patterns, and culture. There is no single portrait possible of the many hundreds of indigenous populations which peopled the Earth two thousand years ago and which continue to figure prominently in nations around the globe. It is important to gain a preliminary insight into this cultural complexity in order to understand better the variations in contact relationships, struggle, and survival in the years after the expansion of European and other commercially driven states. While it is possible to sketch only a relatively small number of these societies, the cultures selected for introduction indicate something of the diversity and continuity of the indigenous reality.

Haida (West Coast of Canada)

Haida Gwaii (Queen Charlotte Islands) is a densely forested, mist-enshrouded series of islands off the west coast of British Columbia, Canada. These lands have been home to the Haida for close to 11,000 years. The people adapted well to a rich marine environment, which focused on hunting, fishing, the collection of shellfish, and the utility of the cedars and Douglas firs that covered the islands. The supply of shellfish was so substantial and reliable that it ensured social stability and provided a foundation for technological, socio-political, and artistic development. Over the generations, the Haida created boats capable of managing the strong winds and seas of the nearby ocean straits, thus enabling them to extend their trading connections with other indigenous peoples. The Haida were well-organized and comparatively sedentary, with seasonal movements to capitalize on valuable resources. The wealth of their land and their knowledge of its capacity enabled the Haida to develop substantial dwellings (long houses), and dramatic artwork. The totem poles of Haida Gwaii are among the most well-known artistic creations of the indigenous peoples of North America.

Inuit/Eskimo (Canada Arctic/Alaska/Greenland)

The inhabitants of the vast, frozen lands of the high Arctic have intrigued outsiders for generations. The people known as the Inuit (in Greenland and Canada) or Eskimo (historically in Canada and currently in Alaska) moved westward into the Arctic regions close to 1,000 years ago, displacing the earlier peoples and establishing a unique culture based on the Arctic seasons and the surprisingly abundant resources of the region. They harvested sea mammals, including whales, and fish and relied heavily in some areas on caribou hunts. The climate was considerably warmer when the first Inuit migrated into the area; subsequent cooling forced the people southward and required the abandonment of the early sod and whalebone shelters in favor of the more familiar hide tents and igloos (snow houses). The Inuit generally lived in small, extended family units, save for occasions when access to substantial amounts of food (through whale hunting or fishing) allowed larger groups to assemble.

Yanomami (Amazon Basin)

The Amazon basin has historically been home to numerous indigenous groups. Those on the margins were contacted by outsiders and developers, who gradually moved into their territories for purposes of mining, logging, or farming. The massive size of the Amazon River basin and the dense impenetrability of the jungle served to protect a number of societies from extensive contact. Among the best known of these indigenous peoples are the Yanomami, who live near the Brazil–Venezuela border, in a region now being subjected to considerable development pressure. The Yanomami organized themselves in small villages, structured around a central communal structure. The people, who now find themselves in conflict with miners and other developers, demonstrated a long and successful adaptation to the local eco-system, which provided reliable hunting and fishing resources and the opportunity for rudimentary agriculture. The Yanomami had little contact with outsiders until the 1980s; challenges to their occupancy and use of traditional lands in recent years have attracted world-wide attention.

Blackfoot (Canada/United States)

The Native Americans/First Nations of the Great Plains are among the best known indigenous peoples in the world, thanks to the representation of plains cultures in hundreds of movies, television programs, and novels. Most of those representations depict proto- or post-contact situations, highlighting the dominance of the horse in plains life. The Blackfoot, like numerous other plains peoples, had a very different existence during the centuries before the Europeans arrived. They lived on an open plain, drawing on wild plants and a few cultivated varieties and building their subsistence around the massive bison herds which migrated across the land. The migrations were not entirely at the discretion of the herds; the indigenous peoples used fire and other methods to shape their migratory patterns. The Blackfoot developed bison pounds, into which portions of a herd were drawn. The surrounded animals were driven over a cliff (or jump) or otherwise trapped by hunters. The bison meat was mixed with fat and berries and dried for winter use. The Blackfoot generally lived in groups of less than 200, moving with considerable regularity as dictated by the movements of the animals or the seasons. They maintained elaborate social activities, rituals, and spiritual traditions, and created strong social networks inside and between groups of Blackfoot.

Mohawk (Canada/United States)

The Iroquois Confederacy, of which the Mohawk (Kanien'kehake or "People of the Flint") were one of the five (later six) key members, is one of the most storied indigenous groups in North America. They played a key role in seventeenth- and eighteenth-century struggles for control of eastern North America and, in the process, established a reputation for political organization and military prowess. The Mohawk lived at the eastern end of the Great Lakes, occupying a strategic location in subsequent battles with the British and French. The land in this region offered abundant resources, including large game (especially deer), fish, and a wide variety of plants, some of which were cultivated by Mohawk villagers. The settlements themselves were more permanent than for many indigenous groups. People lived in large and substantial longhouses. They had, together with their Iroquois Confederacy partners (the confederacy was established close to 1,000 years ago), elaborate social and political codes and well-developed diplomatic relationships with their indigenous partners.

Innu (Labrador/Quebec, Canada)

The Innu lived in the Canadian sub-Arctic, a rocky, mountainous land marked by powerful rivers and numerous lakes. The weather in this region is often extreme, particularly in winter, but the land supports an abundance of big and small game, berries, and fish. The nature of the seasons and the unreliability of food supplies required extensive movement, which in turn supported the development of winter (snowshoes, sleds) and water transportation (canoes) equipment. The Innu, like other northern harvesters, made effective use of the products of their hunts, converting bone, fur, and animal fats into numerous usable items. Individual groups of Innu typically lived within a specific river system, moving along the river as seasons and resources dictated. For most of the year, the Innu lived within extended family groups, gathering occasionally, typically during the summer, for social, spiritual, and ceremonial activities.

Maori (New Zealand)

The Maori are one of the world's best known indigenous groups, identified by their historical combativeness, colourful artwork and tattoos, and the famed *haka*, or war dance, performed by the All Blacks rugby team before competitions. The first Maori reached New Zealand, one of the last major islands in the world to be occupied, around 1200 CE or earlier, likely arriving from islands to the east. The Maori discovered a rich and fertile land, one with abundant large birds, superb fishing resources, and rich agricultural soils. A rich and diverse culture emerged, one with regional dialects and lifestyles, the latter reflecting the widely variable resource base in New Zealand. The richness of the food supplies permitted the Maori to develop an elaborate ceremonial and artistic life, and to create a complex network of social and political relationships. Their culture reflected the Polynesian origins of the first settlers, and developed strong spiritual beliefs, and powerful collective commitments to *mana* (honour) and *atua* (spirits). The Maori were well-organized for war and self-defence, typically building their settlements around fortifications (*pa*) and preparing young men for combat.

Chittagong Hill Tribes (Bangladesh)

Standard western assumptions about indigenous peoples rarely include the numerous groups in the densely populated countries of South Asia. In the Chittagong Hills, bordering Bangladesh, Myanmar, and India, there are some thirteen minority groups, collectively called the Jumma, who have lived in this area for thousands of years. They do not share language, culture, lifestyle, or spiritual beliefs with the dominant Bangladeshi population, and have struggled to maintain a separate identify based on their traditional homelands. The two largest groups, the Chakmas and the Marmas, live in the river valleys and are Buddhists. The Tripuras, the third largest group, are Hindus. The Jummas have faced concerted efforts by the British, Indian, and Bangladesh governments to settle outsiders in their midst and thereby wrest control of traditional territories from the people who have lived there for generations.

Sami (Scandinavia)

The Sami people, long called Laplanders by outsiders, are the famed reindeer herders of the northern reaches of Norway, Sweden, Finland, and western Russia, a vast area they describe as Sampi. Evidence suggests that the Sami have inhabited their territories for some 4,000 years, moving north in pursuit of the reindeer herds. The Sami people adjusted to the various eco-systems of the sub-Arctic and Arctic regions.

Those in the forested areas lived by hunting, fishing, and gathering as food supplies permitted in sizeable villages at key harvesting sites; this was the most common form of Sami subsistence lifestyle. Reindeer herders, who probably settled into this pattern 400 or 500 years ago, inhabited the *fjelds* between Norway and Sweden. A third, maritime group secured most of their subsistence from the ocean. The Sami in western Russia combined fishing and herding. The Sami were, like other indigenous peoples, deeply spiritual, counting on various gods and spirits to guide their lives and their actions.

Bushmen (Southern Africa)

The southern part of Africa is known for its wind-swept desert land-scapes, its stifling heat, and the persistence of the indigenous peoples of the region. The general term "Bushmen" applies to a sizeable number of indigenous groups, all desert-based hunter-gatherers. They have inhabited this area for approximately 20,000 years, surviving and even flourishing in conditions that later adventurers would compare to the harsh lands of the Arctic. The people live primarily off their gathering activities, which require an intense familiarity with the landscape, the fauna, and the seasons. They hunt as well, counting on the occasional kill of small game and antelope to supplement their diet. As with other indigenous peoples living in unappealing geographic surroundings, the Bushmen were protected for many years by the simple harshness of their environment. Limited resources, including water, meant that the Bushmen had to move frequently in order to survive; the same conditions ensured that population remained small and that social groups rarely grew beyond an extended family. They generally lived in small caves and in shelters assembled from wood, grass, and animal skins.

Aka (Central Africa)

The Aka inhabit a heavily forested, swampy section of central Africa. Described as Pygmies, the Aka lived among a variety of agricultural cultures, remaining largely in the wooded regions. They generally oper-ated in small, extended family units in semi-sedentary locations, moving several times a year. The Aka, however, came together during the dry peri-ods for a variety of economic, social, and cultural activities. The society revolved around active hunting, focusing on elephants and other large animals and smaller game. The Aka, like other jungle societies, drew heavily as well on the plant life in the region, harvesting a variety of nuts, root plants, and other edible and medicinal items. Although the Aka engaged in only rudimentary agricultural activities, they nonetheless maintained strong commercial and social relations with other peoples who drew their sustenance from cultivation of plants. This close relationship provided additional sources of food and created opportunities for trade.

Okiek (Kenya)

The Okiek inhabit the highlands of Kenya, and are made up of a small number of interconnected harvesting societies. Like the Aka, the Okeik maintained strong relations with nearby agricultural populations, and merged their forest-based hunting and gathering activity with access to cultivated products produced by other groups. They were noted, in particular, for their harvesting of honey, but they also hunted large and small mammals. Plant products figured minimally in their food supplies. Okiek had well-developed concepts of territoriality, and typically defined family and group lands to incorporate a variety of ecological zones. In this way, they ensured each group had access to reasonable food supplies throughout the year.

Vedda (Sri Lanka)

The Vedda (forest dwellers) have occupied the forested lands on the east-central coast of Sri Lanka for between 14,000 and 16,000 years. They have long inhabited the dry monsoon forests, called *wanni*, of the region, maintaining harvesting traditions and seasonal cycles over thousands of years. Their lifestyle and movements reflected the resources of the land and the rhythms of the year, in particular the ebb and flow of the monsoon season with its strong rains and high winds. They hunted with the bow and arrow, gathered fruits and edible plants, and practised rudimentary agriculture. The Vedda had a rich spiritual life, based on their belief in the power of the *ne yaku*, or ancestral spirits. When migrants arrived from the north, the Sinhala from North India reaching the area in the fifth century BCE and preceding the first Europeans by thousands of years, they characterized the Vedda as wild people, scarcely human in character and action. The Vedda faced the standard challenges when confronted with waves of immigration. Some opted to amalgamate with the newcomers; others retreated into the forests, struggling to maintain their values, lifestyle, and customs in the face of discrimination and competition for resources. Vedda lifestyles have been adversely affected by water-control projects and, in the 1980s, by a campaign launched by the World Wildlife Fund to create a local conservation area.

Jarawas (Andaman Islands)

The Andaman Islands are off the coast of Myanmar, between the Bay of Bengal and the Indian Ocean. Three indigenous groups, the Arioto, the Onges, and the Jarawas, struggle to hold onto land and lifestyles which have flourished in the forbidding and inaccessible areas for countless generations. The Jarawas are dark-skinned, and were long referred to as Pygmies by outsiders. They proved to be intractably hostile to foreigners, and used the dense tropical jungle to protect themselves from intruders. The Jarawas became famed, almost mythologically so, for their ferocity and tenacity, to the extent that several waves of occupiers essentially cordoned off a large portion of the island for their exclusive use. The Jarawas capitalized on the richness of their habitat to develop a stable lifestyle. They hunted, primarily for wild boar, collected turtles and turtle eggs, and found many edible fruits and plants in the jungles. The Jarawas remained largely cut off from contact with the outside world until 1997, when the indigenous group unexpectedly moved out of their forest homelands and established peaceful contact with neighboring communities.

Agta (Philippines)

The Agta live in the mountainous terrain of Luzon, Philippines, following a mixed-economy lifestyle which includes the hunting of mammals (pig and deer), fishing, and rudimentary agriculture. No one food source was sufficient to provide security, the soils not sufficiently rich to support sustained cultivation. And so the Agta developed a seasonal and mobile cycle which involved considerable movement throughout their lands. Food and material not readily available within their territories was often obtained through trade from neighboring groups. The people organized themselves, in the main, in family units but nonetheless maintained a strong sense of being Agta.

Penan (Borneo)

The Penan of Borneo, like the Yanomami of the Amazon, have emerged in recent years as symbols of the continued destruction of indigenous territories and cultures. Their traditional territories now fall within two countries: the Kalimantan area of Indonesia and Sarawak, Malaysia. They live in a vast forested upland district, one marked by numerous valleys and rivers which make movement across the land difficult. Their movements were based on well-placed central camps, from which they moved away temporarily in search of food and supplies. The Penan hunted with spears, harvesting pigs, deer, and other mammals. They relied, as well, on the collection of sago (palm), an important part of their diet. The Penan maintained extensive trade relationships with agriculturalists, selling the products of the forest hunts for foodstuffs and processed materials.

Jahai (Northern Malaysia)

The Jahai people, who live in the rainforest of northern Malaysia, maintained a unique combination of hunting, gathering, trade, and basic agriculture. From very early times, the Jahai found the means of exchanging products which they had in abundance, most notably jungle plants and animals, with external groups who had access to other foodstuffs and materials. The rich and diverse fauna of the jungle terrain provided the Jahai with a wide variety of harvestable plants and made recourse to cultivation less essential. Likewise, a variety of mammals fell victim to their traps, blowpipes, and arrows. Groups had well-defined territories, within which they focused their harvesting activity. Like most hunter-gatherers, they operated in small bands, usually extended families, gathering on occasion for larger group activities and ceremonies. Shelters were rudimentary, for the Jahai moved about with considerable regularity.

Aborigines (Australia)

The first inhabitants of the continent of Australia arrived between 40,000 and 60,000 years ago. Over the thousands of years before the first Europeans arrived, the Aborigines established more than 250 separate and distinct indigenous groups. They varied greatly in subsistence lifestyle and habits, due in large measure to the dramatic differences between the hot, desert territories in the interior, the humid jungles of Cape York and the "Top End" (near Darwin) and the more temperate climates of the south coast and Tasmania. Aboriginal cultures varied substantially across the continent, with the peoples of Cape York adapting to the rich and wet jungle environment, the cultures in the Kimberley responding to the desert-like conditions in that region, and the Tiwi of Melville and Bathurst Islands in north Australia developing social and economic systems in line with the environment of the subtropical marine setting.

In general, Aborigines maintained a rich ceremonial and spiritual culture. The latter was based on a concept described as the "Dreamtime," with spirits filling the physical and supernatural world and with the landscape providing direct evidence of the work of the spirits. The Aborigines developed superb adaptive behaviours, learning to find food and water in the deserts and to cope with the many dangers and uncertainties of life in the tropical regions. The core food supplies typically came from gathering activities, which were more reliable than hunting with spears and boomerangs. The Aborigines developed musical instruments, most notably the didgeridoo, and sophisticated forms of artistic expression, particularly bark and rock painting.

Ache (Paraguay)

The Ache live in the forests of Paraguay, drawing on the rich resources of the near-tropical region to sustain a complex social and economic system. Like other harvesting peoples, they relied on a combination of animals (armadillo, monkey, peccary, paca, and others) hunted by bow and arrow, together with honey and plants. The Ache moved frequently (more so after contact with outsiders) and covered substantial amounts of territory in their various shifts. Groups formed and broke up frequently, in line with available food resources, resulting in considerable social interaction and regular change. Influential hunters dominated the political system, which nonetheless remained very fluid. The Ache were, for many decades, described as aggressive and combative, with attention being drawn as well to their pattern of taking many partners over their life-span.

Yanama (Tierra del Fuego)

The Yanama population has declined precipitously over the past two centuries, one of many indigenous groups to experience such a decline. They live in the southernmost occupied part of the world, a rough, rugged, forested land that nonetheless offered considerable resources for its inhabitants. Their territory provided access to ocean resources (fish and mammals), shellfish, birds, and other resources. Like most indigenous peoples, the Yanama migrated seasonally to take advantage of the availability of foodstuffs, and did not therefore develop permanent settlements or dwellings. They were particularly adept at hunting seals and porpoises and even whales, the latter providing a critical food source. They made effective use of boats capable of inshore navigation, and often used the vessels to move along the coastline in search of food supplies. The Yanama operated, from a socio-political perspective, largely in family and band units, but their system was very fluid and flexible, adapting to environmental conditions and very rarely resulting in large gatherings of the people.

Ainu (Japan)

The Ainu people inhabit Hokkaido, the northernmost large island in the Japanese archipelago. Not recognized by the Japanese government as a distinctive people until the 1990s, the Ainu developed separately from the better-known Japanese cultures on the southern islands. These spiritually intense people organized their lives around their relationships with the *kamuy* (gods). Ainu lifestyles paralleled in many respects the indigenous peoples of northern North America. They harvested large quantities of fish, which they dried and stored (in sheds called *pu*) for the long winter season. Hunting, particularly of the Ezo deer, was also an important part of the seasonal round. Ainu villages, or *kotan*, were typically located near river mouths, where fishing was reliable. There was a small amount of agriculture, but it did not represent the core subsistence activity. They had a strong sense of territoriality (although communities often shared hunting territories) and respected the harvesting and land rights of others.

Chukchi and Yupik (Eastern Siberia)

The vast expanses of Siberia have been home for centuries to a large and diverse group of indigenous peoples. The Chukchi and Yupik peoples inhabited the Chuchki Peninsula, in the far northeast corner of Siberia. The harsh and treeless land is noted, as well, for the difficult inland terrain and fierce winters. Along the coast, however, the rich marine life sustained vibrant and unique indigenous peoples, who learned to harvest migratory sea mammals, particularly whales, seals, and walrus. Inland harvesting activities focused on reindeer herds and a variety of small animals. The Chukchi and Yupik harvested extensively throughout the year, using boats to pursue sea mammals when the ice was off the ocean and, like the Inuit, hunting seals through the sea ice. Whale hunts occupied the core of coastal life, requiring extensive organization and superior hunting skill. The large number and the predictability of migratory whales, each of which represented a large amount of food for a community, permitted the development of sizeable and permanent coastal villages. The coastal peoples moved with the seasons to other harvesting sites, but they maintained the core settlements. Over time, inland groups domesticated the reindeer and moved across the tundra with small herds of the animals. The reindeer herders and whale hunters developed a strong interdependence, and maintained extensive commercial and social contracts. The nature of the seasonal round enabled the development of village cultures and more structured forms of decision-making and ceremonial life.

Nia/Nganasan (North-Central Siberia)

The Nia are one of a number of reindeer-herding peoples located in the northern reaches of Siberia. Their homeland, the Taimyr Peninsula, juts northward into the Arctic Ocean and is located well north of the Arctic Circle. Like the Chukchi Peninsula, the area is largely tundra, and sustains little plant life. The land supports, however, a variety of fish and animal life, including wild reindeer, and the coastal area provides access to a variety of sea mammals. Before the Nia domesticated reindeer in the late seventeenth century, which brought profound changes in lifestyle, they lived on the southern fringe of the tundra, moving slowly across the land and occupying wood and dirt shelters. The Nia drew most of their sustenance from the reindeer. They stored large quantities of the meat for use in winter months; reindeer hides were used for clothing and for the making of portable shelters. They also benefited from the huge flocks of migratory birds that moved through the region each year. The Nia perfected the use of large nets to capture geese and ducks, which featured prominently in their diet.

The indigenous peoples of today represent only a small percentage of all of the indigenous societies that have flourished throughout history. The industrial cultures of the modern era had their origins in subsistence-based economies, and adjusted slowly to opportunities arising out of socio-economic, political, and technological developments. In many parts of the world, indigenous peoples experienced sustainable lifestyles, drawing on the abundant resources of the oceans, rivers, lakes, plains, forests, and mountains. Over millennia, they learned to live with the land and to adapt to its nuances and changes. Life was not easy – for tribal peoples or any others. Starvation was not uncommon among peoples living in desert, high-mountain, or sub-Arctic and Arctic landscapes. Food supplies were not completely reliable, conflict with neighbors occurred with some regularity, and sudden changes of weather could disrupt harvesting cycles. Hardship was a regular part of life. But so, it must be remembered, was it for most people in the agricultural and pre-industrial and early industrial worlds. There, too, life expectancy was short, infant mortality high, starvation far too familiar, and the ravages of war and internal conflict relatively commonplace. The world was not, in the pre-twentieth-century period, a place that offered more than a tiny percentage of the globe's population freedom from uncertainty and fear.

The passage of time transformed and largely obliterated the awareness of the pre-agricultural roots of such cultures as the Europeans, Japanese and Chinese. For many centuries, hundreds of indigenous societies flourished around the world, in contact with immediate neighbors, vaguely familiar with populations some distance away, and virtually invisible to the rest of humankind. Indigenous peoples survived and adapted over the centuries before technology, the search for commercial and political advantage, and the imperatives of Christian missionary zeal forced European and other surplus societies to expand into hitherto unknown territory, that of indigenous societies. Contact between indigenous and expansionist peoples – what Wilbur Jacobs pessimistically referred to as the "fatal encounter" – altered one of the most fundamental equations in human history and launched more than two centuries of struggle and survival. The encounter experience, and the crucial role that indigenous societies played in the unfolding of a global phenomenon, would transform the world in many and profound ways.

3

MUTUAL DISCOVERY: TRIBAL PEOPLES AND THE FIRST WAVE OF GLOBALIZATION

For most of human existence, peoples had little knowledge of other societies, save those located immediately next to their territory. In the centuries before the advent of the written and printed word, long-distance travel, and telecommunications, most societies lived in isolation. Over the centuries, human curiosity, the need for food and new resources, and improvements to technology allowed individuals and groups to venture away from their territories. As they did so, as societies came to know and experience other peoples, they touched off a critical phase of the human experience: that of mutual discovery.

The story of the advance of the dominant civilization – typically the peoples of Europe – has long been understood from one side of the frontier. Original peoples have been viewed as site-bound and uncurious, locked into an unchanging world until newcomers with ships, horses, and military power happened upon their lands. The world's literature is replete with accounts of the baffled indigenous peoples looking in wonderment upon the arriving ships of the great explorers. These celebratory accounts – long the standard in colonial education and collective memory – highlighted the ingenuity of the grand adventurers and the passivity and backwardness of the indigenous peoples.

Far more was at play. These individual encounters, rarely described or recorded from the perspective of the original societies, were part of the long and global process of cultural mingling, conflict, conquest, and social reordering. The phenomenal journeys and events which resulted in the initial peopling of the earth were doubtlessly filled with thousands of adventures, experiences, and discoveries which easily matched the activities of the vanguard of European colonization. But precious little is known about these early adventures, with debate raging over the history, path, and timing of the initial occupations of the lands of the world. Following this stage, when peoples had found their way into most of the ecologically survivable niches on the globe, human societies underwent a series of profound transformations, all of which contributed to the first wave of globalization and the initial occupation of indigenous lands by outsiders from distant lands.

Critical Divisions: Agriculture, Industry and Urbanization

It is now known that the conventional descriptions of pre-industrial and indigenous societies reflect a deeply entrenched western bias. These populations were much better off in terms of security of food supply and life expectancy, more stable, more creative and better organized than the traditional explanations and descriptions would have us believe. But populations tied closely to the land, and peoples dependent upon an intimate understanding of a traditional landscape, lacked the imperative, resources, and opportunity to expand. They still traveled; the idea that only the Europeans were interested in what lay on the other side of a mountain, lake, river, or ocean is both absurd and untrue. Indigenous and pre-industrial populations moved in response both to opportunities and threats. They also, according to oral tradition and as demonstrated by the spread of trade goods, had members who left their midst in order to visit other peoples for the purposes of trade, discovery, or social understanding. Within a relatively narrow band around indigenous territories, therefore, aboriginal travelers ventured out in search of other peoples, cultures, and experiences.

Large-scale movements, either in terms of the length of the distance traveled or the scale of the expedition, awaited other social and economic developments. Larger, more sedentary societies emerged in the Middle East/Mediterranean, South and East Asia, and North and South America. The emergence of large-scale societies in the Americas has typically been obscured by the Eurocentric emphasis on the process of discovery and exploration. When Columbus and his contemporaries provided Europe with a first view of the Americas, the Inca and Aztec empires were as complex, urbanized, and internally diverse as the cultures of

Europe. Ancient, but subsequently vanished, societies in the Mississippi valley were as large as the biggest cities of Europe. The Aztec capital city of Tenochtitlan had a population of close to 200,000, at a time when the largest European cities would have been around one-tenth the size. These cultures tended toward stability in place and, although subject to dislocations through ecological disaster or military struggle, gradually capitalized on agricultural innovation to create formidable, large communities.

Within these societies, social and economic stratification and specialization occurred. Farmers and herders, putting their effort into this one area, produced substantial surpluses, enough to feed their communities, to trade with neighboring and distant communities and to allow them to pay other people for services and supplies. The ability to produce a regular, reliable surplus supply of food provided an essential base for the further evolution of the communities. These societies became, as well, more hierarchical and formally structured, with government and authority systems implemented to provide a measure of control and regulation. As the scale and wealth of these surplus societies expanded, physical manifestations of their power and dynamism emerged. The massive temples of the Aztec, the imposing cities of the Inca, the pyramids of the Egyptians, and the dramatic buildings of Chinese, Indian, and Middle Eastern cultures provided graphic evidence of the scale and ingenuity of the societies.

The time and opportunity provided through surplus production, social stability, specialization, and technological innovation afforded these societies greater flexibility. Some devoted their efforts toward the celebration of hierarchy; leaders used their authority to impose their will on the mass of the citizenry. Because of their physical location, the limitations of agriculture in their immediate vicinity or the vicissitudes of inter-group contact, others placed their efforts into trade with other peoples or on military conquest. Several coastal areas, particularly in the Mediterranean, Spain, Portugal, and China, produced generations of seafarers. These groups started slowly in charting nearby waters, gradually developing the capacity to head further afield, into unknown oceans. These societies, operating independently and usually with no knowledge of each other, challenged technological, social, and cultural barriers, developed the tools of navigation, the ability to mobilize human resources and capital, and crafted the conceptual and ideological frameworks necessary to both justify and motivate their citizens to seek opportunities in new and distant territories.

A critical watershed was crossed with the emergence of a select group of societies with the ability, resources, and determination to grasp for other lands and to dominate other peoples, as did dominant populations in the Middle East, Asia, Europe and parts of the Americas. Most of the world's peoples did not, at this time or subsequently, make this transition. Some had the natural resources and human capacities to do so; others lived on land that lacked the productive capacity necessary to sustain the larger and more expansion model. Many fell into a middle group. The First Nations of the Pacific Northwest, for example, lacked agricultural surpluses, but produced salmon and other resources in great abundance. Drawing on this wealth, they developed stable communities, elaborate artistic and architectural expressions, intricate social structures and the capacity to work, fight, and circulate far beyond the boundaries of their traditional territories. Most of the original peoples, however, lacked the reliable and large-scale surpluses necessary to sustain expansive initiatives. By either not developing agricultural capacity or by limiting their use of farming techniques and lands, these societies effectively restricted their capacity to expand or dominate other peoples. Those, like the Aztecs and Incas, that controlled the wealth and the socio-political organizations, did extend their authority over others.

The world now faced a new development, one originating at several points around the globe. A series of stable, primarily agricultural, surplus-based and more settled societies set themselves on a separate course from other populations. Before these innovations, and the technological and social transformations which accompanied this transition, most societies remained highly localized, with few ambitions of traveling great distances or establishing dominion over other peoples. With a few exceptions, such as the marauding and expansive Mongols of Central Asia, the Greeks under Alexander or the Roman Empire at several different periods, most societies were in conflict or cooperated only with nearby communities. The globe was not, at this juncture, interconnected, although occasional travelers, the excursions of traders, and local contacts gradually spread word of the existence of other, exotic peoples in distant lands.

The slow division of the world's population into surplus societies and those focused on addressing local and community needs represented a critical turning point. It is not, as is often understood, as though the division was between populations with wealth and prosperity and those doomed to a hand-to-mouth existence, the so-called subsistence peoples. Many indigenous populations – the mountain peoples of Papua

New Guinea, First Nations of the Pacific Northwest, Algonquin, and Iroquois peoples of the Great Lakes, and many of the small societies in Central America, the Caribbean, Africa, and Asia – were as stable, well-fed, and as sustainable as the surplus societies of Europe, China, and the Mediterranean region.

Aboriginal groups generally did not have an ideology of domination over land or other peoples. Their spiritual understandings spoke to their specific location; they did not urge their leaders to spread their vision of spiritual awareness and did not assert a special or dominant relationship with the spirits or with a god. Indigenous conceptions of the land and its resources spoke of the need for harmony, respect, and understanding. Where the Europeans and others were told that the physical resources of the world had been created for their direct benefit, indigenous peoples spoke of reciprocity and cooperation with animals, plants, water, and air. Indigenous struggles over land and with other peoples, then, focused on more immediate contests with neighbors and would-be conquerors. A few non-indigenous societies – the Incas, Aztecs, and Chinese – assumed a cultural superiority over other populations and, within the limits of their reach and their technology, established dominion over weaker populations. In Europe, the combination of Christian certainty and the nascent imperatives of the accumulation of profit propelled a continent to see its destiny resting in the conquest and control of distant lands and peoples.

Expansion of Middle East, Europe, and Asia

The ethos of expansionism resulted in the initial integration of the world. The process took more than a millenium, as surplus societies spread slowly from the Middle East and Mediterranean world, from central Africa and central Asia, through Central America and, most dramatically from Western and Northern Europe. The expansions were generally slow, with explorations followed belatedly by processes of incorporation. A few, like the Mongols' spectacular and dramatic invasions, were fast and comprehensive, if not always long-lasting. Other movements, from China toward Southeast Asia and from the steppes of Russia toward Siberia, started later and proved less dramatic in extent, but not necessarily in impact. Through a process of discovery, invention, conquest, and incorporation, the surplus societies had, by the middle of the nineteenth century, mapped almost all of the world, had claimed indigenous lands as colonial adhesions, and had used various economic, military, and administrative techniques to bring the territories and the peoples under centralized control. Expansionist powers wrestled with many intellectual demons. Lands beyond the horizon, intellectual or physical, were mysterious and unknown. For generations, political and spiritual leaders asserted authority over local populations by offering dramatic warnings about the evils and dangers that lurked beyond the seas. Fascinating myths, legends and visions emerged as a result. Reported sightings of strange beasts, odd peoples, and frightful dangers only a short distance beyond the known world ensured that only the brave, brazen and foolhardy dared challenge the barriers of geographical and cartographical understanding. Images varied widely, from notions of an open polar ocean to the north of Europe to lands inhabited by barbarous and frightful creatures to the south of the continent. These imaginings receded very slowly, even in the face of first hand accounts of other territories, providing a foundation for later assumptions about the evils and paganism of indigenous peoples.

Technological challenges and logistical difficulties also impeded efforts to expand into new territories. Societies in the Mediterranean organized armies and supply systems, on a hitherto unimaginable scale, allowing them to expand their control dramatically. Improved shipping helped, as did the gradual development of new armaments, transportation systems and administrative structures. Advancements in navigational tools and knowledge propelled the Portuguese and Spaniards into the forefront of exploration in the fifteenth century. Other European powers capitalized on the new information and, fuelled by Christian zeal, a desire for wealth and national prestige, and sustained by the authority and ambition of expanded monarchies, pressed on to new territories. They moved with urgency, as anxious to deny the newly discovered lands to their rivals and enemies in Europe as they were to identify new sources of wealth and opportunity. Some peoples, particularly the Chinese, had solved many of the technological and navigational puzzles, but nonetheless decided not to expand far from their host territories. They sought, instead, to solidify their control over domestic populations and to focus their efforts on the further development of local resources.

Motivations for expansion varied. Some of the earliest travelers headed out without official sanction, driven as much by a sense of adventure and curiosity as by national ambition or monarchical direction. The initial expeditions generally stuck to well-trodden trade

routes, moving between Europe, the Middle East and Asia and providing greater insights into the mysteries, scale and resources of this largely
unknown territory. The realization that distant territories held hitherto
unknown resources – the exotic and compelling spices of the Far East
were an enormous attraction to the people of Europe – encouraged others to try their hand at exploration. Over time, expeditions headed off
in all directions, with most venturing outward from Europe. Motivations
ranged widely, from a personal search for adventure, fame and wealth to
national determination to secure overland territories for the purposes of
trade with the local population, the identification of new resources, and
the desire to spread Christianity. Once one European power pushed outward, the others felt compelled to follow suit. Portugal and Spain, drawing on the power of the Roman Catholic Church, received papal
sanction for their division of the world into two imperial spheres of
influence. The Kingdoms of France, England, and Holland entered the
global game as soon as wealth and opportunity permitted, sending mercenary expeditions to the north, south, east and west in search of
resources and opportunity. European rivalries gave the acquisition of
new territories yet another level of urgency. To control key passageways
or ports, or to gain control of particularly rich or heavily populated
lands added significantly to national political and military advantage.
Clearly, individual explorers, companies or governments could readily
justify investments in global exploration, on financial, strategic or political terms. And if their arguments and assumptions foundered, they
could fall back on the Christian imperative – the God-given obligation
to take the wisdom of the Scriptures to the unschooled heathens of the
world.

And so, the veil of the unknown lifted slowly, with each new encounter
sparking a process of mutual discovery and, often, misunderstanding.
From the Middle East, travelers moved south into Eastern and Central
Africa, east into Turkey and neighbouring lands, and across the
Mediterranean. In India and China, dominant groups sent traders and
explorers into neighbouring lands, returning with knowledge as well as
items for exchange and sale. Italians, like Marco Polo, traveled to Asia,
returning with spices and descriptions of exotic and strikingly rich lands
and peoples. The Portuguese and Spaniards, capitalizing on critical navigational discoveries, ventured south along the west coast of Africa and
then, boldly, struck out across the Atlantic Ocean is search of faster
routes to China and the Far East. They were joined by the French,
English and Dutch, each of whom sought discoveries, opportunities and

wealth in the New World. North America attracted the Spaniards, Dutch, French, and English. South America fell largely under the control of the Spaniards and Portuguese. On the heels of the circumnavigations by Magellan and others, the Spanish, Portuguese, Dutch, French and English fought over trading niches in South and East Asia. Brand new lands were discovered in the South Pacific, with the British being the first Europeans to capitalize on the realization that the continent of Australia and the beautiful islands of New Zealand even existed. Efforts to find faster trading routes resulted in a variety of British, French, and Dutch expeditions to North America and, heading eastward, into the frozen Arctic waters atop the Eurasian continent.

These initial expeditions nibbled at the edges of newly found territories, leaving unanswered numerous questions about the people, resources and opportunities of the lands. And so, with the same verve and sense of discovery that pushed Europeans onto the world's oceans, they now tried their hand at overland exploration. Gradually, in a process that started in the fifteenth century and was still underway in the middle of the nineteenth century (and was not really complete until the development of airborne exploration in the twentieth century), adventurers and explorers moved slowly into the interiors of Africa, North, South and Central America, Australia, and the remaining uncharted lands of Asia. They came with missionaries, armies, and traders, as the situation and opportunities dictated. Equally important, they came with pen and paper, writing extended descriptions of the newly discovered territories – which they normally described as both intensely dangerous and enormously promising – and the indigenous populations.

The expansionist powers, primarily but not exclusively European, had to come to terms with a differently configured world than that which they had known for centuries. The new world contained many different peoples, adapted to life in strikingly different lands. These new populations often looked radically different, in skin colour, size, clothing, facial hair or decoration. They spoke languages that seemed to defy interpretation and held to values that bore no resemblance to the assumptions that governed life in the explorers' homelands. The indigenous peoples often lived in areas that seemed too cold, or too hot, for human habitation. They flourished in what appeared to be disease-infected jungles and vast, empty desert wastelands. Some survived off fish; others engaged in rudimentary agriculture and herding. Several of the societies they encountered, including those in China, Japan, portions of Southeast Asia, India, Africa, and Central America, were truly impressive in scope and accomplishment. These were not the primordial peoples of myth and legend, barely surviving through acts of endless barbarism and cruelty. The expansionists encountered deeply spiritual peoples, whose temples and religious monuments dwarfed the greatest churches of Europe, and stable comfortable societies which experienced little of the poverty and hardship that seemed endemic in many of the so-called surplus societies. They came face to face, in other words, with populations unlike their own. Understanding and explaining these peoples, time would reveal, proved to be one of the greatest challenges of the Age of Exploration.

The Importance of First Impressions

First impressions matter. Rarely has this been as true as with the initial contacts between indigenous peoples and newcomers. The British were astonished at the seeming dismissal of their arrival by the Aborigines of Australia, who rejected their offer of gifts and new technology, and turned their attentions to the more responsive and interested Maori of New Zealand. Explorers venturing into new lands carried complex expectations, ranging from the anticipated discovery of vast wealth to the prospect that the new worlds contains monsters and other ferocious life-forms. Harsh descriptions of newly identified lands and peoples were the norm, offering readers and other learners highly skewed first impressions of these "different" societies. If a newcomer described a land mass in favorable terms, the area became infused with the characteristics of a paradise of wealth and opportunity to be exploited by those courageous enough to venture forth. More commonly, descriptions tended to be self-justifying, highlighting the bravery, fortitude, and determination of the explorer. They spoke of vast distances, endless hardships, impenetrable lands (holding certain wealth) and, most significantly, ferocious and strange peoples.

In an age of limited literacy in the expansionist countries, particularly in Europe, the ideas about newly experienced land and peoples nonetheless spread widely amongst the population. From the thirteenth to the nineteenth century, even if few people could read the penned accounts of the new worlds uncovered by mariners and adventurers, the stories nonetheless quickly seeped into the public consciousness. They spread, no doubt embellished and misrepresented, by word of mouth and from the pulpits of churches anxious to raise money and volunteers for overseas missions. As printing technologies and reading skills improved, broadsheets, pamphlets, and cheap books circulated widely, consumed voraciously by readers, who often read them aloud for their illiterate friends. Add to this the slowly growing number of individuals with direct experience – soldiers, sailors, government officials, business people, and settlers – and the mechanisms for the popularization of new societies were gradually put in place.

Remember, too, that discoveries of new worlds and new peoples ranked among the most important and interesting revelations of their day. Details and descriptions brought to the Old World by Marco Polo, Christopher Columbus, the crew members from Magellan's expeditions, fishermen returning from the Grand Banks of Newfoundland, or clergy on leave from overseas missions matched in importance almost any other news in circulation. Over a period of centuries, as Europe developed a growing sense of its place on a circular orb, covered by vast expanses of water and ill-defined land forms, learning about the shape of the world and the inhabitants of foreign lands remained a high public priority. Working in an ill-connected and sporadic fashion, explorers, writers, and government officials gradually pieced together the puzzle for the world, filling in empty spaces and offering colorful descriptions of new territories and new peoples. The first explorers ventured forth expecting the best and the worst; many thousands perished in the attempt to define the unknown. Europe, more than any place on the earth, seemed desperate to know about the missing lands and appeared to be genuinely curious about the unusual cultures and lifeways encountered in far distant places.

Outsiders' Descriptions of Indigenous Peoples

The curiosity of newcomers rested in the remarkable "otherness" of the newly encountered indigenous peoples. When Prussians ventured eastward into Polish territory, they discovered societies that looked, in many respects, like their own. Likewise, while the English might have disparaging notions of the Portuguese, they nonetheless met people with a similar level of technology, comparable religious values – even if both Protestants and Catholics viewed each other's spiritual formulations as antithetical – and approximately the same standards of living. This did not hold when they went overseas. They found, instead, people of different skin colours: they described the Asians as "yellow," Africans as "black," and North American indigenous peoples as "red," even though those descriptions scarcely captured the diversity of ethnic composition. They found people, too, who did not hold to European norms of modesty and public comportment. When Pedro Álvares Cabral reached the coast of Brazil in 1500, he and his colleagues were astonished by the public displays of nudity:

> Three or four girls went among them, good and young and tender, with long very black hair hanging down their backs. And their privy parts were so highly and tightly closed and so free from pubic hair that, even when we examined them very closely, they did not become embarrassed.

Cabral was impressed that they stood "so naked and exposed with such innocence that there was no shame there."[1] These formulations, importantly, allowed Europeans to cloak themselves in the puritanical veil of "whiteness," a visual declaration of an intense sense of cultural and racial superiority.

The juxtaposition of the encounter with central Africa and the demonization of the concept of "blackness," created a potent situation. In the age of the Black Death, and at a time when the dangers of Satan were equated with darkness, the black peoples of the African continent seemed worthy of fear and dehumanization. The subsequent discovery that due to the intricacies of African politics, warfare and economics many thousands of these people were available as slaves fit nicely with the visual and cultural impressions of the newly encountered societies. The removal of the young men and women who were most attractive to the slave traders, of course, undermined the local economy and destroyed the ability of the peoples to sustain themselves. Europeans who had been controlling, indenturing, and dominating their own people for generations found it easy to accept the enslavement of such peoples. European religious and cultural values readily discounted Africans as sub-human, allowing the construction of images which encouraged the exploitation of black labor. The expansionists attempted to adopt this same model to North, Central, and South America, interpreting the "other" as being available for commercial use and European control. For a variety of cultural and economic reasons, these attempts failed, forcing the European powers to turn back to Africa and the slave trade for the human resources needed to capitalize on commercial opportunities in the New World.

The societies Europeans encountered did not look at all like the world the travelers left behind. In some places – parts of India, China, and

Central America – the Europeans encountered elaborate and dramatic societies. These select peoples had large cities, often larger than those in Europe, advanced technologies, and complex social organizations. The description by Bernal Diaz of Cortez's travel along the causeway to Iztapalapa conveys the sense of wonderment about the scale of the Mexico civilization:

> [A]nd when we saw so many cities and villages built in the water and other great towns on dry land and that straight and level causeway going toward Mexico we were amazed and said that it was like the enchantments they tell of in the legend of Amadis, on account of the great towers and *cues* and building rising from the water, and all built of masonry. And some of our soldiers even asked whether the things that we saw were not a dream? ... Thus, we arrived near Iztapalapa, to behold the splendour of the other Caciques who came out to meet us, who were the Lord of the town named Cuitlahuac, and the Lord of Culuacan, both of them near relations of Montezuma. And then we entered that city of Iztapalapa, the appearance of the palaces in which they lodged us! How spacious and well built they were, of beautiful stone work and cedar wood, and the wood of other sweet scented trees, with great rooms and courts, wonderful to behold, covered with awnings of cotton cloth.[2]

These people had, too, "strange" religions; clearly God had not visited his graces upon them. In dress, demeanor, and language, they shared little in common with the adventurers who now wandered nervously and uncertainly in their midst. They often marvelled at the richness and diversity of these lands, as the first Europeans did when they reached China and Japan, although they fixated as well on their "barbarism" and oddities. First and foremost, these societies were not European and, with careful attention, the flaws, vulnerabilities, and "uncivilized" elements of the new peoples could be identified.

More often, as they came across smaller indigenous societies, they found peoples who were truly "strange" and "savage." Most did not have the complex urban centers that the Europeans saw as fundamental to their economic and political success. They seemed scarcely more advanced than the animals, for they moved regularly across the land and did not demonstrate dominion over the natural world. In ritual, dress, language, and custom, they showed no signs of understanding the important truths of human existence – God, government, material opportunity, literacy – and hence were readily dismissed as being only an impediment to the development of new territories. Amerigo Vespucci wrote of the Brazilian Indians, in a widely circulated 1503 description,

They have no laws or faith, and live according to nature. They do not recognize the immortality of the soul; they have among them no private property, because everything is common; they have no boundaries of kingdoms and provinces, and no king! They obey nobody, each is lord unto himself. [They have] no justice and no gratitude, which to them is unnecessary because it is not part of their code. They are a very prolific people, but have no heirs because they hold no property.[3]

In many instances, the newcomers feared their ferociousness and nervously described the barbarism which seemed built into the small societies they encountered from Africa to Australia and from Newfoundland to Patagonia, although the aggressiveness often began with the newcomers. Consider the account, written by Gáspar de Carvajal, a Dominican friar travelling with Francisco Orellana along the Amazon in 1542:

This village as situated on a high spot back from the river as if on the frontier facing other tribes who made war on them, because it was fortified with a wall of heavy timbers. At the time that our companions climbed up to this village to seize food, the Indians decided to defend it and took up a strong position inside that enclosure, which had only one gate, and they set to defending themselves with very great courage. However, as we saw that we were in difficulty, we determined to attack them and so, in accordance with this resolution, the attack was launched through the gate. Entering without any loss, our companions fell upon the Indians and fought with them until they dispersed them, and then they collected foodstuffs, of which there was an abundance.[4]

Most European observers, like Carvajal, found little to admire among these societies, save for basic animalistic qualities such as bravery, ferociousness, and skills on the land, and occasionally they discovered ways of using these traits and knowledge to their advantage. In the main, however, they simply discounted the pagan and ill-organized indigenous peoples as non-Europeans and, in the broader scheme of things, as marginally important.

It is incorrect, however, to assume that the newcomers saw indigenous peoples in consistently negative terms. Although the Europeans found much wanting in the societies they encountered, they were nonetheless impressed with many aspects of the indigenous world. José Mariano Moziňo, one of the first newcomers to visit the west coast of North America, wrote of the peoples he encountered:

A languid look is rather frequent among them, but rarely does one find a stupid-looking one. On the contrary, I noticed in many such a lively expression that, through it alone, one could guess many of their thoughts with little question. ... Either because it is natural among them or because they have eliminated all sentiments of modesty entirely, the men frequently abandon this clothing and appear stark naked, without so much as covering their private parts with their hands, even though they might be in a group of numerous women. The women, on the contrary, preserve more decency.[5]

Moziño offered matter-of-fact descriptions of dress, housing, and lifestyle, making it clear that he did not see the people of Nootka Sound as either desperately poor or brutal beyond belief.

But harsh and unkind assessments dominated, as the 1899 description of the "wild men of the woods" in India by Donald McIntyre illustrates:

There are some curious specimens of humanity to be found dwelling among the forests about the Chipla, called "Razees," compared with whom the villagers are quite civilized ... The villagers described these "jungle admi" (wild men of the woods), as they termed them to me, as being almost on par with the beasts of the wilds they inhabit, subsisting chiefly on what they can secure with their bows and arrows, and by snaring

Admitting he had never seen a Razees person, McIntyre offered up the observations of a friend and government official:

The last time I saw a man or woman of the tribe was at Askote in 1866 and they were caught for my special benefit. We gave them a few rupees, but they seemed to value them as much as apes! They would eat anything given to them; and both the man and the woman wore long hair down the back, and used leaves stitched together for clothing.

MacIntyre concluded by commenting "From this, the condition of these remnants of an almost lost race appears to have been still much the same as, we may suppose, was that of Adam and Eve after the fall."[6]

A handful of observers in the years predating Rousseau's conception of the nobility of life attached to the land saw the indigenous peoples' relationship with the land and intense spirituality in positive terms, however. The positive elements of newcomers' descriptions of indigenous societies described an idyllic state of nature; many of the initial commentaries on the indigenous peoples of South America talked about sexual freedom, the absence of greed, and the gentleness of the newly found societies. The image was transformed into public discourse through the writings of Erasmus and Thomas More, Montaigne, Locke, Spinoza, Shakespeare, and many others. Even as Europeans were occupying indigenous lands and conquering original peoples, they found positive elements that were worthy of emulation. In general, however, portraits highlighted the fact that more mobile societies, which newcomers assumed struggled daily for survival, were seen as uncivilized and were deemed an impediment to settlement and development. Caustic and harsh descriptions abound of such groups as the Aborigines, the northern hunter-gatherers in North America, the hill peoples of Southeast Asia, and small societies in South Asia, Africa, and South America. The expansionary powers assumed that their own military and technological prowess proved their superiority, blessed as it was by the hand of their God, and formed little understanding of the dynamics or complexities of the indigenous peoples.

On occasion, however, the newcomers were impressed with the people they encountered. Travelers in the Arctic, for example, marveled at the ability of the Inuit to find sustenance in such a harsh and forbidding land, even though they were initially reluctant to adopt the Inuit lifestyle and material culture. Early French and Portuguese observers wrote favorably about the gentleness, generosity, and sharing cultures of the Brazilian indigenous peoples. Many of the first observers of the Maori feared their warlike nature and saw them, legitimately, as a worrisome but truly impressive military threat. There was, in fact, something of an idealization of the original inhabitants of the Pacific Islands, who seemed to inhabit a tropical paradise and were freed from the worries and struggles of northern countries. Visitors to the west coast of North America described positively the large well-organized salmon-based communities in the region. Many of the early European explorers among the peoples of the American Northeast described such groups as the Mohawk in favorable terms. The discovery of the complex pueblo cultures of the American Southwest likewise generated relatively favorable descriptions. Even in these cases, however, observers quickly identified social elements they described as distasteful – just as indigenous peoples often found newcomers' customs disagreeable. Polygamous marriages, multi-deity world views, seemingly casual attitudes toward life and death, and the absence of material wealth, social stratification, or skills differentiation all provided evidence to the outsiders that the indigenous peoples, however impressive in some aspects, were far from equal beings or cultures.

Tribal Curiosities in the Imperial World

The nations of exploration, particularly in Europe, were entranced by images and stories of the New World societies. Books, pictures, and personal accounts of tribal societies and newly discovered lands remained intensely popular in the Old World. People flocked to public showings of curiosities from overseas. Sailors and their commercial sponsors brought back all kinds of potential trade goods from new lands, ranging from spices and precious metals to never-before-seen kinds of wood, animals, birds, and plants. They brought back, as well, cultural artefacts: weapons, samples of "savage" dress, and artistic work (carvings, jewellery, baskets). Particularly popular were items such as shrunken heads or barbarous paintings, which reinforced written and oral descriptions of the strange and dangerous peoples. The New World artifacts circulated widely, attracting large audiences anxious to learn more of these societies and more than a little nervous about the stories circulating on the subject of the heathen and ferocious peoples who inhabited strange and forbidding lands.

Nothing, however, attracted a crowd so much as a living human being – when Europeans deigned to describe them as such. Starting with the initial adventures into central Africa when travelers returned with startling tales of all-black people, European adventurers knew of the continent's insatiable interest in different men and women. Christopher Columbus brought back several indigenous people from the Caribbean, obvious proof that he had encountered a new and different land. Spanish visitors to the Aztec and Inca empires also brought back several people, captives and friends of the conquerors, and put them on display across Spain. Sebastian Cabot reached the coast of Brazil in the 1520s, and was treated well by the Carijó, who provided food and shelter to the starving explorer. Cabot responded by capturing four sons of the local chief and carrying them to Europe. In 1533, Tupinikin Indians from near Pôrto Seguro voluntarily travelled to Portugal, where they had an audience with King Manoel I.[7] An observer described thus the reaction of three indigenous peoples in France in the 1560s:

> The King talked with them for some time; they were shown our way of living, our magnificence, and the sights of a fine city. [I] asked them what they thought about all this, and what they had found most remarkable. [They said] they had noticed among us some men gorged to the full with things of every

sort while their other halves were beggars at their doors, emaciated with hunger and poverty. They found it strange that these poverty stricken halves would suffer such injustice, and that they did not take the others by the throat or set fires to their houses.[8]

As the British, Spanish, Portugese, and French imperialists expanded across North America and the Pacific, they discovered an innate domestic curiosity back home about the unusual peoples of the New World.

The indigenous travelers rarely fared well as they passed from city to city, country to country, on display as cultural abnormalities. In the most egregious cases, they were caged and highlighted in local fairs and circuses. Museums and galleries also presented the paying public with an opportunity to gawk at these strange human beings from distant lands. They were paraded before the public in their traditional, ceremonial garb, faces often painted to create a frightening countenance, all of this "proving" that the non-European world was inhabited by ferocious societies. Lonely, thousands of miles away from home, dispirited and alienated, the indigenous peoples suffered greatly from their experiences. Many succumbed to European diseases or diet; others, their spirits broken by the punishing combination of entrapment and public display, withered and died. A few, including a number brought over as political emissaries to imperial governments, were treated more favorably, even comfortably, and returned to their homelands with many tales and images of their own (and not as flattering or awe-inspired as the Europeans expected).

By the nineteenth century, visits from strange and distant lands were quite commonplace in public exhibits and fairs across Europe. Ranging from caged "animals" and "sub-humans" to honored chiefs, cultural oddities, and artisans, these visitors provided Europeans with a first-hand opportunity to experience the diversity of the human experience. Okou-Ulah, one of a Cherokee delegation to England in 1730, was clearly impressed with the reception they have received and said:

We are come hither from a dark and mountainous country, but we are not in a place of light. The crown of our Nation is different from that which our father King George wears, but it is all one. The chain of friendship shall be carried to our people. We look upon King George as the sun, and our father, and upon ourselves as his children; for though you are white and we are red, our hands and hearts are joined together. When we have acquainted our people with what we have seen, our children from generation to generation will remember it. In war we shall be as one with you. The great King George's enemies shall be our enemies. His people and ours shall always be one, and we shall die together.[9]

An Aborigine, Bennelong, was transported from Australia to London in 1792, and enjoyed a two-year run as a curiosity in the city. Numerous Maori visited England and Europe in the nineteenth century. One of these, Te Mahanga, journeyed to London in 1806. The man who took Te Mahanga to England, John Savage, said of this companion:

> [N]othing escaped his observation. The church steeples – the shops – the passengers – the horses and carriages, all called forth some singular remark. Of the height of the steeples he observed, Piannah wurrie tauwittee tuwittee paucoora – Very good house, it goes up in the clouds. On noticing any singularities, decrepitude, lameness, or infirmity, in a passenger, he always remarked, Kiooda Tungata, or Kiooda wyeena – Good for nothing man or woman . His eye was constantly seeking articles of iron, clothing, or food. Of some of the streets he observed, Nue mue Tungata, nue nue wurrie, itteee ittee eka, ittee ittee potatoe – Plenty of men, plenty of horses, but very little fish and few potatoes.

Another Maori, Nahiti, traveled to France to visit the king in the 1830s. Tumohe and Paraone made a similar journey to Austria. Entertainers traveled to England, where they played to appreciative crowds. None of this did much to dampen the European sense that they had been specially mandated by God to conquer, incorporate, and dominate these indigenous societies. Even the discovery of artistic talents, cultural distinctiveness, and technological creativity only seemed to add to the imperial continent's disappointment that otherwise gifted people could sink to such levels of depravity and economic irrelevance. The recognition of difference proved, importantly, to be unrelated to the celebration of cultural distinctiveness. Knowing the world was peopled by societies of great variety did little to undermine the Europeans' sense that they were specially entrusted, by God and history, with the duty to spread their religion, values, and lifeways to the far corners of the world.

Indigenous peoples remained of continuing interest and, in many countries, remain so to this day. Public facilities in Australia, New Zealand, and Canada proudly display the work of contemporary aboriginal artists, even as indigenous communities remain on the economic and social margins of the country. Inuit carving, print-making, and soapstone sculpture, introduced as commercial ventures to the Canadian Inuit by government officials in the 1950s and 1960s, remains very popular provided the artwork is restricted to traditional images of seal hunters, Arctic mammals, and traditional northern lifeways. Major fairs and expositions, from the world-famous Great London Exhibition of 1851 to modern world expositions, regularly featured prominent displays of traditional indigenous cultures and art – ironically, often designed to differentiate one European colonial society from another. One rarely sees, however, indigenous peoples paraded before gawking crowds for entertainment purposes; the values attached to the public presentation of indigenous culture are more authentic and positive, and are often designed to generate support for aboriginal causes. Supporters of the Pewan of Sarawak, for example, have introduced community members, decked in traditional clothes, at public speaking events in an effort to gain backing for their anti-logging campaigns.

From first contact through to the present, however, indigenous peoples have generally been viewed as "the other," not as variants on a central theme of humanity. Imperial citizens could scarcely believe that human existence was possible in the vast Arctic expanses and in the jungles, deserts, and harsh tropical environments. Nor could they understand how the indigenous societies in temperate zones – across North America, in Australia, New Zealand, South Africa, and other lands – could make poor use of rich and prosperous territory. Clearly, to the dominant powers, these were lesser societies, less "advanced," less technologically sophisticated, and by definition less "civilized." At best, as the imperialists demonstrated over several centuries, the indigenous peoples were intellectual and social novelties, of interest more because of what they illustrated about the distant past of humanity and what they foreshadowed for dominant cultures which dropped their vigilance and their commitment to colonial expansion.

Indigenous Impressions of Newcomers

European assumptions of their superiority were not, however, matched by indigenous acceptance. The indigenous peoples may have been either awestruck or dumbfounded by their first sightings of the new-comers. The Maori, for example, equated the sailors who arrived off their shores with supernatural beings and thought that they have descended from the sky. When the indigenous peoples of Mexico first saw Cortez, they marvelled at the newcomers:

> And when he [Montezuma] had so heard what the messengers reported, he was terrified, he was astounded. And much he did marvel at their food. Especially did it cause him to faint away when he heard how the gun, at [the Spaniards] command, discharged [the shot]; how it resounded as if it

thundered when it went off. It indeed bereft one of strength; it shut off one's ears. And when it discharged, something like a round pebble came forth from within. Fire went showering forth; sparks went blazing forth. And its smoke smelled very foul; it had a fetid odor which verily wounded the head. And when [the shot] struck a mountain, it was as if it were destroyed, dissolved. And a tree was pulverized; it was as if it vanished; it was as if someone blew it away. All iron was their war array. In iron they clothed themselves. With iron they covered their heads. Iron were their swords. Iron were there crossbows. Iron were their shields. Iron were their lances. And those which bore them upon their backs, their deer, were as tall as roof terraces. And their bodies were everywhere covered; only their faces appeared. They were very white; they had chalky faces; they had yellow hair, though the hair of some was black. Long were their beards; they were also yellow.[10]

Te Taniwha's description of the encounter with Captain Cook's ships at Whitianga in 1769 captures the strangeness of the first contact:

We lived at Whitianga, and a vessel came there, and when our old men saw the ship they said it was an atua, and the people on board were tupua, strange beings or "goblins." The ship came to anchor, and the boats pulled on shore. As our old men looked at the manner in which they came on shore, the rowers pulling with their backs to the bows of the boat, the old people said, "Yes, it is so: these people are goblins, their eyes are in the backs of their heads; they pull on shore with their backs to the land to which they are going." When these goblins came on shore we (the children and women) took notice of them, but we ran away from them into the forest, and the warriors alone stayed in the presence of those goblins; but, as the goblins stayed some time, and did not do any evil to our braves, we came back one by one and gazed at them, and we stroked their garments with our hands, and we were pleased with the whiteness of their skins and the blue of the eyes of some of them.[11]

The Maori reaction mirrored that of the Native Americans of the area later known as New York:

A long time ago, when there was no such thing known to the Indians as people with white skin, (their expression) some Indians who had been out a-fishing, and where the sea widens, espied at a great distance something remarkably large swimming, or floating on the water, and such as they had never seen before. They immediately returning to the shore apprised their countrymen of what they had seen, and pressed them to go out with them and discover what it might be. These together hurried out, and saw to their great surprise the phenomenon, but could not agree what it might be; some concluding it either to be an uncommon large fish, or other animal, while others were of the opinion it must be some very large house. It was at length agreed among those who were spectators, that as this phenomenon moved towards the land, whether or not it was an animal, or anything that had life in it, it would be well to inform all the Indians on the inhabited islands of what they had seen, and put them on guard ... .These arriving in numbers ... concluded it to be a large canoe or house, in which the great Mannitto (great or Supreme Being) himself was, and that he probably was coming to visit them.[12]

Other groups were frightened by the discharge of cannons or firearms and believed that the newcomers had magical and dangerous powers. Still others were astonished by the pale skin color of the newcomers, or their clothing, language, or mannerisms. Put differently, indigenous peoples responded to the arrival of newcomers with much the same combination of puzzlement, fear and uncertainty that governed the other half of the contact experience.

In a late-twentieth-century variation of a common seventeenth- to nineteenth-century phenomenon, Yanomami leaders from the Amazon were brought by their supporters into western view, hoping to generate sympathy and to reinforce their claims to land and resource rights in their homelands. Dressed in their traditional garb, they were paraded before governments, presented to raucous soccer stadiums, taken to electronics shops and otherwise exposed to the material richness of the modern world. Implicitly, many of the government officials and non-indigenous observers believed, like their pre-twentieth-century counterparts, that the Yanomami would be awed by the wealth and technological sophistication of the major cities. Instead, the Yanomami reported considerable distaste for the noise, over-crowding, and material excesses of major centers, and expressed a heart-felt desire to return to their home territories.

So it was in earlier times. The first British settlers attempted – with considerable initial difficulty – to establish colonies in the Chesapeake (Virginia) in the 1570s. Historian Edmund S. Morgan later commented that the lot of the average aboriginal was not dramatically more challenging than the British norm and was, in some areas, more comfortable and dependable. (Robert Hughes, an historian of Australia, made a similar claim about the nutritional standards of the Aborigines compared to Europeans.) Native Americans, it seemed, lived longer, had cleaner and better living quarters, enjoyed greater security of food supply, were less vulnerable to violent death, and lived in a less arbitrary society. Not surprisingly, then, the first Native Americans hauled across Europe did not necessarily gain favorable impressions of the broader society. They might, as their handlers hoped, be awestruck by the beauty and grace of the major cathedrals and state buildings, but these impressions were off-set by the mess and slop of the city streets, the brutality of state justice, the viciousness of European warfare, and the inequities of societies that had not yet established secure food supplies for their people. Indigenous visitors to France, Spain, Italy, and Portugal, if they survived the visit, as only a few did, left with greatly mixed impressions of the Old World. Most simply wanted to go back to their homelands.

The situation did not change much as time passed. Maori visitors to England in the nineteenth century, for example, despaired of the end-less rain, fog, and cold, and found little beyond stately buildings that was more impressive than their Aotearoa homeland. So it was for Pacific Islanders and Asians, the former dissuaded by the inhospitable climate of much of Europe and the later hardly awestruck by public buildings and cities which were often smaller, newer, and less dramatic than those in their homelands. People of the forests, deserts, and Arctic ice experi-enced great hardship in adjusting to the chaos, noise, and disruptions of the industrial age. Minik, an Inuit from Greenland, was brought to New York in 1897 and paraded before audiences by his patron, Robert Peary. The attention only demoralized him, and rendered him ill-suited for re-entry to Inuit society. When his father Qisuk died, in a last act of dehu-manization that tormented his young son, his bones were set aside for scientific investigation and preserved for research and display in a museum in New York City.

If indigenous observers were under-whelmed by their visits to the imperial homeland, they were often even less impressed by their encounters with the newcomers on Aboriginal land. The outsiders clearly had daunting technology; their guns, ships, and metal implements easily overpowered the simpler and smaller armaments of indigenous peoples. They could marshal frightening firepower and powerful armies, and often had little difficulty imposing their military authority over the smaller, more scattered, and less militaristic indigenous peo-ples. But on their own – traveling and living on the land – the newcom-ers were neophytes, often comically vulnerable and unable to adapt quickly to new environments. The speech of a Mik'maq elder, recorded by missionary C. LeClerc, captured the sentiment:

> I am greatly astonished that the French have so little cleverness, as they seem to exhibit in the matter of which thou hast just told me on their behalf, in the effort to persuade us to convert our poles, our barks, and our wigwams into

those houses of stone and of wood which are tall and lofty, according to their account, as these trees. Very well! But why now ... do men of five to six feet in height need houses which are sixty to eighty? For, in fact, as thou knewest very well thyself, Patriarch, – do we not find in our own all the conveniences and the advantages that you have with yours, such as reposing, drinking, sleeping, east, and amusing ourselves with our friends when we wish? This is not all ... my brother, hast though as much ingenuity and cleverness as the Indians, who carry their houses and their wigwams with them so that they may lodge wheresoever they please, independently of any seignior whatsoever?... As to us, we find all our riches and all our conveniences among ourselves, without trouble and without exposing our lives to the dangers in which you find yourselves constantly through your long voyages ... .Which of these two is the wisest and happiest – he who labours without ceasing and only obtains, and that with great trouble, enough to live on, or he who rests in comfort and finds all that he needs in the pleasure of hunting and fishing ... Learn now, my brother, once for all, because I must open my to thee my heart: there is no Indian who does not consider himself infinitely more happy and more powerful than the French.[13]

Several of the major explorers of the Australian interior perished or suffered due to their inability to read local signs. Alfred Gibson (1873) and Ludwig Leichhardt (1848) both died in the effort to describe and explore the "ghastly blank" of the outback. The first expedition to cross Australia from south to north, conducted by Robert Burke and William Wills in 1860–61, ended in disaster when both men perished in the desert. Inuit and Eskimo in the far north occasionally came to the rescue of foundering European expeditions, several of which had collapsed into cannibalism. In the jungles of Africa and South America, newcomers learned very slowly how to handle the heat, insects, and diseases which plagued the area. Pacific Islanders marveled at the outsiders' inability to harvest the riches of the sea and wondered about their capacity to survive in this, the most salubrious of world climates.

Indigenous peoples were comfortable in their traditional places and, like the Aborigines in Australia who turned their backs on the gifts proffered by Captain Cook and his crew, were not overly impressed with the newcomers. A First Nations person in North America said of the difference between his world and that of the recent arrivals:

It is true ... that we have not always had the use of bread and of wine which your France produces; but, in fact, before the arrival of the French in these parts, did not the Gaspesians live longer than now? And if we have not any longer among us any of those old men of a hundred and thirty to forty years, it is only because we are gradually adopting your manner of living, for experience is making it very plain that those of us live longest who, despising your bread, your wine, and your brandy, are content with their natural good of beaver, of moose, of waterfowl, and fish, in accord with the custom of our ancestors and of all the Gaspesian nation.[14]

There were reasons to dislike the colonial representatives. The first newcomers were often not particularly well-behaved. Unprovoked attacks on unsuspecting villages undermined the indigenous' peoples confidence in the newcomers. The soldiers, traders, whalers, and sailors who represented the first wave of European expansion did not always comport themselves in a manner that impressed even the colonial officials. As a French observer wrote about his compatriots in Brazil in the 1550s,

> I must record, to my great regret, that some interpreters from Normandy who have lived eight or nine years in that country accommodated themselves to the savages and led the lives of atheists. They not only polluted themselves with all sorts of lewdness and villainy among the women and girls ... but surpassed the savages in humanities: I have heard them boasting of having killed and eaten prisoners.[15]

It is hardly surprising that many indigenous peoples were dismayed, if not disgusted, with the habits, behaviour and the aggressive interventions of the newcomers.

Europeans, ensconced in their assertion of superiority, rarely noticed that the indigenous peoples were often unimpressed. The newcomers often lacked stamina and were loath to venture far from military bases and settlements. Most of the Hudson's Bay company employees at York Factory, on Canada's Hudson Bay, spent their whole time in the region without venturing far from the post. Many Europeans moved only a few hundred yards from the safety of a government, commercial, or military station during their time in the New World, such was their fear of the unknown. When on their own on the land, they often lost their way or relied on local indigenous peoples to lead them back to safety. In many instances – and historical evidence is fairly limited in this regard – the aboriginal peoples disparaged the sanitation habits of the newcomers – the use of scented powders and regular bathing appalled many non-Europeans – and ridiculed their preference for facial hair. Father Gabriel Sagard-Theodat, recorded in the early seventeenth century the reaction of Huron to the bearded Frenchmen: "They have such a horror of a beard that sometimes when they try to insult us they call us Sascoinronte, that is to say, Bearded, you have a beard; moreover, they think it makes people more ugly and weakens their intelligence."[16] The lonely soldiers, traders, and miners that represented the vanguard of much of European society often drank heavily and lusted after local indigenous women, whom they discarded when they returned to their homelands. Aboriginal peoples often spoke, with some dismay, about the sexual appetites of the newcomers, and of their mistreatment of women. European attitudes to battle and warfare struck most indigenous peoples as uncommonly brutal and vicious. Few indigenous societies around the world – the ones European described so readily as barbarian – came close to the British, French, Spanish, and other European societies in the intensity and destructiveness of their military tactics.

The Europeans who generally described indigenous populations in negative terms – they found many reasons, often rooted in religion, to disparage even the majestic cultures of India and China – were themselves also defined in an unflattering fashion. Indigenous peoples were often impressed with elements of the newcomers' technology, especially sailing ships, navigational instruments, and metal implements. They might, at first, be over-awed by the technology of warfare and destruction introduced by the Europeans. They often subsequently discovered that the newcomers' technological innovations were ill-suited for the battles of the forests and plains and, once they themselves had access to the armaments, the Europeans' aura of invincibility quickly faded. Indigenous peoples did not, as the newcomers expected, simply abandon their established ways and technologies in favor of superior European approaches nor were they awestruck by the manner in which colonizers and invaders entered their lands. They discovered, as did the Europeans, that lifeways, values, and technologies emerged from local conditions and realities; the newcomers soon learned that, without adopting indigenous ways they would suffer and founder in the new lands. Most learned to borrow selectively from the indigenous people.

Early aboriginal impressions of the newcomers varied dramatically depending on the nature of the initial contact. Some outsiders advanced with armies; others came offering trade goods. In many instances, missionaries formed the vanguard of European expansion, sparking reactions ranging from curiosity to horror. Explorers and government officials often commenced contact with gifts, ceremonies, and unclear promises, providing the indigenous populations with a belief that reciprocity and respect were possible in the future. On the economic frontier, the vanguard of expansion rested with soldiers, fishers, miners, and traders, a generally rapacious and culturally insensitive lot. And in virtually all territories, the newcomers came in waves, sometimes overlapping, seemingly endless. Across the globe, favorable first impressions were shattered by subsequent developments. Indigenous impressions and expectations adjusted accordingly and generally in a less positive direction.

The Cant of Conquest: Usable Images of the Original Occupiers of Valued Territories

The images of indigenous peoples carried by the newcomers did not remain fixed over time, although the core assumptions about the superiority of the dominant society remained consistent. At no time – including to the present – did the colonial authorities and population revisit their understandings of the indigenous cultures so as to recast the basic relationship between the groups in a more positive light. What did happen, in many different locations, is that newcomer populations altered their impressions of the original inhabitants to suit their specific needs. Indigenous peoples who were defined in relatively generous terms in the first instance, albeit with a healthy dose of the "noble savage" running through the descriptions, were subsequently presented more negatively.

As numerous scholars have demonstrated, images of other populations reveal almost as much as about the group creating and sharing the impressions as about the people being described. The endless European preoccupation with "heathenism" and "savagery" reflected the Old World debates about Christianity and doctrinal disputes between Protestants and Catholics. Efforts to comprehend indigenous relationships with their land and resources illustrated the growing gap between Europeans and the natural world, for they had by the time of colonial expansion largely destroyed their ancient forests. People, including indigenous societies, defined "others" within frames of reference and concepts that they understood. And as their needs and societies evolved – from a world of kingdoms toward nation-states, from the pre-modern to the industrial, from the spiritual rigidities of the Middle Ages to Protestant and Catholic doctrinal rivalries, from a largely rural existence to urban societies – the Europeans' perspectives on the rest of the world shifted. Non-European societies were defined by their deviations from European norms, with these differences, again, rarely conceived in a positive light.

As European usage of newly found territories shifted, so did their conceptions of the indigenous populations. When colonies were valued primarily for their military/strategic importance, Aboriginal peoples were defined largely in terms of alliances. They were friend or foe, useful allies or intractable enemies. When newcomer expansions required active indigenous participation in order to make colonial economies flourish, as in the North American fur trade, harsh assessments of indigenous societies were tempered by descriptions outlining the "usefulness" of the original peoples. Settlement frontiers, in contrast, tended to view indigenous societies as either potential farmers (a rare phenomenon) or as barriers in the way of "progress." In the latter case, by far the most common, the image of indigenous populations shifted from early and somewhat favorable portraits to more hostile characterizations. The aboriginal communities, in these descriptions, were non-economic, did not make effective use of local resources, and were an impediment to the advance of "civilization."

Images proved to be powerful weapons. Repeated in dozens of memoirs, government reports, and other published accounts, the publicly shared impressions of indigenous populations provided the moral and conceptual justification for the actions of the dominant societies. "Brutal savages" clearly had to be tamed by whatever military might was necessary. Colonial nations preparing for war disseminated descriptions of hostile, malicious, and ferocious indigenous fighters. "Primitive hunters" obviously had no use for lands which could be put to far more productive uses. Agricultural settlements seeking territory for expansion could, with such descriptions in place, take indigenous land with little compunction. "Barbaric heathens" cried out for conversion at the hands of missionaries and, if they stood in the way of the advance of Christianity, the conquering power had both the right and the God-given duty to assume control of their lives.

It often mattered little if the images accorded with reality. In many cases, indigenous peoples did not, even by the European standards of the time, fit the descriptions which filled the popular press. The writers sought to justify their actions – be it conquest, land occupation, missionization, or government administration – not to provide an accurate reflection of the people and societies they encountered. Individuals whom specific indigenous societies thought to be friends and allies nonetheless penned descriptions which would have appalled the original peoples. Authors also picked up on the expectations of their home audiences, who desired descriptions of ferocious, intractable, backward, and pagan peoples. There was less interest in more balanced, sympathetic, and accurate appraisals. Indigenous peoples, then, found themselves entrapped in the cant, or ideology, of conquest and domination, controlled and understood through the portraits painted of them, in word and image, by the agents of newcomer societies.

Racism – The Remnant of First Contacts

Centuries later, the lingering effects of first contacts can still be seen around the world. As Europeans ventured into Africa, they crafted disparaging and nasty images of the black peoples that have shaped subsequent western understandings of an entire continent. General concepts of the exoticism of China, Japan, and Korea, what Edward Said has described as "Orientalism," rooted in first encounters and publicized accounts of new cultures, linger to the present. The images of indigenous peoples from the Pacific Islands to the great plains of North America – a curious amalgam of positive and nostalgic impressions of primordial people living at one with nature and critical and hostile descriptions of peoples lacking the basic necessities of civilization – continue to dominate the unconscious assumptions of many non-indigenous peoples. Non-European peoples similarly formed lasting impressions of indigenous cultures, typically harsh, unfavorable and sufficiently malleable to justify cooperation when travel and military strategy dictated and cooptation or conquest when colonial needs prevailed.

In almost all countries where indigenous and non-indigenous peoples co-exist (Scandinavia being something of an exception here), original societies struggle with the imprecise and pervasive vestiges of historical racism. In its most positive twist, outsiders nostalgic about an intricate cultural connection to the environment, elevate historic indigenous cultures to a level of societal superiority and decry the "modernization" of these peoples. More commonly, the contemporary images speak of cultures unable to adapt to technological change, locked in a non-economic, non-materialistic world that dooms them to irrelevance. The roots of these assumptions rest in the distant past, in the initial encounters and first descriptions presented by outsiders, few of whom offered much more than a superficial gloss about complex, rich, and determined societies. These thin, imprecise, and often inaccurate portrayals often spoke of cannibals and barbarians and introduced portraits of savagery and heathenism to stunned audiences in Europe, which had become immune to surprise at revelations about mistreatment and brutality closer to home. They provided the patina of racism, a veneer of curiosity overlying deeply entrenched hostility and fear, which shaped relations between indigenous peoples and newcomers over the centuries.

4

RESISTANCE AND ADAPTATION: INDIGENOUS REACTION TO NEWCOMER OCCUPATIONS

The process of mutual discovery sparked a critical era in the history of newcomer–indigenous relations. Before the first outsiders happened into aboriginal territory, the original peoples lived in limited worlds. While they typically had extensive contact with neighboring and nearby indigenous populations, these localized peoples had little information on societies from distant lands. Word filtered across indigenous lands as newcomers made first contact with aboriginal societies, spreading news of strange outsiders with new tools, different approaches to war, new spiritual explanations, and promises of economic opportunity. Indigenous responses to the arrival of the newcomers set the stage for decades, if not centuries, of subsequent relations.

Writers who have reduced the meeting of indigenous peoples and outsiders to a struggle between colonizers and the colonized have both emphasized a key element in the process and missed critical aspects of the interaction. Most importantly, the emphasis on the actions, values, and attitudes of the colonial powers effectively stripped the indigenous peoples of their agency. While this was not the intent, the standard refrain that the colonizers pushed, stole, and otherwise destroyed indigenous societies diminishes the active, creative, occasionally wrong-headed decisions that aboriginal peoples made in responding to the arrival of the newcomers. Indigenous peoples have not been hapless uncivilized societies, recoiling in the face of progress, as much of western writing claimed before the 1960s. Nor has the encounter between newcomers and indigenous cultures been characterized by malicious domination and intentional destruction, as much of the writing after the 1960s has suggested. History is a more complex, more messy, and multi-directional process than either argument would suggest.

Violent Occupations: Tribal Peoples at War with Newcomers

Initial encounters with indigenous peoples were generally cloaked in surprise and uncertainty on both sides of the cultural frontier. Indigenous peoples did not know much about the newcomers and were mystified and intrigued by many aspects of the outsiders' material and social world. They were, on first sight, impressed with the technologies of ocean navigation and combat, although they subsequently discovered that the loud and frightening guns and cannons were less threatening than initially assumed. They did not initially understand the imperatives of international trade and commerce, however experienced they were at more localized trades, for the imperatives of sedentary and specialized societies bore little resemblance to their own ways of addressing personal and collective needs.

The newcomers were likewise somewhat daunted by what they saw. The majestic buildings of some of the newly encountered peoples – the Chinese, Japanese, Thais, Inca, and Aztecs – startled outsiders who were used to seeing their societies as being at the forefront of innovation, high culture, and social organization. The lack of rigidity among the indigenous peoples – who followed mobile lives, occupied temporary structures, and appeared without cultural or religious form – bewildered the outsiders, who subsequently assigned them to the bottom rung of the ladder of humanity. Facial markings, clothing (or lack thereof), semi-permanent housing, and the other accoutrements of indigenous cultures were baffling, off-putting to most, curious to some, and to all further proof of the depravity and lack of "civilization" on the part of the original peoples. Add to this confusing array of images, social realities, and the many nuances of new lands – jungles, open plains, rich marine environments, barren Arctic or desert territories – and one can better understand the difficulties that the newcomers had in characterizing or placing the indigenous peoples.

Misunderstanding was a common element in the outbreak of hostilities. Newcomers misunderstood indigenous ceremonies, intentions, or curios-ity. They responded, in many instances, with violent outbursts. Aboriginal peoples, likewise, often reacted out of anger, disbelief, and worry, attacking the newcomers whom they viewed as a major and mysterious threat. The Jarawas of the Andaman Islands, for example, have long used unprovoked attacks on outsiders to keep people off of their territories. Violence often generated additional confrontation. An attack, provoked or otherwise, by indigenous peoples convinced the newcomers of the brutality and untrustworthiness of the original inhabitants. A comparable attack on an individual or a community by newcomers – and the soldiers, sailors, traders, and miners who represented the vanguard of the colonial powers were not noted for their caution and carefulness – demonstrated to the aboriginal peoples that the outsiders were brutal, barbaric, and not to be trusted. Fundamental misunderstandings at the initial stages of contact could, and did, shape relations for generations, with the memories of the conflicts lingering in community consciousness through to the present.

Memories lingered, too, of the brutality and violence associated with the initial expansion of Europeans into indigenous territories. *The Devastation of the Indies* by Bartolomé de Las Casas created a sensation when it was published in 1522 and was quickly translated and circulated around Europe, largely because of its frank and disturbing descriptions of European actions in the Caribbean:

And the Christians attacked them with buffets and beatings, until finally they laid hands on the nobles of the villages. Then they behaved with such temerity and shamelessness that the most powerful ruler of the islands had to see his own wife raped by a Christian officer. From that time onward the Indians began to seek ways to throw the Christians out of their lands. They took up arms, but their weapons were very weak and of little service in offense and still less in defense .... And the Christians, with their horses and swords and pikes began to carry out massacres and strange cruelties against them. They attacked the towns and spared neither the children nor the aged nor pregnant women nor women in childbed, not only stabbing them and dismembering them but cutting them to pieces as if dealing with sheep in the slaughter house. They laid bets as to who, with one stroke of the sword, could split a man in two or could cut off his head or spill out his entrails with a single stroke of a pike. They took infants from their mothers' breasts, snatching them by the legs and pitching them headfirst against the crags or snatched them by the arms and threw them into the rivers, roaring with laughter and saying as the babies fell into the water, "Boil there, you offspring of the devil." ... They made some low wide gallows on which the hanged victim's feet almost touched the ground, stringing up their victims in lots of thirteen, in memory of Our Redeemer and His Twelve Apostles, and then set burning wood at their feet and thus burned them alive ... With still others, all those they wanted to capture alive, they cut off their hands and hung them round the victim's neck, saying, "Go now, carry the message," meaning, Take the news to the Indians who have fled to the mountains.[1]

The viciousness – degrading, demoralizing, and destructive – spread throughout the region and reappeared in numerous sites in indigenous–newcomer contact around the world.

In many situations, misunderstanding was not required; the actions and attitudes of the newcomers provided sufficient spark for a wave of bitter and destructive conflict. The outsiders came into new lands with specific objectives. Whether their goal was the pursuit of wealth, military/strategic advantage, or simply the assertion of political dominance, they often used violence as an initial means of establishing their place in the New World. The Europeans, in particular, came confident of their superiority and found great solace in the reaction of the indigenous peoples to their military technology. Guns, cannons, and iron tools proved of enormous benefit in conflicts with rivals whose weaponry was made out of wood, flint, or bone. Personal imperatives – the desire of a military leader for fame, wealthy, glory, or God's blessing – pushed many outsiders to move aggressively against the typically smaller and less prepared indigenous populations.

The pursuit of slaves motivated Europeans to expand aggressively in Africa and created a foundation for the military conflict which shaped the history of the continent. As recent scholarship has demonstrated, the dynamics of the slave trade within Africa played a major role in determining how this industry and this wave of European domination developed. African tribes raided each other, trading the human spoils of war to outsiders. These internal conflicts, which in turn reflected age-old rivalries, increased in bitterness and intensity in the face of external markets and the seemingly insatiable demand for men, women, and children to fill the holds of slave ships heading for Europe and North, South, and Central America. Europeans moved into the midst of these internal conflicts, using their military prowess and economic might to expand a hitherto small trade into a global exchange network. There were similar experiences in other regions. The Agta of the Philippines had troubles with slave traders well before Spanish colonization brought even more disruptive changes, as did the Batek with the Malays.

Few episodes in world history have matched the African slave trade for brutality and scope. Hundreds of thousands of tribal peoples were captured, transferred within Africa, sold to outsiders, and transported to markets in Europe and the New World. Thousands upon thousands perished in the initial conflicts, were killed on the tragic marches to coastal ports, or perished during inhumane journeys to the slave markets. Many more thousands died at the hands of slave owners or from the punishing cruelty of the plantations. While a great deal is known about the institution of slavery and its manifestations in Europe and the Americas, much less has been written about the impact of slavery on the tribal societies of Africa. Hundreds of indigenous cultures lost many of their people to the slave traders, and suffered from the pain and collective dislocation which followed. Entire regions – the Congo being the best example – were devastated by the rapaciousness of the Europeans. King Leopold of Belgium, for example, launched a malicious and aggressive campaign against the people of his colony in the Congo, aimed at both personal aggrandisement and the creation of wealth for the home country. While the origins of slavery clearly involved inter-African rivalries, raids, and violence, the escalation of the trade to meet the manpower needs of Europe and the Americas brought sweeping changes throughout the continent. More expansively, the institutions of slavery and the racial assumptions which underpinned the demoralizing structures based on notions of civilization and ethnic dominance established a pattern of control, racism, and poverty which the passage of several centuries has not yet erased.

Africa was not the only place where newcomers became embroiled in the intricacies of indigenous rivalries and territorial conflicts. Most famously, the Aztecs had dominated the smaller societies in their region for several generations. Economic and social pressures, including the Aztec need for thousands of human sacrifices each year (the degree of which remains a matter of intense and continuing scholarly debate) resulted in the Aztecs exerting their dominance over surrounding societies. These peoples came under Aztec military control, but had not internalized their allegiance to this aggressive, centralizing power. When the Spaniards arrived under Hernan Cortez in 1518–19, they encountered an Aztec empire in considerable disarray. The smaller peoples rallied around the newcomers and aided them in their subsequent conflict with the Aztecs. The newcomers were strange and small in number. But the weaker peoples of the Aztec empire counted on the Spaniards' technological superiority – firearms, gunpowder, horses, and other armaments – to topple a much-hated regime. Indigenous accounts of the Spaniards aggressiveness in battle captured the frightful brutality of the initial conflicts:

> And when this had been done, thereupon they entered the temple courtyard
> to slay them. Those who task it was to slay them went only afoot, each with his
> leather shield, some, each one, with his iron-studded shield, and each with his
> iron sword. Thereupon they surrounded the dancers. Thereupon they went
> among the drums. Then they struck the drummer's arms; they severed both
> his hands; then they struck his neck. Far off did his neck [and head] go to fall.
> Then they pierced the people with iron lances and they struck them each with
> iron swords. Of some they slashed open their backs; then their entrails gushed
> out. Of some they cut their heads; their heads were absolutely pulverized. And
> some they struck on the shoulder; they split openings, they broke openings in
> their bodies. Of some they struck repeatedly in the shanks; of some they struck
> repeatedly the thighs; of some they struck the belly; then their entrails gushed
> forth. And when in vain one would run, he would only drag his intestines like
> something raw as he tried to escape. Nowhere could he go. And him who tried
> to go out they there struck; they stabbed him … . For this reason were the
> Mexicans very angry; because [the Spaniards] had completely annihilated the
> brave warriors; without warning them they had slain them by treachery.[2]

The original people, even if they were pleased to see Montezuma displaced, did not anticipate – and few peoples have had the prescience to
anticipate the multi-generational impact of initial developments – that
the Spaniards would come in large numbers, establish dominance over
all peoples and, long after the Aztec had been vanquished, rule the
indigenous societies with an iron hand.

Newcomers represented an additional element within complex social,
economic, and strategic indigenous relationships. It is hardly surprising
that the indigenous peoples sought to use the outsiders to their advantage whenever possible. They tried, where they could, to align the newcomers within their political and territorial agendas. Many used
alliances and treaties to solidify – or so they thought – these relationships. Early decisions, including the manner in which the First Nations
in Eastern North America aligned themselves with the English, French,
Spanish, or Dutch, proved to have lasting significance, depending on
the success of their colonial ally in defending their space and authority
on the continent. Maori military leaders likewise sought to entwine
British officials in longstanding local conflicts, as did African peoples in
the messy and complicated colonial apportionment of Africa.

Colonial powers were not averse to shooting indigenous people in large
numbers. In the initial years of contact, small displays of technological

superiority, as with Cortez and the Aztec, could be successful. Over time, larger armies, well-armed and carefully supplied, were required to ensure success against determined foes. They resisted Japanese incursions into Hokkaido, with major conflicts at Kosyamain in 1457, Syaksyain in 1669, and Kunasiri-Menasi in 1789. They managed to slow, but not stop, the Japanese advance into their territories. Their population declined steadily from almost 24,000 in 1804 to less than 19,000 seventy years later. By the early 1870s, the Japanese population on Hokkaido had soared to over 150,000 (and by 1970, the Ainu people counted less than 20,000 while there were over five million Japanese). The Russia expansion into Siberia and Central Europe was marked by the repeated use of military force and, in several instances, the destruction of communities. The Cossacks moved aggressively across indigenous lands, terrorizing the people and generating a strong antipathy toward the newcomers.

Ferocious battles erupted in Central and South America, and along the eastern seaboard of North America. A chilling description of the Dutch attacks on Indians in the region provides a sense of the intense violence of the occupation:

> After midnight, I heard a great shrieking, and I ran to the ramparts of the fort, and looked over to Pavonia. Saw nothing but firing, and heard the shrieks of Indians murdered in their sleep ... When it was day the soldiers returned to the fort, having massacred or murdered eighty Indians, and considering they had done a deed of Roman valour, in murdering so many in their sleep; where infants were torn from their mother's breasts, and hacked to pieces in the presence of the parents, and the pieces thrown into the fire and in the water, and other sucklings being bound to small boards, and then cut, stuck, and pierced, and miserably massacred in a manner to move a heart of stone. Some were thrown into the river, and when the fathers and mothers endeavoured to save them, the soldiers would not let them come to land, but made both parents and children drown – children from five to six years of age, and also some old and decrepit persons. Many fled from this scene, and concealed themselves in the neighbouring sedge, and when it was morning, came out to beg a piece of bread, and to be permitted to warm themselves; but they were murdered in cold blood and tossed into the water. Some came by our lands in the country with their hands, some with their legs cut off, and some holding their entrails in their arms, and others had such horrible cuts, and gashes, that worse than they were could never happen.[3]

There was considerable duplicity as well. According to one analyst, "The English in 1623 negotiated a treaty with rebellious tribes in the Potomac

River area. After a toast was drunk symbolizing eternal friendship, the Chiskiack chief and his sons, advisers, and followers, totalling two hundred, abruptly dropped dead from poisoned sack, and soldiers put the remainder out of their misery."[4]

The battles across North America continued. The Pequot War (1636–37) and King Philip's War (1675–76) in New England devastated numerous Indian communities, who responded to the brutal attacks by using guerrilla warfare tactics. The Indians then found themselves drawn into the equally ferocious English–French conflicts, suffering significant losses in an almost continuous series of raids and wars. Conflict with the settlers erupted again in 1763 during Pontiac's Rebellion and the aboriginal attack on Detroit. With the defeat of the French and the occupation of Quebec, British settlers again pushed westward, sparking conflicts over land and resources with the original inhabitants. Warrior chiefs like Little Turtle and Tecumseh led the resistance against the intruders, but the hope of holding back the settlers disappeared after Tecumseh's loss to the Americans in 1811 and the defeat of the Creek Indians in the south in 1814. There were a few armed conflicts in the east after this time, particularly involving the Seminoles of Florida, but the authority of government and the preeminence of the settlers had been firmly established by this time.

Indigenous peoples learned quickly from these conflicts, many of which reduced their settlements to smouldering embers and left many dead and wounded. Historian Francis Jennings, reflecting on the experiences of the pivotal Pequot War, wrote that the Indians took three main lessons from the conflict. First, they realized that the firm promises and formal commitments of the British could not be relied upon to protect their communities from attack. They discovered, to their dismay, that British military tactics had little place for mercy or compassion and that the battles, once launched, would be total assaults on Indian peoples. Finally, they discovered that traditional Indian weapons and tactics had little chance against the military hardware, tactics, and bloodthirstiness of the newcomers. Not only did the Pequot and their neighbors learn these hard-won and painful lessons, but indigenous peoples far removed from the eastern battlefields found out through trading and social contacts about the vicious and brutal British tactics. Hardly surprisingly, indigenous communities readied themselves for bitter and lengthy conflicts, based on a fundamental distrust for the integrity and reliability of the British state and armed forces.

The most famous indigenous–newcomer conflicts, memorialized in movies, television programs and novels, involved the western expansion of the United States during the nineteenth century. The American West earned its reputation for conflict and brutality. The seemingly inexorable expansion of the settlement frontier, combined with the aggressive actions of miners and the steady mid-nineteenth-century destruction of the buffalo herds, brought conflict between the indigenous peoples and newcomers. The United States army clearly took sides, defending the settlers' and miners' interests, even when these encroached on Indian territory and rights, and working to keep supply lines open to the far west. In a lengthy series of conflicts through the 1850s and 1860s, the United States defeated such groups as the Apache, Kiowa, and Cheyenne. Some of the attacks, like the massacre of the Cheyenne at Sand Creek in 1864, were particularly brutal and soured relations between newcomers and Indians for generations.

The determination and military prowess of the Apache, Comanche, Cheyenne, and Nez Perce struck fear into the hearts of western migrants, who believed that the land and its resources were theirs for the taking. Leaders like Sitting Bull, Geronimo, Crazy Horse, and others became internationally famous for their battles with the US army. The famous Battle of the Little Big Horn, which saw Sitting Bull's Sioux warriors annihilate the 7th Calvary under Lt. Col. George Armstrong Custer in 1876, highlighted the Indians' military ability. Sitting Bull and his people, however, fled to Canada to escape retribution, only to return in despair and hunger five years later. Across the military frontier, indigenous peoples faced attacks against villages (including several bloody massacres), entrapment on small and ill-suited reservations, poor food, and government determination to keep them under control. The Nez Perce fought a bitter and lengthy war for independence in 1877, and were chased hundreds of miles across the west before being forced to surrender and be spilt up by American authorities. The surrender of Geronimo and the Apache in 1886 and the bitter conflict with the Sioux at Wounded Knee that same year signalled the military demise of the Indian fighters on the plains.

Similar conflicts erupted in other regions. The Mapuche of southern Chile waged a long and bitter campaign against the Spaniards, holding them at bay for years through the successful application of the tactics of guerrilla warfare. In New Zealand, wars between the British and the Maori broke out several times during the nineteenth century, with major conflicts in 1845–47, 1860–61, and 1863–66. Although the British forces ultimately prevailed, the military prowess and determination of the Maori made it clear to the colonial authorities that a struggle to the end would result in major losses and great hardship. The larger, well-organized tribes of Africa, particularly in the southern part of the continent, represented a major threat to the newcomers. Several major tribal wars, including the famous battle with the Zulu at Isandhlwana, which demonstrated to a surprised western world both the scale of indigenous organization and their fury at the colonial intrusion, established a socio-military framework for subsequent relations on the continent.

The military conflicts were not always one-sided. In some instances, indigenous peoples used their superior knowledge of local conditions to harass and overcome intended invasions. Military tactics better suited to specific geographical and climatic situations also helped aboriginal warriors to fight against the newcomers. The Maori *pa* or fortifications, for example, proved to be a formidable barrier to British armed forces sent to establish authority over New Zealand. In what New Zealand historians call the First Taranaki War, Maori leader Te Rangitake led a concerted campaign against the British, who seemed determined to take over Maori land. While the British prevailed, the Maori provided to be formidable foes. In North America, Iroquis, Huron, and Algonquin fighters used the guerrilla-like tactics of the forest to inflict considerable damage on British, French, and Dutch troops trained to operate in the "civilized" open field warfare of Europe. Although the final struggles involving the Métis (people of mixed French and indigenous ancestry) in Canada were of comparatively minor scale, the well-trained Métis fighters resisted a substantially larger Canadian force during the 1885 Rebellion before succumbing to the Canadian troops.

In many parts of the world, living in undesirable, inhospitable or inaccessible territories was the only real protection from newcomer invasion and occupations. The Toba of northern Argentina inhabited land that was initially of little interest to newcomers. Left substantially alone, they developed a strong horse-based culture and found themselves in a lengthy struggle with the authorities and, after 1880, settlers and developers. Other groups, particularly the Tehuelche and Puelche, stood in the way of Argentinian exploitation of the Pampas. They were quickly shouldered aside militarily. The indigenous peoples of the North American sub-Arctic experienced little military intervention due to the limited interest in their lands before the twentieth century, when administrative and legislative tools were available to move the original inhabitants off their lands.

Through the course of many conflicts in lands around the world, indigenous peoples discovered both the strengths and limitations of the newcomers' military system. Some elements, such as the use of the horse, were adopted by indigenous groups and soon used against the invaders. In other instances, trading activities with enemies of the colonial power provided the armaments necessary for strong counter-measures against the newcomers. Guerrilla tactics, with small groups of soldiers, farmsteads, and isolated communities singled out for strategic strikes, were implemented with great effectiveness in many parts of the world – all the more successful because the evident brutality of the attacks coincided with the newcomers' fears and assumptions about the original peoples. The prospect for retribution was also considerable. When a newcomer was killed at Coniston Station in the Australian out-back in 1928, the government launched an attack on the Warlpiri which killed between 30 and 100 people. It was only one of many such revenge attacks designed to keep the indigenous communities in line.

The greatest military conflicts – and the ones which appear to have defined for all time the images and assumptions about many indigenous groups – were tied to newcomer attempts to occupy the land for the pur-poses of settlement. So long as contact was limited to traders, govern-ment officials, and soldiers, conflicts were generally strategic and political in nature. Once settlers arrived on the scene, conditions changed rapidly. Governments mustered armies to defend the colonial settlers. Indigenous peoples, for their part, now witnessed for the first time the scale, permanence, and impact of the colonizers' occupation. The desire to oust newcomers from traditional territories was very strong, and resulted in bitter and ferocious struggles. The settlers, aware of the economic and social potential of the various "new worlds" they had encountered, were just as determined to hold onto to the land and opportunity they had been granted by government or had simply taken as their right.

Settlement frontiers were only rarely compatible with indigenous habitation, and the resulting moving line of occupation became a bat-tleground between world views and assumptions about land ownership. The most famous struggles occurred in the east coast colonies of British North America, and then proceeded as the voracious and land-hungry settlers of the newly formed United States of America headed further west. Earlier, the establishment of Spanish and Portuguese control of Central and South America required the dispossession and removal of large numbers of indigenous peoples and their replacement by large commercial land owners. Very often, the contest over land ownership and use erupted into battles and guerrilla wars. The arrival of large numbers of settlers in South Africa, New Zealand and, to a lesser extent, Australia, touched off a variety of local military and police conflicts, most of them ending at considerable cost to the indigenous peoples.

Colonial governments felt compelled to support their settlers, even if the latter had moved in violation of treaties or had undertaken unauthorized expansions onto indigenous lands. They mobilized armies to protect the settlers, established fortified posts to assert their political and military authority, and unleashed their soldiers and sailors on the indigenous peoples if they felt that the settlement frontier was being threatened. The compulsion to protect their settlers meant that the indigenous peoples could count on very little protection from the government and armies, even in the face of misdeeds and malfeasance on the part of the newcomers.

The military conflicts took their toll. Rarely were the indigenous peoples able to repulse the newcomers entirely. Short-term victories were often followed by large-scale attacks and even military occupations. Some groups could and did flee into inhospitable terrain, using geography to keep the invaders at bay. But the scale and technological strength of the newcomers' armies generally wore the indigenous resisters down over time. Chief Joseph of the Nez Perce provided one of the most classic statements of resignation and despair when he said:

I am tired of fighting. Our chiefs are killed. Looking Glass is dead. Toohulsote is dead. The old men are all dead. It is the young men who say no and yes. He who led the young men is dead. It is cold and we have no blankets. The little children are freezing to death. My people, some of them, have run away to the hills and have no blankets, no food. No one knows where they are – perhaps they are freezing to death. I want to have time to look for my children and see how many of them I can find. Maybe I shall find them among the dead. Hear me, my chiefs, I am tired. My heart is sad and sick. From where the sun now stands I will fight no more forever.[5]

Gentle Occupations: Tribal Peoples Co-Existing with Non-Violent Occupiers

The story of newcomer–indigenous contact was not always one of battle, conquest, and dispossession, although these were the most common occurrences. Indigenous peoples were not always averse to the arrival and settlement by outsiders. The colonial powers had metal tools, new military technology, and other material goods, making them valuable as trading partners. Colonial governments, for their part, learned from bitter direct experience or from the costly errors of their rivals that extended military campaigns against the original inhabitants carried enormous costs and rarely resulted in a peaceful settlement and development frontier. As time passed, and particularly by the late nineteenth and early twentieth century, arguments were being mounted that empires had to both enrich the colonial power and contribute to the well-being of the colonized people – it was the white man's burden to share God's beneficence with the rest of the world. On both sides, therefore, there were reasons for more gentle patterns of occupation and coexistence. While these relationships often resulted in significant disruptions in indigenous lifeways and economic activity, they represented a very different attempt by newcomers and aboriginal peoples alike to respond to the changing realities of an inter-cultural world.

The demarcation between periods and sites of conflict and those of cooperation follow no singular logic. Colonial nations which, in one area of the world, experienced violent confrontations with indigenous societies responded very differently in other locations. Indigenous peoples who, in early stages of contact, engaged in bitter conflict with the newcomers, managed more flexible and mutually beneficial relations with the same colonial powers a few decades later. In some instances, the changed approach reflected the realization of the consequences of conflict or, more positively, illustrated a growing understanding of each other. There was no simple pattern from the colonizer's perspective. The Spanish and Portuguese, the first to establish substantial overseas colonies, moved initially with brutality and certainty, only belatedly coming to the realization that their approach to colonization beggared their treasury and slowed the economic development of their overseas holdings. The French had reasonably positive relations with First Nations in northern North America and bitter conflicts in Africa. The British managed to establish respectful relationships in substantial portions of East Africa, waged bitter war against the Maori, and engaged in genocidal behaviour in several of the colonies of British North America. Belgium, late into the colonial game, entered with a vengeance, establishing an unenviable track record of destruction and conquest in central Africa.

Indigenous response to newcomers went through similar patterns. Some, like the Beothuk of Newfoundland, feared the newcomers from the beginning, made very little contact, and perished from starvation, disease, and separation from their traditional harvesting territories. Many of the small tribal societies in the Amazon basin, Australia, Central America, the high Arctic, Siberia, and the mountainous districts of Southeast Asia took comparable approaches, remaining in the safety of their forbidding environments, protected by the difficult terrain from destructive contact with the outsiders. Others fought with the colonial powers until circumstances forced a reconsideration of their approach. The Japanese worried about the potential aggressiveness of the Ainu:

> [They] are a sturdy tribe. Although they seem to be ignorant, it is said that, having solved the problem of death, they have strong characters. If they are not treated with care, they will probably cause trouble in the future. Just recently, a [man] committed suicide because of his anger. We must remember the old adage that a rat when driven into a corner may attack a cat.[6]

For a few, like the Maori of New Zealand, demonstrations of military prowess earned the begrudging respect of the colonizers and resulted in a negotiated relationship which, on paper, held the promise of a reasonable future within a colonial regime. Others, like the Sioux, fought successfully against the newcomers but realized that, even in victory, they had nonetheless lost their land and control over their future. The Aborigines of Cape York, Australia, routinely fought with newcomers, with their acts of violence typically resulting in an equally strong or stronger reaction. Throughout Australia, a series of localized massacres and bitter battles marked the expansion of the ranching and farming frontier. Situations changed with the size of the colonial population, the aggressiveness of the newcomers, and the policies of governments. The indigenous response also shifted over time, as groups oscillated between fleeing from the intruders, fighting with them, welcoming and supporting the newcomers, or seeking a political or administrative accommodation. Some groups, like the Jahai of Malaysia, shied away from direct and extended contact with outsiders, using geography and distance to protect themselves from unwelcome changes.

The expansion into indigenous territories typically involved the search for wealth and opportunity, and the original inhabitants were often viewed as pivotal to the securing of the much-desired resources. The initial colonial efforts in Central and North America, for example, revolved around attempts to use aboriginal labour to produce valuable crops, minerals, or other forms of wealth for the colonial powers. The model established in Central America and portions of South America did not transfer well to the more mobile peoples of North America and much of South America, however. These indigenous peoples did not accept the forcible transition into a commercial workforce. In these cases, much of the economic potential remained unrealized until additional laborers – slaves, indentured servants, and immigrant workers – were imported.

In those parts of the world where the emerging colonial economy drew heavily on traditional indigenous skills of harvesting and traveling, more mutually beneficial relationships developed. The North American fur trade rested on strong and sustained relations between fur traders and indigenous trappers and traders, although much less so during the westward extension of the United States than in the French and British areas to the north. Similar patterns of contact and mutual support emerged during the eastward expansion of Russia into Siberia and with the reindeer-herding Sami people of northern Scandinavia. Russian authorities levied an economically debilitating *iasak* (tribute or tax) on the indigenous peoples, requiring them to provide large quantities of furs to the authorities. They encouraged the development of commercial reindeer herding and, later, commercial fishing, providing the indigenous peoples of the North with an entrée into the market economy expanding from the west. The Ainu of Japan likewise traded extensively with the Japanese, although they often complained about the imbalance in the exchange:

> Lord Matsumae's methods of trade are unfair. We are obliged to buy rice in sacks containing only seven or eight *shō* where they used to contain two *to*. Furthermore, if one bundle of shells is found to be short the next year he charges twenty bundles for it and if one is unable to produce them, his child is taken in ransom. Since all is carried out in the same manner it is a great hardship on the people Bikuni.[7]

The development of the Basho contracting system, comparable to chartered European companies, changed the trading system for the Ainu in the late eighteenth century, but did not strengthen the Ainu hand decisively. In parts of the South Pacific, the early colonial economies relied on indigenous help with fishing, cultivation of crops, and other resource activities. These relationships, while serving to draw the indigenous peoples into colonial and even global trading networks, often proved of lasting duration, sustained in some parts of the world into the post-World War II era.

The arrival of newcomers also ushered in an era of personal contact between colonial and indigenous peoples. With few exceptions, the overwhelming majority of the colonial populations were young men. The dispatch of hundreds of sailors, fishermen, loggers, soldiers, miners, and officials to the far distant fringes of the empire resulted in the creation of incomplete, fragmented societies. The convict societies in several parts of Australia, likewise, shared few social characteristics with the more comprehensive and balanced society of the homeland. Some settlements, like the early communities along the east coast of British North America, Boer communities in South Africa, and British colonies in New Zealand and South Australia, brought men, women, and children, with the goal of providing greater social stability and permanence. But these were exceptions. Most initial colonies were peopled by large groups of young men, with few women among their number.

Although the colonial societies had both legal and social strictures governing relations with indigenous women, the distance from the mother country and the full control of church, state, and community values prevented the full implementation of these rules. Young men, far from the social controls of their communities, sought sexual comfort and companionship from indigenous women. These relationships ranged widely in character, from exploitative and destructive contacts, in which rape and the use of coercion was commonplace, to lasting and mutually beneficial arrangements. Aztec historian Chimalpahin wrote of these experiences:

> Women who came from Spain ... married men of Mexico, and from there came the mestizos. Equally, the daughters of some of our most esteemed Princes, as well as some young women of the servant class, were impregnated by Spaniards and thus more mestizos were born – a thing which happens every day. Some of these keep their mixed origins a secret and hide the fact that they have come from us, the Natives ... . Other mestizos, in contrast, do us honour and are proud to have come from native blood.[8]

Many French and British fur traders in North America entered into formal, if not always permanent, relationships with aboriginal women. Often, these unions solidified commercial or political arrangements. Maori women, likewise, became the partners and wives of non-indigenous men in New Zealand, establishing a pattern of interracial marriage which became a crucial long-term characteristic of the society. Australian Aboriginal women, in contrast, were shunned by almost all non-indigenous Australian people, resulting in a long and bitter history of abandoned women and children. Japanese traders from the mainland imposed themselves on the Ainu women or took them as mistresses, causing dismay among the Ainu men. Many Ainu women married Japanese and, in most instances, integrated into Japanese society, further eroding Ainu culture. Across most of Africa and among the slave populations in the Americas sexual and personal relationships across racial lines were rarely tolerated by the dominant society. These social regulations did not mean, however, that non-indigenous men did not find ways, consensual or otherwise, to satisfy their sexual needs with local women. They did so, in many instances, by generating self-serving images and profiles of indigenous women which labeled them as licentious and sexually promiscuous, and thus limited their personal and collective liability for the difficulties inflicted upon the women and removed their responsibility for the progeny of these typically short-term unions.

Interracial sex and social relations had profound effects on many indigenous and colonial societies. The unions marginalized indigenous women and created additional competition for these women within the aboriginal societies. The sexualization of social relations – with short-term liaisons, rape, and the birth of mixed-race children being key features of indigenous–colonial relations – drove a firm wedge between the groups. Indigenous men were often angered by the treatment of women from their communities and were generally excluded from any comparable relationships with non-indigenous women. Colonial women, in turn, typically blamed their aboriginal counterparts for the failings of the flesh which befell their men folk. Across the Canadian west, for example, observers often complained about aboriginal immorality and portrayed the women as sexual predators who preyed upon the newcomer men. Settlers urged government officials, particularly the police, to keep the women away from towns. As one writer noted, First Nations women were "of abandoned character who were there for the worst purposes."[9] The mixed-race children from these liaisons were rarely raised with contact with their fathers and often found themselves shunned by the colonial society. Indigenous communities were typically more receptive, although mixed-race people often inhabited an awkward and uncertain social space in the evolving order. In Africa, the reality and mythology of black-and-white sex played a prominent role in ethnic relations. Black men were general viewed as sexual predators, a key element in the "black peril" that sat at the core of the colonial order. Many men were persecuted, often without reason, for alleged breaches of the social expectations regarding black-and-white sex. As one scholar wrote of the situation:

> All the world over, both men and women, though perhaps more often and more violently women, who have been kept in stricter bonds, attribute to some dark and shadowy figure which they fear and hate the desires they disapprove of most strongly in themselves. And for Rhodesians that dark and shadowy figure was ready made in the person of "the native," at the same time scapegoat and shadow, while those cellars of the mind were rejected desires were stowed were also the repository for fears, fears that remembered the rebellions in Matabeleland and Mashonaland. And when desire emerged, fear was not far away. So it was that almost every white Rhodesian spoke with horror of the African's lustful immorality, his utter lack of restraint. And he took elaborate precautions to safeguard his women against these tendencies.[10]

In contrast, the vast majority of the offences of white men forcing themselves on black women went unpunished and often passed without comment. As Gabriel Mabeta wrote in 1925:

> O black people? You my esteemed people! You my despised, pauperized and down trodden people! How many more years shall you sleep under a white man's foot? Wake up and rub your eyes and see what he is doing to your daughters. Let us defend our girls and die defending them. A white man has taken our country and has deprived us of all our rights, must he take our girls also? God forbid. A white man's flesh is not of iron, nor is his sinew of wire. Wake up and protect your women and girls ere we are submerged by a wave of half castes.[11]

These contradictory images and expectations were common along the indigenous–newcomer frontiers. Legal prohibitions and social conventions which attempted to prevent interracial sexual relations were a logical outgrowth of these conflicting assumptions about the contact experience.

Sexual relations also often had economic aspects, for the newcomers were frequently willing to pay sizeable sums for access to indigenous women. Edward Markham wrote of the situation in a New Zealand port:

> Thirty to five and Thirty sail of Whalers come in for three weeks to the Bay and 400 and 500 Sailors require as many Women, and they have been out on year. I saw some who had been out Thirty-Two months and of course the ladies are in great request .... These young ladies go off to the Ships, and three weeks on board are spent much to their satisfaction, as they get from

the Sailors a Fowling piece [shotgun] for the Father or Broth, Blankets, or Gowns.[12]

A major sex industry, complete with contracts for the use of Maori women, emerged on the South Pacific islands, as it did among the whalers in the western Arctic. While "half-castes," "half-breeds," and other peoples of mixed newcomer–indigenous ancestry were generally scorned, a cultural group known as the Métis developed in what is now western Canada. With French Canadian fathers and aboriginal mothers, the Métis were defined initially by their participation in the fur trade as laborers and boatmen and, more comprehensively, by their participation in an elaborate buffalo hunt. People of English–indigenous parentage in the region did not establish themselves as a distinct culture, although some individuals and families integrated with the Métis people. The Métis became widely known for their military prowess – their victory over the Sioux at the Battle of Grand Couteau became a key element in their emerging national identity – their tightly organized buffalo hunt, unique language, and vibrant social life. They established themselves as cultural intermediaries between the newcomers, both French and English, and the indigenous peoples, among both of whom they had relatives and strong socio-economic connections.

Social relations were, not surprisingly, also conditioned by racial assumptions and images. Newcomer societies generally portrayed indigenous women as promiscuous, an image which therefore freed them to mistreat and abuse aboriginal females without guilt. The same set of social values made it very difficult for non-aboriginal men to take indigenous women as permanent partners – unless they opted to remain living beyond the edge of settled newcomer society. In the British North American fur trade, where extensive relations between indigenous women and newcomer men were commonplace, a few traders succeeded in taking their aboriginal wives back to the settled colonies to the east or to Britain. Far more common was the process of "turning off" wives to remaining or incoming traders, leaving the new man to look after the women and young children from the relationship. Even these comparatively long-term relationships were quite rare. The vast majority of social and sexual relations between indigenous women and newcomer men were short-term in nature. It is worth noting, in a pattern similar to that of African men and non-African women in Europe and North America, that relations very rarely involved indigenous men and newcomer women.

Within most colonial situations, government attitudes changed when the indigenous peoples were no longer perceived as a collective threat to the functioning of the colony. Relationships that had been managed at arm's length, either through the comforting words of a treaty or through the protection of military power, shifted dramatically when the prospect of an armed conflict dimmed. When the British–French wars in North America ended, when peace was negotiated in New Zealand, and when military adventures weakened the tribal peoples of South Africa, colonial administrators shifted toward a policy of benevolence. Most indigenous communities initially viewed the overtures as signs of cooperation and future partnership, only to discover that they had been pushed toward irrelevance. Only where indigenous peoples remained either economically important or militarily threatening did the colonial administrators continue to maintain a more equitable approach to aboriginal affairs. The shift toward government management of indigenous affairs ushered in a radically different period in the history of aboriginal–newcomer relations.

Indigenous Adaptations

In most instances, aboriginal people and communities exerted significant influence on the contact situation. In those instances where the newcomers swamped the local inhabitants, either militarily or numerically, indigenous people had little opportunity to respond, save by flight or military resistance. In the first instance, they lost control of their traditional lands. They then, by relocating onto the lands of other peoples, imposed themselves on the aboriginal cultures whose territories they entered. Those who fought in such circumstances typically encountered a bitter and disastrous fate, characterized by sharp population loss, dispossession, and cultural disarray. As devastating as these occasions could be, they were relatively rare on the frontier between indigenous and newcomer societies.

Far more often, indigenous peoples adjusted to the arrival of outsiders. At the early stages, when aboriginal communities established their initial assumptions about the non-indigenous peoples, numerical advantage rested with the indigenous cultures and, often, the military balance was either close to even, or to the aboriginal advantage. The passage of time – and particularly the expansion of settlement frontiers – typically tipped the balance toward the non-indigenous side of the power equation, significantly reducing the authority and bargaining power of the original inhabitants. Throughout, however, aboriginal communities responded as best they could to new and disconcerting changes in their human environment. With little direct experience and little evidence at hand about the motives, scale, and long-term impact of the newcomer expansion, aboriginal peoples generally responded to the immediate threats and opportunities, as they understood them within the frame of their society and community values.

For a significant number of indigenous populations, avoidance was the primary means of coping with the intrusions of newcomers. This tactic worked only if there were traditional or other lands available that were of no interest to the newcomers. Otherwise, flight from settlers and development proved to be only a temporary expedient. This transpired repeatedly along the southeast coast of Australia, where Aborigines retreated toward the outback in the face of settlement expansion, and along the east coast of North America, where indigenous peoples discovered that there were few places truly secure from incursions. Aboriginal populations in sub-Arctic and Arctic lands and in tropical jungle regions had more success, for non-indigenous interest tended to be highly focused and site-specific. The Beothuk of Newfoundland fled in the face of non-indigenous activities; the entire population died off by the nineteenth century without ever establishing regular contact with the newcomers. Various groups in the Amazon, the Akuriyo of Surinam, the Jarawa of the Andaman Islands, and other residents of tropical areas used the veil of the jungle to avoid contact for hundreds of years. The Pygmies in the Belgian Congo refused efforts to settle them on plantations, and remained in the jungle areas that the Belgian settlers found both intractable and unattractive. Although the forests provided the Pygmies and others with protection for several generations, post-World War II logging and industrial activity eventually placed these previously isolated lands in the path of development. Among the Nenets of central Siberia, the indigenous peoples resisted, and even revolted against, the intrusions of Russian and Soviet agents. Interestingly, the Nenets who had adopted sedentary lifestyles generally accommodated the Russian agendas and administrative systems. Those who remained on the land, following the reindeer herds as was their tradition, resisted more regularly and proved troublesome to the national government. They identified a series of grievances against the Russian and, particularly, the Soviet governments – complaints which resonate with the global experience of indigenous peoples. The specific grievances included the taking of their reindeer, the occupation of indigenous lands, persecution of shamans, forced labor processes, restrictions on political rights, and the removal of children to boarding schools, where they lost traditional knowledge and language skills.

Indigenous participation in the surplus economies was quite common across the globe. In some areas, such as the northern Canadian fur trade, the economic relationship was often mutually beneficial and supported by indigenous peoples. Likewise, the Maori of New Zealand participated actively in the whaling, mining, and early farming activities on the islands. The Maori were aggressive consumers and traders, demanding fair return from the storekeepers and finding ways to capitalize on the new technologies and material goods available to them. In many parts of North, Central and South America, newcomers attempted to press indigenous peoples into plantation work, an effort that also failed with many of the mobile societies in Africa. In the face of indigenous resistance, desperate employers, supported by their governments, intervened more directly. Across the South Pacific, for example, plantation operators used all measure of trickery and compulsion to secure Islander and Aborigine workers. Outrage in Britain about the mistreatment of indigenous peoples resulted in government intervention in the early twentieth century to stop the impressment of aboriginal labour.

The indigenous–newcomer economic exchange was often very uneven. Indigenous peoples typically had limited material needs and lacked the determination to enhance their financial position that dominated most newcomer communities. Companies found, however, that trading with indigenous peoples could be extremely lucrative, whether it be for furs in North America, spices and plants in South East Asia, fish products in various coastal regions, or precious stones and minerals in South Africa and across Australia and North America. The traders worked hard to generate demands for new products, and when they failed to interest the indigenous peoples in more material goods, they introduced consumables like tobacco (if not native to the area) and alcohol. New economic systems were implemented to tie individuals and communities to a specific trading firm, with many companies offering loans to the harvesters in order to ensure their commercial loyalty. Alcohol quickly became a highly desired trade good, quickly consumed and enticing to the indigenous peoples. Numerous commentators observed that the indigenous peoples acquired a taste – and a demand–for rum, whiskey, and other such drinks, creating a more diverse trading environment and introducing alcohol into the social and personal worlds of the first people. Some of the companies – the Hudson's Bay Company in Canada is perhaps the best example – worked fairly cooperatively with indigenous peoples and struck a balance that, most often, served both partners in the trade. In most other areas, particularly under the influence of competitive trading conditions, companies were rapacious and aggressive in seeking commercial advantage. So, too, however, were indigenous peoples, who sought ways to exploit isolated traders, competitive options, and the newcomers' lack of familiarity with local conditions.

The key, however, is that indigenous communities did respond. Indigenous people reacted with wide variations to the intrusions and actions of newcomers. Some groups fled into traditional territories, using distance and geography to shield themselves from the newcomers. Others, more optimistic and enthusiastic about the outsiders, sought economic integration and settled among the new arrivals. Many groups expressed considerable faith in the new authorities and negotiated or signed treaties and other accords with the colonial powers. Many other groups dug in and resisted the occupation of their territories. And a large number of indigenous peoples went, in distinct phases, through most if not all of these stages, as they attempted to respond to the ever-changing and seemingly never-ending intrusions by outsiders.

Newcomers and Indigenous Peoples

The rhetoric of contemporary indigenous politics suggests that the arrival of newcomers was an unvarnished disaster for the aboriginal peoples and their lands. While there is much truth to this assertion – there are relatively few examples of positive, well-developed and mutually beneficial relationships along the cultural frontier – it is also true that some non-indigenous peoples wrestled with and even agonized over the impact of expansion on the original societies. Missionaries were, of course, foremost among this group. But there were other outsiders, including soldiers, government officials, and other observers who were upset about the destruction and dislocation of indigenous cultures as a result of exploration, settlement, and development.

By the early nineteenth century, when all but a few indigenous societies had been eliminated as major military threats, philanthropists and moralists began to contemplate a more positive sense of responsibility for original peoples. Criticism mounted of violent military campaigns and broken treaties. Advocates for the indigenous peoples generally shared a belief that rapid assimilation and incorporation into the developing mainstream was in the best interests of the indigenous cultures. As a consequence, these same commentators lobbied extensively for the protection of government reserves, health and education services, and a more respectful approach to the responsibilities of national governments and colonial authorities. The most important of these organizations was the Aboriginal Protection Society, created in 1836 with the mandate of critiquing British colonial involvement with indigenous peoples. The organization lobbied hard for fair and just treatment of indigenous peoples, including their right to be protected from the intrusions of outsiders. The Aboriginal Protection Society, like the churches, assumed that the indigenous peoples would be affected by settlement and industrial development; they sought to ensure that the local residents benefited from the transitions. Atrocities in the Congo attracted the attention of the APS, who protested loudly against Belgian actions. Their publicity campaigns generated widespread condemnation and demands that the imperial powers stop the exploitation. These organizations were joined by numerous missionaries, who often devoted a great deal of their effort in the field to urging the protection of indigenous rights and the preservation of aboriginal societies. They were not, as followers of the Christian church, averse to the cultures being changed radically in the process, but many were staunch defenders of the rights of the marginalized minorities.

Other organizations and indigenous advocates focused on protecting the integrity of indigenous cultures. They were drawn, often through the evocative descriptions of explorers and early anthropologists, to the characterizations of the unique, mobile populations inhabiting the isolated corners of the world. These commentators, described by John Bodley as the "Idealist Preservationists," advocated substantial reserves where the indigenous peoples could live without the intrusions of outsiders. Large tracts of land were set aside in Australia, New Guinea, several areas in the Amazon, and a few reserves in Africa, with the express purpose of protecting the indigenous way of life. Even here, of course, outsiders set themselves up as the arbiters of indigenous futures, deciding for the peoples how they should relate to the rest of the world.

In the haste to criticize the racism and expansionism inherent in the expansionist process, commentators have often underestimated the importance of newcomer advocates in the indigenous struggle. L.F.S. Upton, an analyst of the ill-fated Beothuk of Newfoundland, argued that the group died out, in large measure, because they had too little contact with the British settlers and thus failed to be drawn under the protective grasp of the church and to a lesser extent the state. In numerous other regions and countries, missionaries and government agents worked to protect indigenous harvesting, demanded government support for education and rudimentary medical care, and criticised the incoming non-indigenous population for their rapacious behaviour. More than a few of these representatives of newcomer societies "crossed over" and became outspoken advocates for the rights of indigenous peoples. The same churches which spawned aggressive attacks on aboriginal languages, spirituality, and cultural values also produced the first wave of indigenous rights advocates, giving national and international voice to people without the skills or connections to take their stories to a broader audience.

Cultural Persistence and Indigenous Survival

The first decades of contact with outsiders brought dramatic changes to the indigenous world. Violent occupations upended centuries-old relationships with traditional territories and left greatly diminished populations to cope with the mass invasion of their lands. Indigenous peoples were enslaved by the thousands and, as will be shown, killed in the hundreds of thousands by imported diseases. Even where relations were more mutually beneficial, the advent of metal tools, new economic systems, intense social contact with newcomers, and the arrival of government administrators and agricultural settlers meant major changes for the original peoples in these areas. There was no single reaction and therefore no single outcome to this world-wide process of cultural encounter.

Very often, the newcomers spoke wistfully of the once proud and once formidable indigenous populations, declaring them incapable of adapting to the many influences associated with colonization and occupation. The outsiders assumed, from Australia to the Arctic and from Brazil to Hawaii, that the arrival of the outsiders would, invariably, result in the demise of the local population. That exact result happened in places, with the violent dispossession or other dislocations resulting in the collapse of the indigenous societies. More often, the aboriginal communities faced enormous pressures to change. They lost assured access to land, faced great competition for resources, and struggled with the complexities and depredations of the newcomers. Indigenous cultures changed in ways large and small. Some learned the languages of the colonizers; others accepted incorporation into new economic, social, and political systems. Interracial sex and intermarriage blurred the lines between newcomer and indigenous populations. Falling under the control of government meant that authority passed from traditional leaders to external agents, resulting in less attention to the needs and nuances of aboriginal culture. But forecasts of the imminent collapse of indigenous values, customs and world-views proved to be wrong-headed.

Yet so, too, did the idea that indigenous cultures would remain intact. Roger Sandall, in a book entitled *The Culture Cult*, critiques what he called "designer tribalism" and accuses western liberals of "romantic primitivism." He accused academics and writers from Karl Polanyi to Margaret Mead of over-glorifying the less savoury aspects of indigenous life – be it coming of age rituals or attitudes toward women and human life – and of romanticizing the thus-censured social portrait. Sandall's description cut to the bone, for the indigenous-rights and aboriginal-support networks count among their number many people who offer uncritical definitions of original people's social ways. And as he points out, few of these people would choose to live themselves, or have their children live, under the strictures and values of indigenous societies that they support so wholeheartedly.

This critique of indigenous societies is hardly new. For decades, opponents of indigenous people's rights (or supporters of their assimilation into the social mainstream) have pointed out the imperfections of indigenous societies in the modern era – the absence of individual freedoms in some cultures, restrictions on women, the value attached to communitarian decision-making in most, the violence of some societies, the reality that indigenous peoples did not always live in harmony with nature and the non-materialist values of societies trapped in a materialist world. Sandall and others, while correctly pointing out the improvements in the human condition attributable to the same western industrial order which produced imperialism and the colonial system, make two fundamental errors. First, they fail to acknowledge that many of the elements which they critique in indigenous cultures were, at one time, integral to western belief and social systems. Second, they do not recognize that, like all human organizations, indigenous societies change over time. Just as western society stepped away from the brutality of religious persecution which marred much of its history and from the excessive poverty of serfs, slaves, and the working poor, so too have indigenous societies moved beyond aspects of their cultures that were in place when first contact occurred.

Adaptation, therefore, is a central theme in the history of indigenous response to the arrival, advance, and activities of newcomer populations. The responses raged widely, from confrontation to retreat, from economic integration to maintenance of traditional harvesting ways. Indigenous societies learned from the outsiders, just as the outsiders learned many important lessons from the original peoples. This messy, often violent, occasionally mutually beneficial meeting of cultures, societies, and values shaped the human history of much of the globe and established the foundation for efforts by indigenous peoples to make their way in a complex, integrating and often aggressive world.

5

BIOLOGICAL CHANGES: ECOLOGICAL IMPERIALISM AND THE TRANSFORMATION OF TRIBAL WORLDS

For generations, understanding of the impact of colonial expansion focused on the most obvious elements of the intrusion. Writers celebrated the work of explorers and chronicled the adventures of soldiers and traders. They often memorialized the lives and times of the early settlers and spoke warmly of the efforts of missionaries and government agents to "civilize" the frontier districts. Little was said or known about an equally dramatic transformation that accompanied the mingling of peoples and the crossing of oceans. The newcomers brought with them animals, plants, and an ideology of land and resource use which quickly altered the natural landscapes of the newly identified territories. Less visibly, but no less powerfully, the exchange of microbes – diseases and germs – ushered in a profound reordering of indigenous realities. The newcomers carried, as well, radically different ideas about ownership of the land, concepts which quickly clashed with indigenous understandings of the human–land relationships.

The impact of the ecological change rested largely on a simple but crucial reality. Parts of the world were biologically distinct from other areas. Because they were contiguous, there was considerable exchange over time between Europe and Asia, Asia and Africa and North and South America, with the limits imposed more by climate and geography than by human movements. But distance provided other parts of the world with a substantial buffer. Unique environments, such as the Galapagos Islands in the eastern Pacific Ocean, provide the most telling evidence of the impact that isolation can and did have on the evolution of the biological setting. New Zealand, long separated from the

Australian continent, did not host any mammals, save for a warm blooded bat, and therefore had few predators. The plant, bird, and fish life on the islands reflected this ecological separation. So, too, did the unusual flora and fauna of Australia, home to dozens of unique species and, following the era of European discovery, a source of wonderment to the newcomers. North America likewise had very little biological contact with the European continent, and the indigenous peoples inhabited a very different epidemiological space than did the inhabitants of the Old World for a period of some 12,000 years.

The movement of human beings across vast distances during the periods of exploration and expansion bridged these ecological gaps and transferred all manner of plant life, animals and diseases between regions. To add to the misunderstandings of this complicated biological process, the world's people had no knowledge of the role of germs in the spreading of disease and no ecological understanding of the impact of new plants and animals on human and physical landscapes. Few people thought much beyond personal and community needs and economic opportunity when considering the importation of plants, animals, and fish, and scarcely any attention was given to the potentially harmful or transformative effects of these exchanges. In both indigenous and other worlds, healers, farmers, and others had developed the capacity to respond to familiar phenomena; the New and Old Worlds shared a limited ability to cope with new diseases, new plants, and animals and the inevitable but unanticipated transformations associated with biological exchange.

Ecological change associated with human movements is a longstanding and familiar process. While the greatest and most dramatic transitions accompanied the expansion of Europe to colonies around the world, human migrations have always brought about shifts in land and resource use, the distribution of plant and animal life, and the transformation of the existing ecosystems. The question of the ecological impact of indigenous populations has generated a great deal of debate in recent years, particularly as the idea of aboriginal peoples over-harvesting local resources and disturbing the ecology flies in the face of the stereotype of the indigenous peoples being at one with the environment. But there is considerable evidence that the original inhabitants of North America, South America, New Zealand, and other locations had a decisive impact on the local ecology. In New Zealand, for instance, the large, slow, and easily harvested moa birds disappeared quite quickly after the arrival of the Maori. Across North America, significant mega-fauna, large, often slow-moving animals, were apparently hunted to extinction or otherwise displaced by the arrival of human beings in their midst. According to Paul Martin, many species of large animals became extinct across North America. Furthermore, Martin argued, the last ice age could not account for the disappearance of these animals, and he argues that wasteful hunting by newly arrived human populations destroyed a great deal of wildlife.[1] These transformations, which remain the subject of considerable debate, demonstrated no ill-intent or deliberate desire to transform the ecology, but represented instead the inevitable and normal changes that accompanied human settlement in previously unoccupied areas.

The same kind of ecological transformations, not surprisingly, accompanied demographic and political change in Europe. The expansion of commercial agriculture out of the Middle East and, over centuries, throughout Europe and beyond brought about enormous changes in local forests, river systems, and animal life. By the age of European expansion, much of Europe had been deforested to make room for crops, large portions of the agricultural land had lost its fertility, and the flora and fauna had been dramatically over-harvested. As Kirkpatrick Sale wrote:

> But no alteration of the landscape was so profound or purposeful as the erasure of the European forests. There are no statistics on this destruction – the medieval age was not one to think that way – but considerable circumstantial evidence points in the same direction, and it is not even a matter of much controversy. Europe's was a civilization literally made of wood: wood was used to build its houses, ships, mills, machinery, plows, furniture, plates, pipes, tools, carriages, even clocks and (at times) watches; wood and charcoal provided the fuel for heating and cooking in homes and shops, castles and cottages and in all industries from bakeries and glassworks to ironworks. ... All the great forests with which it had been blessed – an essential energy resource denied, incidentally, to the civilizations of the Middle East and much of Asia – were steadily and recklessly depleted to serve that civilization, and by the sixteenth century there were virtually no old-growth areas, no natural ecosystems, left.[2]

And yet the population of Europe continued to rise. The impetus to explore and to identify new sources of food lay, in part, with the despoliation of the European ecosystem. The arrival of Viking settlers on the uninhabited shores of Iceland, likewise, resulted in the substantial recasting of the landscape for purposes of farming, herding, and other activities. The logic is simple. The expansion of human activity disrupts the ecology, bringing many unintentional and often little understood transformations. The greatest environmental change in world history, one with dramatic implications for indigenous peoples, commenced with the expansion of Europe and the subsequent mingling of peoples from across the globe.

Environmental Changes

Historian Alfred Crosby referred to this process as "The Columbian Exchange," or the "biological consequences of 1492." His basic observation was a simple one: the crossing of the Atlantic Ocean sparked a hitherto little understood biological transformation of both worlds. In the early years of the twenty-first century, the implications of these shifts remain very much in evidence. Kudzu (imported from Africa) and Eurasian milfoil plants migrate northward in North America from the equatorial zones, displacing native species. Strange Asian fish, released into the wild by pet owners or restauranteurs, show up in eastern American states. European mussels, transported on the bottom of ocean-going ships, are deposited in inland waters, with devastating effects on local watersheds. Across Australia, millions of rabbits, descendants of introduced species, continue to wreak havoc on the landscape. In New Zealand, environmentalists wage a seemingly unwinnable struggle against the opossums which attack the unique flora and fauna on this long isolated archipelago. At a different scale, human attempts to reshape landscapes through the construction of hydro-electric and irrigation dams have had massive and unintended impacts on vast stretches of territory. Resettlement schemes in Irian Jia, Indonesia, and forestry projects in Sarawak, Malaysia, likewise, failed to anticipate the immediate and long-term effects of rapid and ill-planned development. These modern examples, however, pale in comparison to the long and complex history of the ecological changes associated with the expansion of newcomers onto indigenous lands.

When the first European explorers set out, they wisely brought substantial amounts of supplies with them. In the holds and on the decks of their ships, they carried plants and animals, planning to use them in the unknown and potentially inhospitable lands on the other side of the ocean. Unintentionally, these same ships carried hundreds of rats, which managed to get to shore, carrying both disease and the capacity to upset local ecosystems. Upon arrival, finding lands that ranged from the harsh and frightening islands of the far north to the densely forested territories of the temperate zones of North America to the jungles of the

Amazon and Africa, the early colonizers worked assiduously to transform them into farmland and settlements. This was particularly true in the temperate zones of North and South America, southern Africa, and portions of South America which attracted the vast majority of the European migrants. Few gave more than a passing thought to the ecological impact of their decisions. Those who did saw the transformations in a positive light, believing that the changes added to the diversity of plant and animal life and made alien spaces more habitable as, indeed, they did.

The most dramatic European addition to North America was probably the horse, an animal that had once inhabited portions of the continent but which had been extinct for centuries. The introduction of the horse transformed the very foundations of indigenous life in many parts of North and South America. The widely held image of the plains Indians astride their war and hunting ponies is, in fact, an artefact of the post-contact era. The first horses of the modern era arrived via Spaniards, who used the mobility thus afforded to extend their control over much of Mexico and Central America. Horses quickly passed through indigenous hands and spread across the Great Plains. The domesticated animals proved to be an enormous boon to the prairie hunters, for the horse improved the efficiency of the bison hunt, made travel much easier, and quickly transformed the nature of warfare in the region. By the time the first Europeans ventured into the western regions, horses had figured prominently in indigenous life for several generations. The newcomers typically assumed that the horse was a permanent part of the aboriginal way of life, as indeed it now was.

Other animals carried with them significant economic and social implications. The arrival of a variety of domesticated animals, particularly cattle and sheep, resulted in the expansion of herding and ranching, thus competing for land and resources with other large game and, over time, forcing indigenous peoples away from their traditional hunts. The need to manage stock in plains areas from North America to South America and Australia brought the newcomers once more into conflict with the original inhabitants. Across South Africa, for example, Boer ranchers shouldered African peoples aside by extending their grazing range, gradually encroaching on indigenous land. Local hunters were used to harvesting what was needed from the land. The new animals were, however, viewed as personal property by the newcomers and were protected with considerable force. The arrival of herds of cattle and sheep meant, as well, greater competition for the grass and water resources of the region, resulting in a further diminishment of the open range for wild game. When, faced with hunger and potential starvation, indigenous peoples killed the domesticated animals, they incurred the wrath of the rangers and herders, thus adding to already tense situations. The list of imported animals connected with the "Columbian Exchange" is substantial indeed. The seemingly quaint and harmless decision to carry English and European song-birds to North America resulted in the rapid diffusion of the new birds across the continent. The massive flocks of starlings that, by the nineteenth century, became a permanent feature of the continental landscape originated in this process, which capitalized on the transition of much of the land mass from forest to cultivated farms. So it was, too, with a wide variety of plants, fish species, insects, and other forms in life. In many cases, these new plants, animals, and birds found attractive climates and geographic surroundings, often shouldering aside local species in the process.

Few areas on Earth were transformed as dramatically as Australia and New Zealand. The latter was home to virtually no mammals; the birds had very few defences against predators for the simple reason that there were none. Australia is home to a wide variety of unique animals, from the kangaroo to the koala, but there were large ecological niches that remained unfilled. The rabbit, already mentioned, spread dramatically across the Australian continent, causing enormous disruptions in the wake of the invasion. Similarly, water buffalo brought in from Asia for agricultural purposes escaped and soon left their mark in many northern regions. New Zealand suffered through successive introductions of "exotic" animals and plants. Fur traders brought over possums from Australia, believing (correctly) that they would flourish in the island nation and (incorrectly) that they could be harvested profitably for their pelts. Rats that swam ashore from boats wreaked havoc on bird populations. And the many plants that the newcomers cultivated in New Zealand spread rapidly in the near-perfect growing conditions, threatening to overwhelm the native bush. One positive development, in the eyes of many, was that trout species introduced in the nineteenth century flourished in New Zealand, creating over time one of the world's best sports fishing industries.

The ecological transformation did not continue endlessly. Geography and climate restricted the adaptations of numerous species, some of which were being deliberately transplanted into newly occupied lands. The frigid lands of the far north, with short growing seasons and ferocious winters, proved impenetrable to many imported forms of life. Mountainous areas, likewise, proved more resistant than lowlands and coastal zones. Desert areas were also inhospitable and only the hardiest plants and animals could make the necessary adaptations. Many of the plants, animals, and other items carried from northern and western Europe did not flourish in tropical regions.

Animals transported for domestic purposes often escaped, establishing the foundation for large and disruptive feral populations. Pigs introduced by Europeans often flourished in the wild, as did thousands upon thousands of wild horses. The rabbits that overran much of Australia were initially intended to be raised for food; once allowed to roam free in the outback, however, their population exploded. Camels brought to the same continent to assist with transportation proved ill-suited to the task but those freed into the outback survived in a feral state. And so it was, in numerous locations, with cats, dogs, cattle, sheep, and other imported animals, freed to move across lands with few natural predators and therefore with limited checks on their population growth.

The sharing of biomass was not all in one direction. Plants were returned to Europe and other nations. Several New World plants particularly potatoes and corn (or maize), flourished in the Old World and became the foundation for a major population explosion. There is a tendency to idealize these more profitable biological exchanges but, as Felipe Fernández-Armesto has pointed out, the sharing of maize within North America and overseas carried significant costs:

> [Maize] did not make people longer or stay healthier; on the contrary, the exhumed bones and teeth of maize eaters in and around the Mississippi floodplain bear the traces of more disease and more deadly infections than those of their predecessors. When Old World invaders adopted maize, they showed similar reluctance and even worse effects. ... Wherever it took over, similar tyrannies accompanied it: collective effort to plant, harvest, process and store it, and elites to organize its product and regulate its distribution. Soil had to be prepared in various ways according to the genus of place: earth might have to be ridged or raised; forest might have to be cleared. Surplus food demanded structures of power. Storage had to be administered, stockpiles policed.[3]

Different conditions in the Old World prevented the transplantation of a variety of highly valuable plant species – tobacco, cotton, and most spices – which could be produced much more cheaply and effectively in the land-rich colonies. Sailors carried valuable plants from the South Pacific to the Caribbean and found new places for commercial production. Rubber, tobacco, and cotton plants, for example, were moved to new colonial locations, where growing conditions suited the cultivation of the crops, where there was abundant land for commercial production and where administrative structures provided capitalists with assurances of freedom to prosper from the new economies. Animals from the various New Worlds were more curiosities than substitutes for existing domesticated species in Europe. The new and unique animals figured prominently in the fast developing zoos across Europe and were a welcome addition to fair and circus circuits across the continent. In general, however, Europe and the densely settled parts of Asia had few ecological niches available for imported animals and plants, and only a small number of commercial crops became part of the Old World ecosystem.

The rapid expansion of settlements on indigenous territories resulted in increased competition for local resources. Miantonomo, a Narragansett, said of the newcomers, "since these Englishmen have seized our country, they have cut down the grass with scythes, and the trees with axes. Their cows and horses eat up the grass, and their hogs spoil our bed of clams; and finally, we shall all starve to death."[4] Newcomer agricultural settlements typically began along the coast and gradually moved inland, soon engulfing the temperate zones that were best suited for commercial cultivation. This meant that one aboriginal group after another found itself shouldered aside. The newcomers hunted and fished from the same resource pool that had sustained the indigenous peoples for generations. They generally did so with less discrimination and forethought than did the long-time residents, often resulting in a rapid depletion of game for all people in the area. When shortages occurred, and they often did as a result of poor planning on the newcomers' part, tensions arose and conflict could easily follow. The net long-term effect was that there were fewer resources to harvest and pressure on the indigenous peoples to move further afield, typically into the territory of another indigenous group.

At times, the attack on local resources was deliberate. Pastoralists saw little value and considerable threat in the continuation of indigenous harvesting. In various parts of the Australian outback, particularly the Kimberley district, local animals were shot or poisoned to make room for sheep and cows. Across the American West, massive bison herds interfered with the development of railways, ranching, and farming; at the same time, new tanning techniques increased the value of the bison for trade. Commercial hunters began to attack the herds. The bloodthirsty destruction of these animals, for profit and for sport, stands as perhaps the single best example of the incompatibility of the needs of the local ecology, traditional harvesting practices, and commercial agriculture. According to an estimate by Francis Haines, close to 6.3 million bison were slaughtered in the Kansas to Texas region in 1872–74 alone, with some 400,000 killed by plains Indians and the rest by commercial hunters. Estimates of the decline of the herds suggest that the number of buffalo fell from over 60 million before the Europeans arrived to less than 1,000 by the end of the nineteenth century. The farmers and ranchers did not mourn the destruction of the buffalo herds, for their disappearance into tiny, protected herds left vast stretches of prairie open for agriculture. This tension between mobile indigenous populations and sedentary farmers and ranches played out in many locations around the world, as one group struggled to survive with a diminishing land and resource base and the other, sincerely believing themselves to be on the vanguard of progress and prosperity, sought the ways and means of solidifying their hold on their newly occupied and legally titled lands.

The destruction of the buffalo herds increased tensions between the plains Indians and the traders and newcomers. The conflict peaked in 1874, when Comanches in the Texas Panhandle laid siege to the trading post at Adobe Walls. A war party of some 700 warriors attacked the buffalo hunters, only to be met with a withering counterattack. The Comanches were forced to retreat, and although they and other plains Indians continued to harass the hunters, the Adobe Walls battle marked the last significant attempt to turn back the buffalo hunt. Within a decade, the buffalo had been wiped out in vast portions of the American West, driving the Indians into a state of desperation and clearing the way for cattle ranchers and farmers to move into the area.

The expansion of the surplus-based societies generated enormous ecological and therefore socio-cultural change. Newcomers came looking for wealth and opportunities to prosper. Amongst their vast arsenal they carried a seductive and misunderstood tool – land-tenure systems which rested on the codification, registration, and legalization of individual property rights. At its very root, this system (with its multiple variants) stood in sharp contrast to the communal, fluid, and non-proprietarial concepts of land tenure that existed among the indigenous peoples. On top of this conceptual and organizational change, the newcomers brought plants and animals which, when released into the wild to breed and compete for ecological niches, often forced out local species and thereby upset local harvesting patterns. Given that the indigenous world was based on a sophisticated and culturally entrenched understanding of the natural environment, the transformations wrought by the introduction of new land-tenure systems and new species often proved to be extremely dramatic.

Disease and Epidemics

The ecological impact of newcomer expansion had another equally profound and dramatic element: the spread of new diseases. In the years before the age of expansion, it is hardly surprising that the various societies evolved with very little biological contact. While there were many diseases, such as yellow fever and malaria, which are specific to particular sites and ecological conditions, others developed and flourished within human societies. When a disease worked its way into a population, the people gradually developed immunity to it, turning an often-fatal ailment into a childhood disease, rather like chickenpox among the Europeans. So long as the populations remained geographically separate, diseases rarely spread between one and the other. Once exploration, trade, travel, warfare, and contact expanded, however, the biological risks expanded dramatically.

Historian Alfred Crosby has argued that the peoples of North and South America and the Pacific regions lacked immunological resistance to European diseases. In these circumstances, "virgin soil epidemics" swept through the local population, killing many, many people and undermining indigenous societies with shocking rapidity. The diseases proved exceptionally frightening to the aboriginal peoples, for they had no way to explain them within their spiritual or medicinal conceptual frameworks. Shamans or spiritual leaders, once believed to be all-powerful, had their weaknesses exposed as they failed to solve the dilemmas posed by the new illnesses. People stricken with the disease, often watching dozens of their community members die within days from the sicknesses, typically fled to neighboring settlements. Unwittingly, they took the disease with them, thereby spreading it to yet another vulnerable group. And so, with the speed of a prairie fire, the diseases sliced through indigenous populations. Wilbur Jacobs would later refer to the "fatal impact" of European expansion, in which disease devastated and undermined indigenous peoples. Some indigenous peoples shared the view that there was little that they could do to stop the destruction: as a Maori writer observed "As the clover killed the fern, and the European dog the Maori dog; as the Maori rat was destroyed by the Pakeha rat, so our people also will be gradually supplanted and exterminated by the Europeans."[5]

While the indigenous peoples were not without disease in the generations before contact, they had no experience of numerous European illnesses. A Yucatan commentator said, rather uncritically, of the years before the newcomers arrived:

> There was then no sickness; they had no aching bones; they had then no high fever; they had then no smallpox; they had then no burning chest; they had then no abdominal pain; they had then no consumption; they had then no headache. At that time the course of humanity was orderly. The foreigners made it otherwise when they arrived here.[6]

There are countless documented examples of the impact of introduced diseases – and there would be more save for the fact that many of the outbreaks occurred in advance of the arrival of newcomer chroniclers of the deadly events. Smallpox, the most deadly killer in human history, cut an enormous swath through indigenous societies. Smallpox devastated the peoples of Central America following the arrival of Cortez. Bernardino de Sahagún described the consequences:

> [A]t the beginning of the year 1520 the epidemic of smallpox, measles, and pustules broke out so virulently that a vast number of people died throughout this New Spain. This pestilence began in the province of Chalco and lasted for 60 days. ... During this epidemic, the Spaniards, rested and recovered, were already in Tlaxcala. Having taken courage and energy because of reinforcements who had come to them and because of the ravages of the [Mexican] people that the pestilence was causing, firmly believing that God was on their side ... they began to construct the brigantines that they would need in order to wage war by water.[7]

It is important to understand the sense of trauma and turmoil associated with the outbreak of a hitherto unknown disease. Thomas Herriot, writing about the impact of imported illness on Roanoke Island, said:

> [B]ut that within a few dayes after our departure from everies such townes, that people began to die very fast, and many in short space; in some townes about twentie, in some fourtie, in some sixtie, & in one six score, which in truth was very manie in respect to their numbers. ... The disease also was so strange that they neither knew what it was, now how to cure it; the like by report of the oldest men in the countrey never happened before, time out of mind.[8]

The massive losses associated with the epidemics in Mexico touched off widespread suffering and panic:

> It was [the month of] Tepeilhuitl when it began, and it [smallpox] spread over the people as great destruction. Some it quite covered [with pustules] on all parts – their faces, their heads, their breasts, etc. There was a great havoc. Very many died of it. They could not walk; they only lay in their resting places and beds. They could not move; they could not stir; they could not change position, nor lie on one side; nor face down, nor on their backs. And if they stirred, much did they cry out. Great was its destruction. Covered, mantled with pustule, very many people died of them.[9]

Disease, it soon transpired, was a powerful weapon that eased the conquest of the region. The Iukagir and Nia of Northern Russia, for example, succumbed in large numbers to smallpox outbreaks in 1669, 1690–93, 1884, and 1889. The same disease swept across the Great Plains of North America in 1780–81 and again in 1837–38, killing thousands of people each time. One observer said of the 1633 smallpox outbreak, that "it pleased God to visit these Indeans with great sickness, and such a mortalitie that of a 1000 above 900 and a halfe of them dyed, and many of them did rott above ground for want of burial."[10] The Pueblo of New Mexico saw their population collapse, in the face of a smallpox epidemic, from 130,000 in 1539 to less than 6,500 in the first decade after 1700. South Australian Aborigines incurred the wrath of smallpox in 1814 and 1831, with estimated population losses of 90 percent. A smallpox outbreak in California in 1830–33 destroyed close to three quarters of the Yokut and Wintun population. The Timucuans of Florida lost an estimated 98 percent of their people by 1800; in that region, in fact, within 250 years of initial contact, all of the indigenous people had disappeared. Among such diverse groups as the Ache of Paraguay, the Soriano of Bolivia, and the Akuriyo of Surinam, smallpox exacted a serious toll. Even such isolated peoples, far removed from newcomer settlers, experienced rapid population losses due to imported disease.

Epidemic disease created sweeping devastation on its own, spreading quickly from person to person, village to village, but many indigenous people concluded that the destruction was deliberate. They attributed the outbreaks of illness to sorcery by the newcomers, superior "medicine," and any manner of supernatural or practical actions. In one of the most famous statements about the use of disease as a form of government policy, Lord Jeffrey Amherst instructed: "Infect the Indians with sheets upon which smallpox patients have been lying, or by any other means which may serve to exterminate this accursed race."[11] Contemporary indigenous observers have repeated these claims – not always accurately – reflecting the disbelief and anger with which indigenous peoples confronted the impact of disease.

Smallpox was the most severe and most virulent killer, but it was not the only disease to cause serious difficulties. Measles, mumps, whooping cough, influenza, and many other illnesses were brought to indigenous territories by newcomers. There are stories, some of them accurate, in many different areas about poisoned blankets or other supplies, left behind deliberately to destroy the local population. The substantial truth of the matter is that disease rarely needed a helpmate. The illnesses had a profound impact on people who lacked the immunity or resistance that other societies had built up over the generations. Many societies suffered crippling losses. Some were wiped out altogether or suffered such grievous losses that the survivors amalgamated with other societies. In numerous locations around the world, population declines of between 75 to 90 percent were commonplace. As Henry Dobyns once observed, the American frontier was not a virgin land, as the settlers described it. Rather, it was best understood as widowed territory.

Debate continues to rage about the severity of the disease-related population loss, although most analysts argue in favor of a significant, even cataclysmic decline. Russell Thornton, in his study of the extent of population loss in North America, estimated that the decline was in the order of 90 percent or more, a massive devastation of the original peoples of the continent. The Huron of the Great Lakes region in North America were virtually wiped out, leaving a small remnant population behind. The impact was uneven. Losses do not appear to have been as severe in the Pacific Islands and New Zealand as they were in North and South America. Similarly, there is often more discussion of mortality among the newcomers to Africa than among the indigenous populations. Throughout Africa, diseases like yellow fever, malaria, and other tropical maladies killed many members of the immigrant communities, turning assignments to military stations, missions, or government posts into death watches. There appears, in the case of Africa, areas in Asia, and portions of South America, to have been less indigenous population loss as a result of the importation of disease than the destruction of newcomer life through exposure to tropical illnesses.

While the precise numbers will remain lost in the fogs of historical analysis, the reality is that the diseases introduced, unintentionally or otherwise, among the indigenous peoples of the world had enormous consequences. As oral societies, these populations relied on elders to protect and preserve their traditional knowledge. A quick and deadly outbreak could and often did carry off a large percentage of the elders in a single devastating blow. It is impossible, however, to determine the precise loss in cultural and social terms, except to assume that it was typically considerable. Some indigenous communities rebounded from the population loss, particularly if the deadly illnesses killed mostly the young and very old. In many instances, however, the individuals exposed to the newcomers were principally those in their childbearing years, precisely the ones that the indigenous communities could least afford to lose. There was also a cumulative effect from the impact of disease. Successive epidemics – sometimes as many as one a year for a decade – devastated the societies' belief in their spiritual leaders and healers, opened indigenous minds to the potential power of the newcomers' God, and so weakened the population as to make resistance to the occupation of their lands virtually impossible. The dispiriting impact of wave upon wave of biological attack – particularly to illnesses that seemed to leave the newcomers unscathed – demoralized indigenous populations and undermined their ability to respond as they wished to the intrusions and opportunities associated with the immigrants.

The destruction caused by introduced diseases had significant conceptual consequences. Because a large percentage of the population loss often occurred before the newcomers made face-to-face contact, it became easy for the new arrivals to assume that the indigenous people had very small populations, even though living in bountiful lands. This, in turn, contributed to the notion that aboriginal societies were small, inefficient, marginally sustainable, and constantly scrambling for survival. Sick aboriginal people could obviously not travel, work, fight, or otherwise contribute as much as individuals who were well. As the newcomers met yet another indigenous group reeling from the effects of a major disease outbreak, they could readily assume that the sick state was the norm. Newcomer rhetoric quickly described indigenous peoples as diseased, unkempt, and unable to care for themselves. Given that no one then understood the relationship between newcomer expansion and the outbreak of diseases among the indigenous people, it is perhaps not surprising that they reached these conclusions. These images, however, became deeply entrenched in the public's imagination and would prove extremely difficult to change in subsequent generations. Perhaps most significantly, the frequent appearance of epidemic diseases and the massive population losses experienced by the indigenous peoples in many parts of the world fed the notion that the aboriginal populations were dying and would soon disappear.

It is impossible to ascertain the precise impact of the importation of diseases into indigenous territories, in part because of other losses associated with war, acts of genocide, and the consequences of forced removals or starvation associated with the destruction of game. Because of the manner in which disease was spread between indigenous groups and in advance of newcomer settlement, it is often difficult to know the size of the pre-contact population and hence the scale of depopulation. Consider the North American situation. Before the 1960s, scholars assumed that depopulation was relatively small and, equally important, that there were very few indigenous peoples on the continent. Research by Henry Dobyns and others forced a reconceptualization of indigenous population, with the challenging assertion that the pre-contact numbers were as much as ten times higher than generally thought and, consequently, that some 90 percent of the people died through the first generations of contact. These numbers remain a matter of debate, with some suggesting that the depopulation estimates are over-stated and others arguing that the introduction of foreign diseases represented, in Russell Thornton's deliberately provocative phrase, an "American Holocaust." A collective estimate prepared by anthropologist John Bodley argues that the global indigenous depopulation was on the scale of 90 percent, representing close to 30 million people.

Not all population loss can be attributed to disease. In many parts of the world – Latin America, Africa, and portions of Asia – the newcomers forced the indigenous peoples to work in mining camps or as plantation slaves. The aggressiveness of the new bosses, who evidenced little concern for the health and well-being of the indigenous peoples, was matched by the unsuitability of the indigenous population for the new work environment. The rapid expansion of the rubber industry in Brazil, Peru, Bolivia, and Ecuador between 1880 and 1910 had massive impacts on the local population. The extension of ranching, logging, mining, and other industrial-age activities in many areas also had profound effects. Thousands of indigenous peoples died in various work settings, their spirits often weakened by incarceration, enslavement, and brutal working conditions. In an era when conquering imperial powers gave scant thought to mass death in work situations – heartlessness towards workers was widely in evidence in Europe and parts of Asia at these times – ruthless exploitation of indigenous peoples only added to the steadily mounting death toll.

There will never be a precise definition of the full demographic impact of imported diseases. In areas as diverse as Tasmania, Australia, and the eastern Arctic in Canada, from the southern tip of South America to the Congo, careful research has documented dramatic population losses. Some groups – the Beothuk in Newfoundland, the Aborigines of Tasmania (in this case a widely repeated claim that is now disputed), the Yahgan of Tierra del Fuego, and others – were wiped out entirely. Many groups collapsed to the point of demographic unsustainability; the Huron of the Great Lakes, for example, succumbed in large numbers to disease and warfare in the seventeenth and eighteenth centuries and disappeared as a distinctive culture. Many cultures were reduced to greatly depleted remnants, struggling to survive after living through the debilitating effects of smallpox, measles, or some other disease. It is clear, as well, that the impact of disease was complicated by other transitions, ranging from spiritual uncertainty to competition for land and resources, contributing to substantial population declines.

The demographic holocaust did not end with the introduction of better medicines, or more humane imperial regimes. In the post-World War II era, indigenous groups in Brazil, Papua New Guinea, and other isolated areas who had extended contact with outsiders for the first time experienced the same "virgin soil epidemics" that had decimated other populations. The Yanomami, whose contacts with outsiders have been extensively documented, suffered through a series of debilitating diseases with large population losses. At the same time, missionary and governmental organizations had the capacity to respond more effectively to these outbreaks than their seventeenth- and eighteenth-century counterparts, thus ameliorating the full impact of the diseases. That the issue of biological encounter remains a matter of active concern and interest in the contemporary word is a somber reminder of how potent and destructive a force epidemic disease has been among the indigenous peoples of the world.

Land and Land Ownership

While the arrival of outsiders transformed the biological world in ways that are still substantially unknown, a profound and sweeping ideological revolution likewise accompanied the mingling of cultures and peoples. Land and questions of land ownership stood at the center of this remarkable transformation, one which continues to bedevil indigenous populations around the globe. It may well be the most fundamental distinction between tribal and non-tribal peoples. The manner in which different societies understood and understand their relationship to the physical world and the resources upon and within it sits at the heart of being indigenous and, likewise, is one of the defining characteristics of surplus and industrial societies.

The Bible has often been evoked to defend the Christian assertion that human beings have dominion over the land. This simple concept is rife with ideological meaning, for it speaks directly to the separation of the human beings from the natural world and asserts the right of human population to use the land and its resources for their purposes. Indigenous peoples, in contrast, identify themselves as being "part" of the land and, at best, as having stewardship responsibilities for their physical environment. Their obligation is to pass on the land to future generations much the same as they found it. In non-tribal societies, in contrast, land ownership is generally assigned to individuals or groups of individuals, or the state in the case of communist and selected socialist countries in the twentieth century, many of whom, it must be noted, hoped to pass it on to future generations in good and profitable shape. Through a variety of technical structures and processes, individuals or groups gained the right to exploit the land and its resources for personal or collective benefit. That the land and resources might be dramatically transformed in the process is, again, well with the rights of the owner(s) of the land.

These concepts of land tenure and control sit at the center of the transition of many peoples around the world from mobile, harvesting societies to sedentary, specialized, and surplus-producing cultures. Indigenous peoples, in contrast, resisted many of the changes, often in the face of dramatic pressures and incentives to accept the new order. That they did so rested, in large measure, on their conceptualization of their community's relationship to the land. Indigenous peoples considered themselves part of their natural environment, not separate from it and certainly not in dominion over it. This does not mean, as is often suggested, that aboriginal societies lived in perfect harmony with their physical setting. They were, as human beings, capable of mistakes, vulnerable to unpredictable changes in resources, weather, and intergroup relations. Indigenous peoples occasionally over-harvested local resources, as appeared to have happened in several locations across North America, where indigenous migrants encountered easily harvested wildlife. In general, however, indigenous peoples conceived of themselves and their communities working within a spiritual world which encompassed the animals, plants, land, and other forces and works of nature.

Europe and other agrarian and highly structured societies approached questions of land and resource use very differently. They had no difficulty finding moral justification for their exploitation and use of whatever natural resources came before them. Agriculture flourished only where there was a suitable land-tenure system in place to ensure continuity of ownership and appropriate control of the land and its bounty. As a consequence, societies from China and Japan to England and Spain developed elaborate land-tenure systems which, in turn, served to maintain the strength and position of a relatively small number of land owners. A cant of ecological domination quickly emerged. Forests represented convertible wealth, and were cut down rapidly either to clear land for agriculture or to produce wood products for use or sale. Mineral deposits were excavated for the purposes of the state or the individual owners. As explorations pushed out to new lands, the value of the territories was determined in large measure by the ability to produce crops or other natural resources for export back to the sponsoring colonial power.

The concepts of individual ownership and private property which accompanied the colonial expansion conditioned the initial contact experience. Most indigenous societies had a generalized sense of individual responsibility for and use of specific territories, be it family trapping grounds, community fishing sites, or effective use of a sizeable tract of land for ceremonial and subsistence purposes. This did not accord readily with the introduction of the idea of state-sanctioned land-tenure systems and with the assertion of the new claimants that they could use the land and its resources for their private benefit. To the largely communitarian indigenous peoples, the emergence of societies in their midst where individuals could amass large land holdings and generate considerable personal wealth made little sense. The newcomers did not bring a single land-tenure system. Some societies, as in parts of North America, Australia, and New Zealand, introduced freehold land and allowed selected individuals to own specific and comparatively small pieces for their personal use. More common throughout North and South America were larger landholdings, assigned to an individual, often through personal ties to the monarchy or government, and worked by others. In Central and South America, the control exercised by the landowners, oligarchs with strong connections to colonial and national governments, established a cruel domination of the indigenous peoples throughout the region. These large holdings, in places like New York, Mexico, and through much of South America, established among the newcomer societies an hierarchical order which provided little room or flexibility for the indigenous peoples. If they had a role, it was as lowly paid laborers, forced or voluntary, on large plantations, farms, or ranches.

The ideology of colonial land-tenure systems swept through societies around the world. In India, the introduction of fixed land allocations interfered with land use by indigenous peoples, who saw their territories assigned to and used by others. The disruptions were not all due to the actions of the British imperial authorities. Local Indian business people recognized commercial opportunities and joined with the new commercial system, setting themselves at odds with communally oriented peoples. The result, running throughout the nineteenth century, was a series of local revolts and skirmishes, launched by indigenous communities attempting to prevent the alienation of their land. The British reacted to the protests in a few areas by taking small steps to protect local access to the land.

The imposition of new ideologies of land ownership and resource control altered dramatically the foundations of the tribal world. As outsiders entered onto "unused" and "unclaimed" aboriginal lands, they saw few of the normal signs of land occupancy and use. Outside governments declared the land, as in Australia, *terra nullius*, and asserted the right to assign ownership of land and resources to newcomers. They chided, in the process, the indigenous societies for failing to capitalize on the evident potential of the vast lands, often covered in forests, well-suited for agriculture, or rich in minerals, and considered themselves fortunate that the "backward" indigenous societies had ignored the wealth at their very feet.

In many colonies, the arrival of settlers ushered in an age of unchecked growth and expansion – and greater conflict with indigenous peoples. Many colonial officials, from New Zealand to British Columbia, worried openly about the avariciousness of the newcomers and sought ways to protect indigenous rights and resources. David Abernathy summarized the situation:

Adding to the problem colonial governors faced, settlers threatened the indigenous population. Given their intense interest in appropriating land and using it in new ways to make a profitable living, settlers were generally far more destructive of indigenous ways of life than even the most exploitive of governors. Indeed, officials in pure and mixed settlement colonies often felt that in order to maintain peace and assume some measure of justice they had to limit settlers' proclivities to undermine if not exterminate indigenous societies. In such situations tensions developed between colonial bureaucrats, whose power reflected the spatial stretch of a European government, and a community whose presence marked the partial diffusion of Europe's activist way of life.[12]

The new ideologies effectively interpreted tribal concepts of stewardship and resource control out of existence – and even late-twentieth- and early-twenty-first century efforts to reestablish a tiny measure of indigenous responsibility have made few inroads. All of the world, save for the ice-covered reaches of Antarctica (which falls under a unique multinational political arrangement), falls within the jurisdiction of a nation-state. These states, in turn, have procedures for allocating land and resources to individuals, collectives, or corporations, with the expectation that these lands will be used for "productive" purposes. Most of the world's agricultural production now comes from privately held lands, ranging from the complex rice terraces of Bali, Indonesia, and the barren dry lands of the Sudan to vast corporate farms in North America, and even larger ranches in the dusty outback of Australia. In only a small number of places, such as the largely inaccessible highlands of Papua New Guinea and the densely forested areas of Sarawak, do significant numbers of people continue the mobile, basic agriculture and harvesting patterns of the past.

In explaining what he described as the "explore–control–utilize syndrome" of European expansion, David Abernathy argues that there were fundamental misunderstandings between indigenous peoples and newcomers around the human–land relationship. Not having a sense of fixed land ownership in accordance with European concepts, indigenous peoples had more flexible arrangements regarding the use of land and resources. The idea that the land could be sold, alienated, bargained away through treaty, or otherwise passed permanently into the hands of the newcomers was not familiar to them. Settlers and governments saw any land transfers as permanent and irrevocable; indigenous peoples saw such discussions and arrangements as part of a fluid, ever-changing relationship, in which the land and resources could be returned to indigenous control as needs warranted. This fundamental misunderstanding would, of course, dominate indigenous–newcomer relations in many parts of the world.

Land and resources controlled by indigenous peoples have increasingly come under the sway of imposed concepts of land ownership.

Reserves in Canada and reservations in the United States, typically involving small amounts of marginal and uneconomical land, seek to define a balance between collective and individual ownership, but with little success. There is some recognition of collective rights and, in a few nations, large blocks of land set aside for exclusive indigenous use, such as Arnhem Land in Australia and substantial tracts of tribal territories in the Amazon basin. In most areas, however, the hold of indigenous peoples on their traditional lands and resources, if they have one at all, is tenuous in the extreme. Instead, personally and corporately controlled land and resources dominate much of the world.

Tribal Worlds Reconstructed

Over several centuries, indigenous territories and ecosystems had been transformed by the arrival of outsiders. More had changed than the ethnic composition of the population; much more had happened than the marginalization of the tribal peoples whose roots on the land often went back for thousands of years. The process of ecological globalization brought sweeping alterations to the physical world, particularly through the introduction of animals, birds, plants, and fish to new territories. Equally, as we have seen, the spreading of microbes which accompanied cultural encounters resulted in the destruction of tens of thousands of indigenous peoples, making colonial conquest and occupation far easier than might have otherwise have been the case. The effects of the biological encounter lasted for generations, with the indigenous communities weakened, in some cases to the point of extinction, by the advance of newcomers. At the same time, the imposition of ideologies of land ownership and management carved up the landscape in ways the original inhabitants could scarcely have imagined and could not control. What had once been vast tracts held in common, available for the use of the many, became private holdings, controled by the powerful and fortunate few. The physical manifestations of the ideology of land tenure and ownership – fences, survey marks, national boundaries, and the like – asserted human domination over the land and ensured the newcomers could record their control of specific territories.

New concepts of domination and authority accompanied the more direct transitions associated with the expansion of newcomer societies. European countries, in particular, debated concepts of sovereignty over the lands. Individual nations asserted through the act of discovery, the authority of the church, military conquest, treaty, or other method that they had dominion over the newly found territories. In the process, they dismissed, often with little consideration, the reality of indigenous use and control. For generations, Australian courts upheld the concept of *terra nullius*, the idea that the land was unoccupied, even though Aborigines had walked on the continent for more than 40,000 years. The Ainu, likewise, found their generations-old use of the land swept aside by a Japanese government that denied their control of the land. In New Zealand, the Maori were granted tracts of land for personal use, but lost the community control and tribal regulation which had long dominated their land-use system. Governments of the new nation-states placed a premium on the proper use of land and resources and, unilaterally, deemed aboriginal use to be "inefficient." New legal systems, involving courts, land registries, and a variety of concepts of land tenure, provided the administrative manifestation of the ideas that land was divisible, that it could be owned and used for the benefit of individuals, and that the original owners could be dispossessed with little concern for their longstanding relationship with their territories.

The global process of expansion, conquest, and occupation transformed the world in ways that are only now become fully understood. Biological conquest, combined with ideologies of land holding, effectively turned the natural world and its relationship with indigenous societies on its head. The age-old system of living and working with the ecology was displaced by an aggressive assertion of humanity's capacity and willingness to exercise control over the landscape. Scientific knowledge was not sufficient to warn the expansionary powers of the ecological consequences of transporting plants and animals to the newly discovered worlds. Medical understanding did not alert the newcomers to the reality that their presence in new worlds unleashed epidemic diseases of devastating power. The cultural significance of the imposition of new land-tenure systems meant little to newcomer authorities who assumed that the indigenous peoples would simply adopt the lifeways and economic means of the newly dominant societies. Only the passage of time would awaken nations and peoples to the full impact of the biological transformation.

There is a tendency as well to see the transformative effects of ecological imperialism and the new approaches to land tenure as artifacts of the past. Much of the literature and discussion, save for that produced by the indigenous support groups and aboriginal organizations, suggests that historic acts created the contemporary problems. The implication appears to be that modern governments have avoided these difficulties, that the errors of the past have been acknowledged and that a new order is emerging. There is, however, a fundamental continuity between the past and the present regarding biological, epidemiological, and land issues. Imported diseases continue to cause significant difficulties for indigenous communities, particularly in the Amazon basin, Papua New Guinea, and other regions where there has been limited contact with outsiders. The sharing of the globe's biological resources continues apace, with plants, aquatic life, animals, and birds still being introduced to areas outside their normal habitants. The struggle to control this biological imperialism is ongoing, with little prospect for an early end to the dislocations and transformations.

The creation and imposition of approaches to land and resources in conflict with indigenous uses likewise remains a feature of the indigenous–newcomer relationship. In Botswana, for example, the conflicting imperatives of a national park, conservation, and traditional indigenous land use have caused considerable strife and the relocations of the !Kung off their territories. The expansion of oil exploration in northern Canada resulted in the carving up of the land through seismic lines and other access routes, upsetting harvesting and community life. Mining, ranching, and logging operations in the Amazon, all controlled by non-indigenous operators and organizations, have challenged indigenous activities and undermined local harvesting and community structures. Post-World War II preoccupation with hydroelectric development and grand water-diversion schemes flooded vast tracts of indigenous lands, destroyed harvesting opportunities, and caused incalculable disruptions to aboriginal societies.

The struggle continues in more recent times, owing to the continued expansion of industrial societies and settlers onto indigenous territories, the sweeping effects of global warming, which carry grave risks for the island peoples of the Pacific and the harvesting societies of the far north, and the intrusive impact of international pollution. Scientific investigations in remote regions have documented the spread of industrial pollutants into the indigenous food chain, particularly in the North, and serious concerns have emerged about the continued utility of country foods. The explosion at the Chernobyl nuclear plant in 1986 resulted in the spread of radiation across Scandinavia and, in particular, the contamination of reindeer and fish – the cornerstones of Sami harvesting and economic activity. The disaster forced the destruction of thousands of reindeer and the undercutting of the economically important commercial reindeer market. Throughout indigenous territories, environmental change, poor management of resources, and the spread of pollution continues to harm indigenous harvesting activities. The expansion of surplus societies into the lands of indigenous peoples caused enormous changes in the global biosphere. For indigenous peoples, these often subtle, occasionally dramatic, transitions in their natural world provided yet another challenge to which they had to respond. In some instances, most notably epidemic disease, there was very little that they could do to protect themselves. In other cases, as with the arrival of the horse in North America, adoption and adaptation was swift, creative, and culturally dynamic. The sharing of resources added to the complexity and diversity of foodstuffs, improved the quality of life in many quarters, and generated new economic opportunities. This often-neglected aspect of the encounter process has been a persistent influence on indigenous peoples and played a significant role in shaping the response of aboriginal communities to the arrival and settlement of newcomers.

6

SPIRITUAL CONTESTS: MISSIONARIES, CHRISTIANITY, AND INDIGENOUS SOCIETIES

Human societies devote an enormous amount of social and cultural energy attempting to understand and explain the nature and authority of the spiritual world. Highly structured and ceremonial religions like Christianity, Buddhism, and Islam have left their mark on history through prominent spiritual buildings, central religious texts, and elaborate codes of social and public conduct. Much less well-known are the hundreds, if not thousands, of spiritual expressions found among indigenous peoples. These rich and complex societies revolved around strong spiritual understandings and associated social regulations and expectations.

Throughout human history, spiritual differences generated enormous conflict, as members of one religious order sought to establish or impose dominion over another. Spiritual conceptions, which explained how the world emerged, how human beings related to the rest of the environment, and how humans should relate to each other, have often formed the centerpoint for social organization, political action, and even economic behavior. It has really only been in the recent past – in the more secular, scientific times of the industrial age and beyond – and then only in selected nations that spiritual and religious considerations have receded into the background.

At one very important level, the contact experience between indigenous peoples and newcomers was conditioned by spiritual considerations. Expansionary powers, particularly Christian nations, buttressed their plans for political and economic incorporation with commitments to bring news of God and the Christian way to pagan populations. In other instances, the Chinese occupation of Tibet being a good example, colonizing powers sought to undermine or destroy regional spiritual or religious systems in order to solidify their authority over the local people. But it is wrong to reduce the spiritual conflict to one of instrumentality, to see the religion and spirituality as essentially a tool of economic or political authority. While this was clearly part of the process – nations routinely called on representatives of the church to support political campaigns and acts of conquest – there was also a fundamental conflict between indigenous and newcomer concepts of the spiritual world. These conflicts and misunderstandings had a considerable impact on shaping the nature of cross-cultural relationships and, ultimately, of determining the acceptability of indigenous peoples by the new dominant societies.

Faith is, ultimately, based on the belief that it is possible to understand and explain human relationships with the spiritual world and, in particular, with the deities (god or gods) which defined and dominate creation. People who truly believe typically focus on their relationship with or responsibilities to the Creator and, through the formal structures of religion, participate in a local faith community. But a significant number, particularly among the various Christian denominations, have felt personally called to share the good news of salvation, eternal life, and their understanding of human existence with other peoples. These proselytizers, or missionaries, carried their convictions with them to societies in distant lands. They did so with the firm conviction that they were doing God's bidding and had a profound moral and spiritual obligation to convert those without faith, and therefore without understanding, to their religion's conception of life and spirituality. The Bible provided necessary evidence of God's instructions in this regard.

The Christian Missionary Drive

The historic roots of missionary endeavor are very deep indeed, beginning with the work of Jesus and his disciples. In 52 CE, for example, the missionary St. Thomas carried news of the new Christian faith to India. Over the next two hundred years, Christians carried the message to new lands, including southern Spain, Ethiopia, Ireland, and China. After Christian efforts to solidify the faith's claim to much of Europe, the effort spread further afield, moving through Denmark, Sweden, and

Norway between 800 and 1000 CE and into Russia and Poland by the end of that period. The Christian church subsequently consumed much of its evangelical fervor and resources on a series of brutal and bloody crusades in the eleventh to thirteenth centuries, as the faithful attempted to retake control of the Holy Land. Much removed from these efforts, early Catholic missionaries, including the Franciscans, attempted in the thirteenth and fourteenth centuries to establish a foothold in China.

The major missionary expansion occurred in league with the grandiose Spanish and Portuguese explorations of the fifteenth century. Catholic priests accompanied all campaigns of exploration, discovery, and conquest, and carried the expectation that they would share the faith with whomever they encountered, working in league with the official representatives of the Portuguese or Spanish authorities. Portuguese missionaries reached the Azores (1431) and the Congo (1483). Faced with growing competition between the Spanish and the Portuguese, and blissfully unaware of the human and geographic scope of his actions, Pope Alexander VI issued a Demarcation Bull (edict) in 1493, assuring Portugal of control of Africa and the East Indies (Brazil was added the following year); Spain was granted access to the remainder of the "New World." The Pope's imperial edict did not end the competition. Within the Catholic faith, a series of orders operated, each with a specific commitment to missionary work. The Franciscans, Dominicans, Augustinians, and Jesuits often worked at cross-purposes and struggled to be the first to reach new land and new peoples.

The sixteenth century saw the rapid expansion of missionary effort and the establishment of the churches as a major influence in both colonial affairs and the lives of indigenous peoples. Throughout the early part of the century, Catholic missionaries established missions throughout Central and South America, playing a major role in the solidification of colonial control over the regions. The Franciscans arrived in Florida in 1526. The Dominicans moved into Columbia in 1531 and Peru the following year. The Jesuits, soon to be known as the most dogged, austere, and determined of the Catholic orders, established missionary projects beginning in 1540. And so it continued, with the Jesuits reaching India in 1542, the same year the Franciscans established a presence in Mexico. By 1555, Christian missionaries could be found throughout the West Indies and Central America – in Columbia, Ecuador, Peru, Brazil, and numerous other locations in the western hemisphere. Their effort was not restricted to the Americas, although this region attracted the most attention. The

Augustinians and Jesuits reached the Philippines in the mid-1560s, the Dominicans arrived in Mozambique in 1577, and the famed Jesuit missionary Matteo Ricci arrived in China in 1583. Ten years later, in 1593, Franciscan priests entered Japan. The process continued, with the missionaries continuing to accompany explorers and joining with the first wave of European settlers. The Franciscans reached California by the beginning of the seventeenth century and Quebec in 1611, while the Jesuits headed for Paraguay (1610) and also Quebec (1615) where they sought to expand westward into indigenous lands. Ursuline nuns also joined the missionary work in Quebec while the Vincentians established operations in Madagascar in 1648.

While the Catholics had much of the early mission field to themselves, their monopoly on evangelization did not last long. The emergence of dissenters within the Catholic church resulted in a splintering of the faith and the emergence of a series of Protestant traditions (noted, in large measure, by a lengthy debate about questioning the authority of the church). In 1585, for example, Thomas Herriot attempted to spread the English version of Christianity in the Virginia region of North America. When the Pilgrims arrived in Massachusetts in 1620, they assigned one of their number to spread the gospel to the local indigenous peoples. The primary Protestant thrust was, however, tied to the Pietist movement in Germany, dated to the mid- to late seventeenth century. If Protestantism was a reaction against the perceived theological shortcomings of the Catholic church, Pietism was, according to historian Herbert Kane, "a revolt against the barren orthodoxy and dead formalism of the state churches of Protestant Europe."

A number of Protestant churches soon joined in the rush for indigenous and foreign souls, although they lagged far behind the Catholics in terms of human and financial resources, putting and sustaining far fewer missionaries in the field. Anglicans worked among the indigenous peoples on the margins of English settlement in the Americas. Danish missionaries reached India in the early years of the eighteenth century. Moravians expanded globally, particularly in the 1730s, moving into the Caribbean, Greenland, British Guiana, Surinam, and South Africa. Aggressive moves by the Protestants soon displaced the Catholic missions in Africa. Led by several new missionary organizations the British churches undertook a systematic expansion. The formation of the London Missionary Society in 1795 was but one of several institutional developments which gave organizational substance to the growing Protestant determination to spread the non-papal version of Christianity around the globe.

The northward and eastern expansion of Europe also resulted in the spread of western spiritual traditions to additional indigenous groups. As early as 1526, the Swedish Church was working among the Lapps. Almost a century later, in 1621, the Russian Orthodox Church instituted an archbishiporic for Siberia in Tobol'sk. The Orthodox Church continued to push eastward, establishing centers in East Siberia in 1682 and Kamchatka in 1705. They eventually expanded as far as Alaska in the 1830s. During the eighteenth century, the church in Russia, backed by the government, moved very aggressively, organizing mass and mandatory baptism, destroying indigenous religious icons, disempowering shamans, and otherwise undercutting indigenous spirituality. They faced considerable resistance, particularly from the Nenets, who protected their traditional spiritual activities from Russian Orthodox Church intervention. The efforts in Russia and Scandinavia matched the fervor and intensity of the Catholic and Protestant campaigns to take the Christian gospels around the world. Even in these northern regions, however, bitter memories remain. As one Sami activist said of the Christian advance,

> The conversion of Samis often involved violence, for the priests hung on to their privileges, disciplined the people with all sorts of weapons, and introduced spirits into Samiland. The best known is probably "Tuderus, Christ's clergyman, hated here in Samiland." He banished the shaman drums. Sometimes he took his wife with him, and had the Samis give her rides and presents.[1]

By the early years of the nineteenth century, the missionary enterprise had enveloped much of the globe and had brought Christian values, traditions, assumptions, and teachings to hundreds of indigenous groups. Some of the old orders faded, including the Jesuits, who were disbanded for several decades. Others joined the spiritual fray, including the Church Missionary Society (1799), American Board of Commissioners for Foreign Missions (1810), and the Hawaiian Evangelical Association in Micronesia (1852). While the greatest effort was typically directed at densely populated areas, including slave-holding regions of Central and South America, China and Africa, mobile indigenous groups attracted considerable attention. The urge to expand had many roots, including the desire to support European settlement, a firm belief in the efficacy of Christianity, and an intense, hate-filled competition between Protestants and Catholics. The missionary enterprise did not always work. The Japanese expelled the Christian missionaries and retreated into isolation. It was not uncommon for individual missions to fold, often for lack of a suitable missionary, and for years to pass before contact was re-established. Missionaries were not always necessary. The Christian church took hold in Korea in the 1830s without the active intervention of outside missionaries.

The impulse to mission did not begin to abate until the mid-twentieth century, and even now efforts to spread faith to "heathen" and "pagan" peoples continue. Missionary organizations, often aligned with national attempts to control particular regions or populations, spread into the most remote corners of Africa, Australia, North America, and South America. Missionaries carried the message of the colonial churches into the distant lands of Siberia and the tiny islands of the South Pacific. Efforts continued to focus on large populations where possible, but the scattered mobile populations continued to hold particular fascination for the national missionary organizations. There were areas of dramatic conversion activity, such as the spread of Christianity throughout sub-Saharan Africa where a rapid growth in Christianity was noted before 1950 and an even faster expansion after that time.

Indigenous Spirituality and Newcomer Impressions

During the age of expansion, particularly as European powers reached throughout Asia, South America, and Africa, they encountered a complex array of societies. Some, like the Mughals in India, the Aztecs in central America, the Han in China or the Japanese were large, complex and sedentary peoples. The European newcomers recognized them as "others"; they were clearly not "civilized" in European terms, but they were formidable enemies, capable of majestic architectural, literary and artistic accomplishments, and therefore deserving of cautious respect. The spiritual formulations in these societies were typically codified, with substantial organizational structures, written codes and elaborate rituals. They were dismissed out of hand as inferior to Christianity – derided as superstitions in most instances – but were none the less accorded a measure of grudging respect due to their evident complexity and hold on the population. Newcomers often found, even more helpfully, that the institutions of theocratic states, where religious personalities either led the society or influenced the national leadership, could be used for the purposes of colonization and domination.

Smaller societies, in contrast, elicited a much less favorable response. Whether the tribal peoples lived in the Amazon basin or on the North American plains, on the tundra of Siberia or the Australian outback, indigenous cultures were viewed in a very different fashion. Their spiritual concepts, deeply embedded in their relationship with the physical world, lacked the structures and forms that outsiders expected. These mobile populations, small in number and generally without permanent base or large buildings, lacked the basic prerequisites of what the expansionist nations viewed as civilized peoples. They were described as "pagans" and "heathens," and held up to contempt by the largely Christian explorers, soldiers, government officials, settlers, and traders who made the first forays into their territories.

The initial impressions and descriptions stuck. Once described as "backward" and "uncivilized," the tribal peoples had secured a label which proved extremely difficult to dislodge. Only a tiny handful of people, the precursors of contemporary anthropologists and social scientists, took the time to learn much about the spiritual foundations of indigenous life. Their descriptions, generally few in number, were typically riddled with evidence of the observers' cultural superiority. The newcomers chided the tribal societies for the child-like simplicity of their spiritual beliefs, for their seemingly irrational belief in the spiritual authority of animals and other elements in the natural world, and for the absence of formal structure. These peoples had no written equivalent of the Bible or the Koran. They could point to no great spiritual leader, like Jesus Christ, Muhammad, Buddha, or Confucius. Instead, to the jaundiced and unsympathetic eye of the colonizer, they put their spiritual faith in witch doctors, not learned priests, counted on unscientific explanations for natural phenomena, and spoke of a life beyond death which drew no insight or connection to the "great" religions of rest of the world. Moreover, their sacred sites were trees, mountains, winds, and animals; there were precious few signs of the temples, cathedrals, and dramatic spiritual centers which dominated religious observations in sedentary societies.

The newcomers placed their impressions of indigenous spirituality alongside their understandings of tribal lifeways and saw little of value. They did not see peoples steeped in cultural tradition, with a remarkable understanding of local ecosystems, and a deep appreciation for both the spirits of the living world and the life hereafter. Instead, they saw societies bent toward savagery and brutality, tied to unintelligible concepts of social structure, collective responsibility, and material wealth. They saw peoples who, in the famous words of Thomas Hobbes, lived lives which were "nasty, brutish and short." The newcomers could marvel at the temples in India, the medieval castles in Japan, and the architecturally stunning sites of worship in China, even as they disparaged the "superstitions" which underlay their beliefs. Confronted with the reality of small-scale tribal worlds, these same newcomers rarely had more than contempt for what they viewed as the pitiful dwellings, disorganized social systems, and vapid, animist religious formulations.

The expansionist ethos of the Christian faith stood at the center of the contest between tribal and newcomer spirituality. Largely alone among the world's major religions, Christianity has from its earliest days been suffused with a zeal for proselytizing. Beginning with the disciples, selected and charged with the responsibility for spreading word of Jesus's life, Christianity has been engaged in a now two–millennia-long search for lost and wayward souls. The founders of the faith – unlike Islam, Confucianism, Judaism, and Buddhism – did not believe that one's entry into the Christian world was a matter of birthright or was something that was restricted to any one people or culture. Christians were drawn by their faith to spread the word, to seek converts, and to endeavor to save the souls of those who did yet profess complete belief in the life and teachings of Jesus Christ. For centuries, Christianity's struggles focused on asserting dominance in Europe and, thorough a series of bloody and vicious Crusades, regaining control of the Middle East. The battles started as a struggle against European pagan traditions and rudimentary spirituality, with the Roman Catholic church gradually beating back the forces of superstition. The church used close alliances with the princes and monarchs who controled the continent to entrench their authority and enhance the wealth of the institution.

There is a wide-ranging debate about the expansive tendencies and proselytizing aspects of Islam, an understandable question given the dramatic expansion of the faith over the generations. While some have argued that Muslims were called, through words or lifestyle, to attract people to the faith, other commentators have argued that Islam's spread was largely a result of military action. The association of the faith with military power, administrative authority, and trading prowess drew adherents to Islam:

> This ambience gave to the Muslim proselytizer a distinct psychological advantage. In conquered lands the Muslim could always speak from a position of power. This is in stark contrast to the situation of Christian and Buddhist

missionaries, who were often forced to testify in grovelling submission before the authorities of China, Japan and other countries. In certain geographical locations Muslims were considered superior because of their literacy, their powers of magic and healing, and their wealth. Here again is see a contrast with Christian and Buddhist proselytizers, who were considered "running dogs" and "foreign devils" – in short, supremely *inferior* peoples.[2]

The Islamic faith expanded alongside the territorial extension of the Muslim world, drawing in many adherents and growing far beyond its Middle Eastern base. By the eighteenth and nineteenth centuries, the growing strength of Europe served to cap Muslim expansion, which had earlier been crucial to the spread of Islam. The faith – and the Muslim people – became more defensive and sought to consolidate its hold on territories and peoples and played a comparatively minor role in the subsequent contacts with indigenous peoples.

Missions and Imperial Expansion

Returning to the Christian world, internal struggles escalated over the generations, peaking in a contest led by Martin Luther in the early sixteenth century between Catholic religious leaders who believed in the God-given infallibility of the pope and Protestant dissenters who saw Christianity as a more personal and human institution. The Protestant–Catholic struggle ultimately became a dominant factor in the imperial race to claim newly discovered portions of the world. Each denomination fervently believed God to be on their side, and ridiculed, derided, and chastised the other for the audacity and aggressiveness of their vision of world domination. In the initial stages of European expansion, with the emphasis on retaking the Middle East and Eastern Europe from Muslim control, the goal was simply to replace non-Christian beliefs with the "proper" Christian understanding of the world and the hereafter. The animosity between Catholic and Protestant nations, colonies and peoples knew few bounds. At best, they treated each other with suspicion and spiritual contempt; at the worst, culturally based contests resulted in bitter and violent confrontations. Much has been written about the Catholic–Protestant rivalry, which resulted in frantic and occasionally foolhardy rushes for souls in indigenous territories. As one historian observed, however, too much should not be made of the competition:

> In any case, sectarian historical traditions have ludicrously exaggerated, or actually invented, the cultural differences between Protestantism and Catholicism. Of course, *odium theologicum* was a powerful influence on the mutual perceptions of colonists from different parts of Europe, which, at the relevant time, were developing mutually hostile religious traditions. And of course, Catholic missionary efforts proved more committed and sustained than those of the Protestants. Crucial similarities, however – "common differences" – balance and in some respects outweigh these divergences.[3]

On numerous occasions, however, indigenous peoples found themselves caught between Protestants and Catholics, trapped in a doctrinal struggle not of their making.

Christianity, therefore, became a critical underpinning for European expansion – the ideological equivalent of the communist/capitalist thrust of the twentieth century – and the churches emerged as handmaidens for empire. From the churches' perspectives, Christianity carried a responsibility to spread the message of the gospel to "lost souls" wherever they were to be found. Within each denomination, religious orders or church missionaries societies were formed, with special responsibility for carrying the world of God to heathen and pagan peoples. While scholars have subsequently derided much of the Christian effort as being little more than a cover for imperial designs and aspirations of conquest, it is vital to recognize that a very real and deep spiritual conviction underlay the missionary impulse. Men and women by the thousands signed up for a life of deprivation and hardship – a small number finding considerable power and personal wealth – and committed themselves to overseas mission work. The motivation to devote one's life to the service of the Lord, as understood within the Christian denominations, was a critical element in the expansion of Europe and influenced the relationship between indigenous and non-indigenous peoples.

In launching their colonial initiatives imperial powers were quick to seize on the power, organizational ability, and service functions of Christian denominations. They did so, in part, due to the Christian imperatives and authority structure which rested very close to the halls of power in imperial Spain, Portugal, and France. England, dominated by the non-Catholic (Anglican) Church of England had a somewhat more distant relationship between church and overseas activities, but the two arms of empire still reached simultaneously for new lands and new peoples.

The churches and national governments discovered that both stood to gain from cooperation. There were occasions when church and state stood at odds, as in some of the early settlements in the American colonies. Most often, however, the relationship was symbiotic. Governments needed the churches and their missionary armies to reach indigenous peoples in distant regions. The missions served, as well, as effective demonstrations of imperial sovereignty and provided an important adjunct to trading, military, and settlement activities. Imperial governments came to rely on missionaries as a vanguard of the settlement process, introducing indigenous peoples to the ways of the Christian world and thus preparing them for adaptation to the new order. Anglican missionaries played an important role in convincing the Maori to sign the Treaty of Waitangi in 1840, with Archdeacon Henry Williams producing a Maori-language version of the document to reassure the Maori. His version, however, downplayed the full transfer of sovereign control of the land to the British, a rather major consideration for the Maori. British missionaries likewise helped induce the Ndebele to sign agreements with the British South Africa Company, once more masking the full impact of what the Ndebele were conferring on the British. Missionaries also played critical roles in the negotiation of major treaties across the Canadian west, using their cultural role with the aboriginal communities to reassure the signatories, and often serving as translators for the actual negotiations.

The churches, in their turn, benefited from a close relationship with national governments. The protection provided by imperial armies provided a check against indigenous aggression. Related to this, the church basked in the aura, authority, and power of the colonizing power – just as the colonial government capitalized on indigenous awe and affection for the Christian message. In numerous instances, church officials traveled with government convoys, received supplies from official sources, and, in the settlement era, often secured financial assistance from the government in return for providing such services as education and medical care.

Missionary Approaches and Indigenous Peoples

The missionary enterprise varied enormously. Within the Catholic tradition, missionaries ranged from the zealots and martyrs of the Jesuit order to more state-focused organizations of priests and nuns. Protestant missionaries likewise covered a broad spectrum. Some groups, like the Puritans who settled in the New England portion of the American colonies, believed in personal relationships with God and challenged indigenous peoples to demonstrate the same connection with the Lord. The Church of England, in contrast, viewed its responsibilities as being strongly in league with the British Empire, and worked closely with state authorities. Even within the Anglican faith, approaches to missionary endeavors differed greatly. The Society for the Propagation of the Gospel in Foreign Parts enjoyed the support of the "high" or conservative branches of the denomination; the "low" church organization, the Church Missionary Society, drew its inspiration and financial sustenance from the more evangelical elements of the Church.

The work of spreading the gospel varied widely. Catholic orders established model farming settlements in Brazil and sought to integrate Algonquians into the new agricultural communities in New France. In remote portions of Africa, Catholics and Protestants struggled to overcome climatic, disease, and cultural barriers in determined attempts to bring the gospel to isolated groups. Formal efforts to educate the Chinese on the wonders of Christianity, often through the good works of medical missionaries, stood in stark contrast to itinerant clergy who traveled hundreds of miles across the Canadian sub-Arctic or the Australian outback in search of souls to convert. The central themes running through the missionary endeavor were a firm belief that agricultural settlement was the root of cultural transformation and that the education of the young was a requirement for the successful and long-term conversion of the indigenous population. Many missionaries devoted an enormous amount of effort to translating the scriptures into the local language or dialect, in the process introducing the indigenous population to the written word. In several instances – such as the Inuit in Greenland and the Maori in New Zealand – the presentation of the indigenous language in script form resulted in a burst of literacy and the rapid development of reading and writing skills. Missionaries encouraged their congregations to learn the language of the colonial regime, although the most effective were those who quickly learned to converse with the indigenous peoples in their own tongue. Those who followed the missionaries often faced major challenges. The Yanama of southern South America, for example, moved into central mission settlements and experienced profound disruptions to their seasonal rounds. The new communities, for the Yanama and many others, became breeding groups for epidemic diseases, killing many of the people in the process. Many tribal groups were loath, for cultural and economic reasons, to abandon their mobile ways and shunned the missionaries' appeal to settle down in a permanent location. In such instances, the missionaries either traveled with the indigenous peoples or resigned themselves to having minimal contact with their putative congregations.

There was, ultimately, no single approach to missionary work. Europeans were fascinated with stories of overseas missionary heroism and martyrdom. Many threw themselves into their work with messianic zeal, sacrificing themselves in the pursuit of lost souls. The famed Jesuits of New France sought out martyrdom in the service of the Lord; graphic descriptions of painful deaths at the hands of indigenous peoples stimulated great interest in their North American work. Protestant missionaries in Africa died by the score, victims of a climate and ecology ill-suited to denizens of the northern temperate zones, their passing hailed as evidence of their devotion to Christian service. Missionaries sought the inhospitable, the dangerous, and the unappealing, believing that God had called them personally into his service and that pagans from China to the Amazon deserved the blessings of the Bible.

More prosaically, some clergy called on the "hellfire and damnation" messages of the Old Testament and used harsh threats and foreboding sermons to cajole indigenous people into communion. Others drew heavily on the New Testament, and the more optimistic Jesus story, to convince tribal communities of the beauty of the Gospels. They were extremely persistent, celebrating decisions like that of Wanalancet, Pennacook chief, who surrendered to Puritan preaching in 1674: "I have, all my days, used to pass in an old canoe and now you exhort me to change and leave my old canoe, and embark in a new canoe, to which I have hitherto been unwilling; but now I yield myself up to your advice, and enter into a new canoe, and do engage to pray to God hereafter."[4] For every missionary who attempted to build a congregation through lofty intellectualizing, there were many others who used hard toil, traveling and dwelling alongside the tribal peoples to show them, in living form, the meaning of God's word. Some, particularly Catholics, insisted on adherence to a social and cultural code, using individual and group punishments to hold congregations to the Christian line. Convert communities, called *aldeias* in Brazil and *reducciones* in the Spanish colonies, attracted sizeable populations. Other mission stations sought to create "ideal" villages, like William Duncan's Metlakatla on the Northwest Coast of North America and several Maori settlements in New Zealand, where communicants were re-crafted in the image of the colonial state. There were missionaries who attacked indigenous spiritual traditions with vigor and determination, desperate to eradicate all vestiges of the "pagan" order. Others, in sharp contrast, took a much more flexible approach, tolerating a number of indigenous traditions while celebrating every sign that the people had accepted key elements of Christian practice. Indigenous peoples only rarely responded with aggression to the missionaries. The spiritual interventions were more subtle and less dramatic than the intrusions of miners, farmers, and soldiers. But as their work took root, and particularly as divisions emerged within aboriginal societies, criticism emerged. One Seneca said of the missionary organizing among his people that "my continuance there would be distructive of the nation, & finally over throw all the traditions & usages of their Forefathers & that there would not be a warrior remaining in their nation in the course of a few years." An Algonkin said that as a result of the Christian prayers, "Now, our dreams and our prophecies are no longer true, – prayer has spoiled everything for us." Another, from New England, said, "Our forefathers ... taught us nothing about our Soul, and God, and Heaven, and Hell, and Joy, and Torment in the Life to come ... .We are well as we are, and desire not to be troubled by these wise new sayings."[5]

Throughout the European colonial world, Christian-based denominations capitalized on the expansion of empire to spread the word of Christian salvation. They sought, because they saw no contradiction in doing so, to link their faith to the material culture of their country of origin. They linked salvation to agriculture, Christianity to trade, spiritual bliss to military alliances. To the missionaries, the European continent represented the embodiment of God's wisdom and accomplishments; all other nations, peoples and religious formulation were, by definition, inferior and suspect. National and doctrinal conflicts figured prominently in the church's work. Catholics and Protestants, in particular, competed aggressively for communicants, deriding each other's workers and message. The competition occasionally became intense, with the priests and pastors engaging in unseemly rushes for souls, baptizing any who would stand for the ceremony in the hope of securing government recognition of the church's hold over a particular individual or group. In addition, various denominations or orders competed within the faith, setting Protestant against Protestant, Catholic against Catholic.

The Christian churches were aggressive, interventionist, and often culturally insensitive, but they were not working on a *tabula rasa*. Missionaries viewed indigenous spirituality as superstition and aboriginal religious practices as pagan. But they quickly discovered that the indigenous beliefs and values were deeply held, and were formidably connected to the indigenous way of life and environment. As in economic, military, and political affairs, aboriginal communities responded creatively to the advance of the Christian frontier, and found unique and innovative ways of drawing the missionaries and their work into their world. The pattern should now be familiar. Indigenous peoples were occasionally overwhelmed by the new forces, but more often adapted selectively to the new system. They made a concerted effort to sustain that which was most central to their lives through many decades of attempted cultural transformation. Missionaries were, on occasion, very aggressive and demanding. They expected the indigenous peoples simply to accept the wisdom and wonder of Christianity. Most often, however, they discovered a far from passive people who, however intrigued they were with the Christian ways, held tightly to the values and assumptions which had ordered their world for generations.

Indigenous Responses to Missionary Efforts

Indigenous peoples faced a wide variety of Christian intrusions, ranging from all-encompassing Catholic and Protestant communities of faith to occasional visits from itinerant preachers. As with many of the other wonderments associated with the initial arrival of newcomers, there was a sharp and often bewildered reaction to the first appearance of the missionaries. Some individuals and groups quickly came to see the religious interlopers as intertwined with the power of the newcomers. When, as often happened, indigenous peoples succumbed to newly imported diseases, it is hardly surprising that some wondered if the missionaries had a source of power denied to aboriginal healers. In some areas, as among the Mi'kmaq of the east coast of North America, this conjunction encouraged many to seek succor from the church in times of illness. At other times, such as among the Iroquois, the fact that most who received the last rites from Catholic priests died shortly thereafter generated enormous suspicion and even hatred. Others were drawn to the church by the prospect of stronger military alliances, better trade relations, or other practical considerations. In many other areas, particularly Catholic-dominated Central and South America, the authority of the colonial state empowered the Catholic missions to impose theocratic order on the indigenous peoples, stripping them of their freedom and demanding adherence to Catholic precepts.

Importantly, missionaries also moved into indigenous territories as a direct consequence of concern related to the negative effects of development. When miners, loggers, and others moved into the Cape York region of Australia, the Aborigines were severely dislocated. News of the socially destructive impact of newcomer activities resulted in the dispatch of missionaries into the area, with the clear expectation that the clergy would both protect the indigenous peoples and prepare the Aborigines for adaptation to the new order.

Over the decades, particularly as non-indigenous settlement and development encroached on aboriginal territories and contact with missionaries and church communities increased, indigenous adherence to the newly introduced faiths increased. Thousands of indigenous peoples became practising Christians, of varying degrees of formality and conviction. They faced a church which expected, if it did not demand, adherence to new social norms. Communities which had long practiced polygamy were ordered to desist. Burial practices were supposed to adhere to Christian norms. Traditional spiritual beliefs were derided and criticized; public expressions of belief in the old order were discouraged and even suppressed, typically with the assistance of government.

Indigenous participation in the Christianization of their world varied dramatically. The churches sought to recruit indigenous spiritual leaders, relaxing their educational requirements in remote regions in favor of ensuring that someone – anyone – was keeping the church alive among the indigenous peoples. The Catholic Church's insistence on unmarried priests severely limited the attractiveness of the priesthood (aided by Protestant criticism in areas of competition) and kept the number of indigenous priests very small. Protestants, in contrast, were more flexible on marital status and recruited a sizeable number of aboriginal clergy and church support workers. The translation of the Bible into dozens of languages and dialects, from Maori to Inuktitut (Inuit), allowed believers to carry the tools of the faith with them on their travels. Aboriginal artists lent their skills to the creation of Christian symbols and ceremonial artifacts.

Many thousands of indigenous peoples became active Christians, a phenomenon that has rested uneasily with descriptions of the missionaries as aggressive and unforgiving colonizers. They attended church services whenever they could. They learned the liturgy and the hymns. They donated money to the church, assisted with the construction of new buildings, and provided sustenance to the missionaries. They followed the social strictures of the Christian church, were married before a priest (when possible) and buried their dead in Christian rituals (often with an indigenous element or two). They were devout and enthusiastic; missionaries often remarked that the indigenous congregations could not sing well, but did so with conviction. Many groups managed, within a generation or two, to put aside public displays of those customs and traditions that missionaries found offensive. In the most extreme cases, entire communities threw themselves into the creation of worshiping communities, built around theocratic principles and typically dominated by Christian missionaries.

Patterns of conversion and faith had disruptive influences within indigenous societies. Those who believed or professed the Christian faith – whether they came to their loyalty out of pragmatic or spiritual considerations – often found themselves at odds with others. Jesuit communities, including large settlements in Paraguay and smaller congregations in North America, were particularly adept at building barriers against the rest of the world. The Huron of the North American Great Lakes region found themselves engulfed in a series of bitter internal struggles centerd on disputes about the authority of the Christian church. Delaware Native Americans divided into converts and traditional peoples and lived in separate settlements. Indigenous peoples who opted for Catholicism over Protestant offerings often picked up the intense and at times ferocious rivalries of these denominations. Maori communities tended to adopt one denomination or the other, thus rendering the rivalry into an inter- rather than intra-group affair. Missionaries generally encouraged these struggles, supporting the adherents in their efforts to separate themselves from non-believers. In recent years, fundamentalist Christian groups, which emphasize the importance of personal salvation, have encouraged a separation of communities into those who have experienced God's grace and those who have not.

Scholars have struggled to explain the pattern of indigenous participation in Christianity. Seemingly putting aside the idea that they became Christians because they believed in the new faith, analysts have argued that cultural colonization contributed to the acceptance of the church. They pointed to the conjunction of church and state and to the indigenous peoples' desire to gain access to the material and other wealth of the newcomers. Others have asserted that conversion and baptism followed the devastating impact of introduced diseases and the other political and economic dislocations accompanying the newcomers. This argument – what Canadian historian John Webster Grant presented as the "moon of wintertime" hypothesis – holds that indigenous peoples turned their attention to Christianity when their spiritual leaders failed to heal the people dying from these illnesses. The analysis, however, does not explain the numerous instances when indigenous peoples joined the Christian church at a comparative high point, when they were participating actively in the new economies and holding their own in the face of colonial expansion.

There is no simple explanation for indigenous adherence to Christianity, if only because there was no single pattern of engagement. Some aboriginal people joined the new faith for entirely pragmatic purposes. They were drawn by the power of the newcomers, as seen in their technology, military prowess, and material wealth. Having access to the Christian God, some believed, would provide access to the accoutrements of the western industrial world. The mystique of the newcomers often faded, particularly when the indigenous peoples discovered that the outsiders lacked the knowledge, skills, and technology to flourish in their often difficult surroundings, but the initial and positive impressions often lingered. Perhaps the most significant element of indigenous conversion is the realization by many that adherence to Christianity did not require an abandonment of traditional values, beliefs, and practices. Across many different cultures, syncretic patterns of spiritual beliefs emerged, with the missionaries adapting their message to suit local realities or the indigenous peoples maintaining key customs and spiritual assumptions. Even in communities where the priests declared indigenous traditions to have been eliminated, as in Central America, many core elements of the old belief systems remained within the communities.

Religious alliances were often tied to diplomatic and military agreements. Joining the French, Portuguese, or Spanish fold brought indigenous peoples under the watchful and hierarchical eye of the Catholic Church. Those within the British Empire, in contrast, were often exposed to a broader range of ecclesiastical options, often marked by intense competition among Protestant denominations and a decidedly unchristian rivalry between Catholics and Protestants. (The small peoples of the Siberian North came under the control of the Soviet state after 1917, its communist orthodoxy supplanting Christian proselytizing.) Given the manner in which the preeminence of a specific faith accompanied the religious alliances of the imperial power, it is hardly surprising that the pattern of indigenous contact with organized Christianity generally mirrored the colonial structures of an expanding Europe.

Likewise, the manner in which epidemic disease accompanied the expansion of the Christian colonizers created an important precondition for conversion. In the initial decades of contact with newcomers, most indigenous societies suffered through a series of devastating epidemics, with high levels of mortality. In most instances (save for Africa, where this general pattern was largely reversed), the newcomers were only minimally affected by the diseases that they carried to the new worlds. Before the arrival of the outsiders, shaman – medicine men, spiritual healers, and experts with traditional medicines and procedures – looked after the ill. Faced with imported epidemics, these traditional healers seemed powerless, certainly in contrast with the newcomers who seemed impervious to the sickness. Missionaries often served as doctors and nurses to the ill and appeared to have strong healing powers. In such situations, it is hardly surprising that many aboriginal peoples turned to the Christian God for succor and safety. They were, of course, encouraged in this transition by missionaries who themselves equated the peoples' desperate conditions with the failure to accept Christianity and implied that prosperity and good health would follow conversion.

The argument that indigenous communities accepted Christianity only when at a low point in collective health and spiritual well-being does not apply universally, however. In many parts of the world, aboriginal peoples welcomed the missionaries, appeared intrigued by their religious ideas and ceremonies, and even became enthusiastic adherents. For such groups, there appears to have been a conscious and deliberate decision to become practicing Christians and to develop an intellectual and spiritual affinity with the foreign faith. It is ironic, in fact, that historians who have been pleased to demonstrate that aboriginal peoples exercised considerable agency over economic, political, social, and diplomatic interactions with newcomers have often been reluctant to assume that comparable influences governed indigenous involvement with organized Christianity.

There is abundant evidence of aboriginal interest in Christianity, ranging from the development of indigenous clergy to generations-long adherence to individual denominations in numerous communities. While critics of the missionary enterprise tend to argue that coercion, manipulation, and imperial domination account for the aboriginal acceptance of a colonial religion, other forces were also at play. Beyond the pragmatic economic or diplomatic considerations identified earlier, aboriginal people were drawn by the charismatic authority of individual preachers, found solace in the stories and lessons contained in the Bible (many of which resonated with the collectivist impulses of indigenous societies), enjoyed the ceremonial trappings and traditions of Christianity or, as with many non-aboriginal people, fell into the habit of church attendance for more community and social reasons. The efforts of Christian missionaries to learn local indigenous languages and to translate the Bible into the vernacular (which had the additional impact of creating a visual representation of hitherto oral languages) earned support and understanding in many quarters. Whatever the motivations for joining the church – and most baptisms of indigenous communications appear to have occurred before spiritual conversion was assured – the Christian faith took firm root in aboriginal communities around the world.

Christianity found its most ready adherents in indigenous communities that practiced very flexible, polytheistic (multiple gods or spirits) spiritual beliefs. The missionaries' doctrine offered a compelling contrast to traditional beliefs, in that they posited an all-powerful God, with a demonstrated life on earth, and a full complement of theological, religious, and cultural practices. Highly localized spiritual beliefs were extremely useful in explaining natural and human phenomena that related to a specific locale. These formulations did little to explain, let alone control, the much broader material, technological, cultural, economic, and epidemiological influences associated with the arrival of the newcomers. Old spiritual beliefs helped cope with the known world; it is hardly surprising that many indigenous people sought solace and insight in new, broader spiritual explanations to help understand a more complex and varied new world order. The fact that Christianity offered a sacred text – a clear, systematic exposition of basic beliefs and moral lessons – also helped in approaching those peoples whose spiritual beliefs were not compiled in a single such document.

The Christian church which remained, however, had often been molded or shaped by aboriginal influences. However doctrinaire a missionary might wish to be, it was difficult to preserve doctrinal purity hundreds if not thousands of miles away from the nearest sizeable European settlement. Faced, often, with resistance from indigenous peoples who were reluctant to abandon all of their traditional customs and practices, missionaries in the field typically showed restraint and flexibility. Efforts to eliminate polygamy, a particular evil in the missionaries' eyes, typically moved slowly. Burial practices often remained a combination of Christian and indigenous traditions for many years. Biblical stories, hymns, and symbols were merged with the iconography of the aboriginal society in order to make Christianity more understandable to indigenous audiences. Complex biblical concepts were simplified and rendered visually, often in images that made sense to indigenous congregations. Aboriginal clergy were particularly given to adjusting biblical ideas to local situations. The Christian churches which emerged in the indigenous communities, therefore, shared much in common with the broader Christian faith and the specific denomination. They also reflected in ways large and small the values and spiritual understandings of the indigenous peoples.

Indigenous Revitalization Movements

The missionary advance also sparked an indigenous counter-response. Not all indigenous peoples accepted the new faith and some resented the presence of the proselytizers in their midst. Various revitalization or nativist spiritual movements emerged in many societies, often drawing on Christian models of preaching and spiritual gathering. Powerful aboriginal spiritual leaders, some of them traditional shaman seeking to maintain their authority in a changing religious environment, offered a counterpoint to the Christian church. Handsome Lake, a Seneca Iroquois chief, sparked a major revitalization movement in his territory, responding to the cultural demoralization of his people and the uneven reaction to Christianity. Handsome Lake had fallen into a trance while ill and recovered, declaring that he had had a vision for his people. He encouraged both a return to traditional Iroquois values and greater adaptation to western norms. Comparable individuals and movements, designed to rebuild cultural confidence and lift people from despair, emerged in other areas, including Black Elk's work among the Lakota Sioux. Messianic movements erupted in indigenous territories in India, capitalizing on demoralization associated with the occupation of tribal lands and involving powerful leaders who claimed god-like authority over their people. Mission supporters also often clashed with indigenous groups which remained outside the missionaries' orbit. Among the Cuiva of South America, for example, locals associated with the Jesuit missions often fought with those Cuiva who resisted the priests' overtures. There were many revitalization movements across the indigenous world, often led by messianic leaders who blended elements of Christian thought with a strong appeal to indigenous spiritual traditions.

Aboriginal revitalization movements often generated a sharp rebuke from missionaries and government officials, and some lingered underground for years if not generations. Indigenous spirituality did not disappear, even in the face of decades of missionary work and countless attempts by government and Christian workers to suppress the unwanted aspects of indigenous spiritual expression. Aboriginal groups maintained a strong commitment to traditional values and assumptions, despite determined government and missionary opposition. Where missionaries were more accommodating, indigenous ceremonies and spiritual ideas gradually melded with Christian values in a syncretistic fashion. While some of the major missions endeavored to recreate European settlements and sought to convert indigenous peoples in lifestyle as much as spiritual belief, most missionaries had limited contact with their mobile communicants. In such circumstances, missionaries aimed for superficial adherence and formal political attachments. Circumstances and resources simply did not permit the missionaries to do more than make occasional contact, perform ceremonies where possible, and pray for their souls. In such situations, it was impossible for Christianity to force out completely the indigenous world views.

That aboriginal spirituality would continue should hardly be surprising. Indigenous spiritual understandings reflected an ancient relationship with the environment and the spiritual world. The largely animist spirituality of the indigenous world viewed all things – human, animal, flora, physical landscape, air, fire, lightning, and so on – as having a spiritual essence. These understandings were deeply embedded in aboriginal life, informing harvesting activity, seasonal movements, ceremonies, and other rituals. Christianity, in contrast, was presented largely as a human-centred faith system, speaking earnestly about individual and collective relationships with a single God, but not providing a counterbalance to the inclusive and comprehensive spiritual world envisioned through indigenous spiritual conceptions. So long as the people maintained their relationship with the land, and so long as the communities kept the stories and teachings alive through their language, songs, stories, ceremonies, and collective activities, indigenous spiritual assumptions remained active and, in many instances, impervious to Christian interventions.

The Lingering Effects of Spiritual Intervention on Indigenous Peoples

Missionary work had other, perhaps unexpected, elements. The missionary enterprise was, at heart, paternalistic, in that the missionaries believed that they knew what was best for the indigenous peoples. Few missionaries hesitated in introducing culturally and spiritually aggressive programs for the transformation of indigenous peoples. At the same time, in many parts of the world, the missionaries emerged as the primary, albeit self-appointed, spokespeople for the indigenous population. Before aboriginal communities gained the linguistic, cultural, and political skills to represent themselves before the colonial, imperial, or world community, the primary voices raised in defence of indigenous peoples came from missionaries. They couched their interventions in the interventionist and culturally superior language of their day. They spoke, often, without consulting their congregations. Their messages were often tinged with self-interest, in that supporting missionary work was, in the minds of the missionaries, of direct benefit to the aboriginal peoples.

But at a time when colonial people had little time for indigenous interests, the missionaries offered an often forceful, effective, and well-connected outlet. The same connections to government and the military while propelled the missionaries into the field and often sustained their operations provided a conduit for appeals on behalf of the indigenous peoples. Jesuit Antonio Vieira of Brazil attacked the enslavement of Indians and convinced the government to retract its policies. The missionaries, who developed refined skills at addressing broad, public constituencies in the interests of raising funds and attracting men and women to the field, used these same skills and contacts to bring indigenous issues to the attention of the public at large. They spoke out, on occasion, against military aggression against indigenous peoples and against government neglect of aboriginal communities. They called on governments to negotiate treaties and to honor them when they had been signed. They asked the authorities to keep "bad whites" away from their indigenous congregations, to staunch the flow of liquor into the communities, to provide funds for (often mission-run) schools, and to be fair in the allocation of land, food, and other supplies to indigenous communities. The missionaries were not always successful. Government officials routinely complained that church officials intervened too often and too aggressively on behalf of indigenous causes. But missionary communications and efforts to encourage government attention often stood alone in publicizing the crises in aboriginal communities and in securing attention to their needs and rights.

Christian enthusiasm for missionary work waned throughout the twentieth century. The emergence of the social gospel tradition in the Protestant denominations and less prominent variations in the Catholic Church turned the emphasis from conversation to social and economic well-being. Missionaries also acknowledged that their interventions had not always been beneficial and had caused disruptions. As the British colonial-fragment states – Canada, Australia, New Zealand, and others – matured, interest in addressing the spiritual needs of national indigenous peoples declined in favor of aggressive moves into the densely populated areas of India, China, and Africa. It was easier to find missionaries to send to the Orient than to the marginal zones within these countries, although local, national, and international missionary organizations continued to press for interventions with aboriginal societies.

The impulse to mission and the indigenous response to proselytizing continue through to the present. Long-term Protestant and Catholic missions remain active in tribal territories and thousands of indigenous peoples around the world are active and proud members of their faith communities. A sharp backlash against spiritual imperialism and western efforts to undermine aboriginal cultures challenged the traditional missionary enterprise. The mainline churches moved more cautiously than in the past, demonstrating respect for indigenous spirituality and culture, working to incorporate indigenous leaders into the organizations, and apologizing formally for the aggressive interventions of the past several hundred years. Much of the contemporary mission effort is devoted to "good works," from education and medical assistance to community economic development and the empowerment of women. In tribal territories around the world, however, the Christian churches remain an active and prominent presence.

Aggressive missionary work continues on a variety of fronts. Pentecostal church workers, propelled by a personal relationship with God, have expanded operations among aboriginal communities in North and South America. The Summer Institute of Linguistics (affiliated with the Wycliffe Bible Translators) has been, and continues to be, a significant base for missionary activities among indigenous peoples. It is an extremely large and active Protestant organization, with a particular interest in indigenous populations. In 1974, the Colombian Asociacion National de Usuaerios Campesinos said of the Summer Institute:

> We study the way in which the evangelical missions and the Summer Institute of Linguistics works. They claim to be interested only in the Bible and come to study our languages. In this way they can penetrate easier into communities which are already forewarned against the traditional methods of the Church. But in many area we have removed the Summer Institute of Linguistics from our lands because we have realized that it is they, also, who

are destroying our culture, traditions and customs. As well as this they exploit their knowledge of ourselves, of our lands and the riches of our earth in order to help the "gringos" (Americans or foreigners in general) who follow them to open oil wells, to extract timber and gold, etc.[6]

In a number of instances, the establishment of a fundamentalist Protestant church has created sharp divisions within the communities, as doctrinal and social differences drive wedges between and within families. Pentecostal churches opened in northern Canada, for example, have caused bitter divisions. The Church of Jesus Christ of Latter Day Saints (Mormon) church has also been actively seeking converts; their work in the South Pacific has been particularly pronounced and, in terms of adherents, markedly successful. The Mormons have extended their expansive genealogical work to indigenous communities. Other missionary groups have been active among indigenous groups in the Amazon, seeking to bring these peoples into the Christian fold, often with extremely disruptive results. One commentator reacted with dismay to the response of a missionary to the outbreak of disease among the Ayoreos:

> There can be no doubt that it would have been possible for the missionary, who had a jeep, an aeroplane and funds at his disposal, to save the lives of these people. But [William] Pencille was convinced that "It's better they should die. Then I baptize them (on the point of death) and they go straight to heaven."[7]

Norman Lewis, speaking to a missionary working among the Achés, was puzzled by the missionary's assertion that the indigenous peoples were destined to be consigned to hell unless he could translate the Bible and introduce them to God. "There is no salvation," the cleric said, "for those who cannot be reached. The Book tells us that there are only two places in the hereafter; Heaven and Hell. Hell is where those who cannot be reached will spend eternity." Lewis reflected on the discussion: "It seemed to me unreasonable that divine retribution should be visited on the Achés because Mr. Stolz had been unable to learn their language, but the missionary shrugged his shoulders. Such things were beyond his jurisdiction, he suggested."[8] Overall, the impulse to spread the gospel to indigenous peoples has diminished in the traditional Catholic and Protestant denominations, but remains active among other Christian groups.

Indigenous groups, themselves, have worked very hard in recent years to sustain and, in places, revive, aboriginal spirituality. Much of this has been accomplished at the local level and within the spiritual traditions of individual groups. Elements of pan-Indian (in North America) and pan-indigenous spirituality have been emerging, part of the longstanding process of cultural adaptation among indigenous peoples. In North America, rituals such as pipe-ceremonies and sweat-lodges have become more commonplace, expanding beyond initial cultural boundaries often through the use of pan-aboriginal practices within prisons and other institutions as part of a process of rebuilding cultural confidence among indigenous peoples. Aboriginals looking for a broader structure for their spiritual expression have either worked with Christian and other faiths to find a place for their practices and beliefs or, more globally, have found a welcoming home within the Baha'i tradition. There is, as well, growing non-indigenous interest in aboriginal spirituality, particularly in Europe and North America, as non-aboriginal people seek a stronger connection with the natural world and endeavor to repair a generations-long antagonism between western and indigenous thought. At its best, this effort represents a sincere attempt to understand indigenous traditions; at the other extreme, it is little more than cultural or spiritual tourism.

The longstanding tradition of missionaries serving as advocates for indigenous peoples also continued after the 1970s, somewhat coloring the critical portrait that many activists and analysts have painted of church groups. In many areas, missionaries are among the most outspoken supporters of indigenous rights. With the Huaorani of Ecuador, the Summer Institute of Linguistics played a major role in securing the establishment of a "Protectorate," which assured the indigenous community of some measure of autonomy within a small portion of their traditional lands. Conservative Christian groups remain active throughout Latin and South America, although the focus is often on the adherents to other Christian denominations. The traditional or mainstream Protestant missionary groups have shifted much of their emphasis from proselytizing to "good works," such as economic development, health services, and education. The Baha'i, a culturally inclusive faith, has expanded its presence among many indigenous peoples and has hosted major congresses of indigenous spiritual leaders. There are major differences between the historic pattern of missionary intervention and the contemporary situation, including a great sensitivity (at times) to indigenous culture and spiritual understanding and a growing role for indigenous peoples within the missionary enterprise and the broader church.

The attack on aboriginal spirituality, it should be said, was not always associated with the expansion of Christianity. The Ainu of Japan, for example, were not aggressively proselytized by Christian missionaries, but found their spiritual beliefs mocked and marginalized by the national government. In the northern regions of the Union of Soviet Socialist Republics:

> In many cases cultural traditions of the indigenous peoples were violated. A campaign was started against shamanism and family rites, sacred objects were taken away by force and people became subject to moral pressure .... This is how one way of life, one world-view, and one system of values is crushed by other ones. When a people loses its feeling of being master in its own house, it also loses its feeling of worth and dignity, and this loss is irreparable.[9]

Spirituality has, for several centuries, been a centerpiece of the encounter experience. Often intrusive, occasionally inclusive, and typically intellectually challenging, the clash between western, Christian beliefs and indigenous spiritual and religious practice helped divide and separate tribal and colonial populations. Indigenous peoples were not slavish in their adherence to the new spiritual order, although some groups did initially see the Christian faith as being the embodiment of the newcomers' power. Instead, the spiritual encounter was one of mutual exploration, aboriginal adaptation, attempted (and often successful) non-indigenous-directed cultural change, and collective misunderstanding. Religion and spiritual encounter reflected the complexity of the indigenous–newcomer experience, and demonstrated as well the determination and ability of aboriginal peoples to adjust to new intellectual and social currents.

7

ADMINISTERED PEOPLES: INDIGENOUS NATIONS AND REGULATED SOCIETIES

Indigenous peoples proved to be obstacles to colonizing powers in many parts of the world. Periods of economic cooperation and military alliance often proved short-lived, particularly when the expansionist powers dispatched large numbers of settlers or economic migrants to the new lands. So long as the newcomers did not need indigenous territories or could not find a productive use for the land, they tended to leave the aboriginal peoples alone. This phase often lasted for a very long time, until after World War II in the case of aboriginal populations living in the most remote, isolated, and climatically challenging parts of the world. For those indigenous peoples living in temperate zones or in areas with large quantities of easily harvestable resources, the time of being ignored before being integrated into the new economies often proved very short-lived. Colonial powers were anxious to capitalize on any potential opportunities within their new possessions.

Beyond the phase of mutual discovery, a period which saw responses ranging from bitter conflict to wonderment, benevolence to greed, generous humanity to stunning brutality, lay an even more complex era of administration. Once the initial surprise of discovery and initial contact faded, and once military struggles and diplomatic alliances had been settled, military and civilian authorities faced a curious dilemma. The original belief that these populations could easily and quickly be incorporated into the orbit of the colonial power proved illusory. Governments from England in the seventeenth century to Russia two hundred years later, from nineteenth-century Japan to modern Indonesia wondered what could be done with the aboriginal peoples who inhabited their colonial territories. Authorities wondered if these peoples would survive the onslaught of modern influences; they also worried that the pre-industrial societies would stand in the way of productive and profitable exploitation of the newly claimed land and resources. Some colonizing powers, like Belgium in the Congo and Japan with Hokkaido, devoted little administrative or political effort to the rights and needs of indigenous peoples Others, most notably the British, committed a great deal of effort to conceptualizing and implementing policies for indigenous peoples. In the mid-1830s, for example, the British House of Commons established a Select Committee with specific responsibility for evaluating British colonial policy toward the aborigines throughout the Empire.

The colonial authorities faced a formidable challenge, from their perspective. Few of the tribal peoples showed much of an interest or aptitude for the new resource or agricultural economies – the Inuit and the Arctic whaling industry, Native Americans and the fur trade, and the Maori and the South Pacific whaling industry being among the best examples where there was substantial adaptation. The outsiders brought trade goods, and most indigenous groups sought opportunities to trade for the new items, particularly metal goods, firearms, and the other accoutrements of the industrial age. Most of the tribal peoples, however, maintained their commitment to the mobile, harvesting lifeways that had served them well for centuries, and showed little interest in much more than a tangential connection to the newcomers' activities. The recalcitrance and lack of interest in commercial agricultural pursuits among indigenous peoples in the Americas, for example, proved to be a crucial element in the development of the transatlantic slave trade, for the newcomers found the tribal populations unwilling to contemplate work in the plantation fields that sprang up along the east coast of South, Central, and North America.

Asserting Control

Underlying the expansion of colonial powers and, later, national governments into indigenous territories were clear assumptions on the authority of the western and dominant states to assert ownership over under-utilized aboriginal land. There was a handful of philosophers and commentators who defended the right of indigenous peoples to sovereignty over their territories. The arguments of people like early Spanish commentators Franciscus de Victoria and Bartolomé de Las Casas could not stop the more aggressive positions taken by imperial authorities. Faced with the demands of settlers and ranchers for lands and miners for access to minerals, governments assumed that they could move forward without securing full approval from the indigenous owners of the lands. In the United States and Australia, in particular, governments brushed aside aboriginal claims that they had sovereignty over their lands.

The newcomers had to assert, as a top priority, their dominion over the indigenous populations. In nineteenth- and early-twentieth-century writings, authors declared that the tribal peoples had been overwhelmed by the military power and technological prowess of the expansionist powers. Their subsequent defeat at the hands of the colonial armies, where armed intervention proved necessary, or their acquiescence in accepting incorporation, appeared preordained and obvious. Historical analysis has now overturned these assumptions. Newcomers were often ill-prepared for the new worlds, and suffered grievously in the heat of the jungles and the cold of the Arctic. They had trouble adapting to the climatic and biological conditions in their new territories. Early European settlements on the east coast of the Americas, throughout Africa, and in Asia often experienced strikingly high death rates. Indigenous peoples often came to their assistance by introducing local medical treatments, giving them food, and otherwise assisting the newcomers with their adaptation to strange lands. But the period of maladaptation passed, faster in some areas than others.

Governments extended their military, economic, and political dominance, often over populations seriously weakened by the importation of foreign diseases or the ravages of prolonged armed combat. With the primary struggles out of the way, and with their formal control of land and resources asserted to the satisfaction of other colonial powers, if not the local indigenous peoples, authorities now had to determine how best to manage the tribal societies. While there was no fixed pattern for the way this relationship evolved, governments were generally effective in stripping the autonomy and authority of the indigenous peoples. Incoming immigrations found that they could count on the power of the colonial authorities to back their plans to capitalize on the wealth and opportunities of the new territories.

Treaties with Indigenous Peoples

In the initial phases, governments often negotiated treaties or peace agreements with the indigenous peoples. Spanish authorities signed treaties of voluntary obedience with chiefs of Central America, like that accepted by the Cacique Queco in 1510. Queco averred

> that he wanted to be the vassal, servant, and *churiga* of Their Highnesses, and that all his *principales* and Indians did also. He said that he did not come the first time they sent for him because he was greatly afraid. He said he did not want the gold they had taken from him, but gave it willingly for Their Highnesses and the Christians, and that all he wanted from now on was to eat, drink, and plant maize, and that he and his people would make houses, plant fields, and build roads for the Christians, and that he wanted the wives they had taken from him returned.[1]

While the passage of time would reveal a striking imbalance in power between the small, widely scattered tribal peoples and the well-resourced and militarily powerful colonial governments, the distinctions were not immediately evident. Only a small number of newcomers – explorers, traders, and soldiers – typically formed the vanguard of the colonial power; and indigenous populations, in their pre-epidemic state, generally outnumbered the migrants by a substantial margin. Similarly, the later military dominance of the newcomers was, after the shock and surprise of the first encounter with firearms had passed, more assumed than real. Tiny outposts of soldiers and traders, often thousands of miles from homelands and typically existing for months without new provisions, were surprisingly vulnerable, a reality the immigrants and the tribal peoples both acknowledged.

As a consequence, and because of the uncertainty about the legal authority of colonial authorities in the new worlds, several colonizing powers signed treaties with the indigenous peoples. The treaties varied widely, and played a particularly prominent role within the British Empire and its colonial fragments. At one end was the hastily crafted pact between the Dutchman Pieter Minuit of New Netherlands and the Metoac of Manhattan in 1626, which saw the Dutch gain the island for a pittance. There was, as well, the famous Two Row Wampum treaty that the Iroquois signed with the British in the 1640s, and which drew the two sides together in what the Iroquois saw as an agreement to operate in parallel in the future and the British referred to as a "Covenant Chain," or intertwined relationship of mutual respect and reliance. At the other extreme was the more complex, bilingual resolution of Maori claims in New Zealand in 1840, which resulted in the Treaty of Waitangi, signed for the British by Captain William Hobson and by more than forty Maori chiefs, led by the influential Tamati Waka Nene. The treaty process, as will be discussed later, is far from complete, as aboriginal groups continue to negotiate land claims and rights with national governments, resulting, in a few countries, in agreements worth hundreds of millions of dollars, land and resource rights, and considerable powers of government and decision-making authority. The 3,000 members of the Tli-Cho Dene (Dogrib First Nation) of the Mackenzie Valley in Canada, for example, signed a modern-day treaty in August 2003, gaining over $150 million in financial compensation, annual payments of close to $3.5 million, broad powers of self-government, a share in future resource revenues from traditional lands, and effective management control over an area roughly the size of Switzerland (39,000 square kilometers). In Canada and other nations, governments have found it much easier to deal with indigenous groups in remote, non-agricultural regions than with communities in more densely settled parts of the country, where there are competing demands on the land and resources.

A compelling statement by the Cherokee orator Onitositsah outlined the complex indigenous response to the demand for treaties:

When we enter ... into treaties with our brothers, the whites, their whole cry is *more land!* Indeed, formerly it seemed to be a matter of formality with them to demand what they knew we durst not refuse. But on the principles of fairness, of which we have received assurances during the conducting of the present treaty, and in the name of free will and equality, I must reject your demand .... Let us examine the facts of your present irruption into our country, and we shall discover your pretensions on the ground. What did you do? You marched into our territories with a superior force ... your numbers far exceeded us, and we fled to the stronghold of our extensive woods, there to secure our women and children ... You killed a few scattered and defenceless individuals, spread fire and desolation wherever you pleased, and returned again to your own habitations ... The great God of Nature has placed us in different situations. It is true that he has endowed you with many superior advantages; but he has not created us to be your slaves. *We are a separate people!* He has given each their lands, under distinct considerations and circumstances; he has stocked yours with cows, ours with buffaloe; yours with hogs, ours with bear; yours with sheep, ours with deer. He has, indeed, given you an advantage in this: that your cattle are tame and domestic while ours are wild and demand not only a larger space for range, but art to hunt and kill them. They are, nevertheless, as much our property as other animals are yours.[2]

The motivations for the treaties varied widely. Some of the agreements were imposed on weak and already dislocated indigenous peoples;

others were negotiated from positions of mutual strength and shared interests, with aboriginal peoples securing considerable concessions from the colonial authorities. In many instances, the treaties either ended or prevented armed conflict and brought peace into regions inflamed by indigenous–newcomer conflict. In northeast North America, the overlapping claims and ambitions of the French, British, and Dutch resulted in the negotiation of treaties designed to commit specific aboriginal groups to colonial alliances, thus defining the military and political balance of power in the region. A significant number of the treaties were negotiated or imposed at the end of a period of armed conflict, and were accepted by the indigenous peoples as unavoidable. As the British victories over the French in Acadia (now the Maritime provinces of Canada) mounted in the mid-eighteenth century, the Mik'maq and Maliseet signed treaties with the British, at least in part to head off further destructive conflicts with the clearly superior British armed forces.

In the broad history of British treaty-making, the Royal Proclamation of 1763 holds particular pride of place, certainly in defining aboriginal rights across North America. The British, having finally vanquished the French in the Seven Years War, sought to cap the expense of running the costly North American colonies. The Colonial Office was anxious, as well, to keep settlers in the eastern regions of the vast continent, and hoped to avoid further and expensive conflict with the aboriginal peoples in the interior. The Royal Proclamation established a notional western boundary of settlement and required that treaty negotiations with indigenous peoples be concluded before settlement proceeded on their lands. The Royal Proclamation was not observed closely. Colonists, freed from fear of French retaliation, spread to the fertile lands of the west. Even more importantly, the American Revolution, which followed little more than a decade after the Proclamation, rendered the document of much lesser importance in the former British colonies that now formed the United States of America. In the remaining British North American colonies, authorities paid some attention to the document and endeavored to clear away potential indigenous claims before permitting settlement and development to occur.

More than anything, the Royal Proclamation provided dramatic and high-profile evidence that at least one major European nation accepted the idea that aboriginal people had a legitimate claim to their traditional territories. And while the sovereignty of the nation-state and colonial authority was assumed to trump indigenous claims, it was nonetheless made evident that British officials respected the rights of aboriginal peoples. The British followed their Proclamation, however, only in selected instances. They made no effort to negotiate for the land rights of the Aborigines of Australia, believing that these mobile and pre-industrial peoples had no substantial claims to the land. The militarily impressive Maori, on the other hand, forced Britain's hand. The British did not negotiate with the aboriginal peoples of the Canadian west before transferring land to the Canadian government in 1870; the task of signing a series of treaties, Number 1 to Number 11, negotiated between 1871 and 1921, fell to the newly formed Dominion of Canada. The British signed a small number of treaties on Vancouver Island, but refrained from extending the treaty process to the mainland colony of British Columbia. The later treaties in northern Canada, particularly Treaty 11, were signed in unclear conditions; subsequent investigations revealed that the Dene of the Mackenzie River valley had not been properly consulted about the agreement.

Few of the treaties ended up defining subsequent relations in a profound or systematic way. For a wide variety of reasons, only a handful of indigenous groups had the authority and presence to compel compliance by colonial officials or national governments. The newcomers, for their part, generally revealed both a shallow collective memory and considerable bad faith. Loron Sauguaarum, commenting on the unhappy experiences with the Casco Bay treaty (Maine), said:

> My reason for informing you, myself, is the diversity and contrariety of the interpretations I receive of the English writing in which the articles of peace are drawn up that we have just mutually agreed to. These writings appear to contain things that are not, so that the Englishman himself disavows them in my presence, when he reads and interprets them to me himself … . What I tell you now is the truth. If, then, any one should produce any writing that makes me speak otherwise, pay no attention to it, for I know not what I am made to say in another language, but I know well what I say in my own.[3]

The broad promises and seemingly solid assurances contained in the documents rarely stood up in the face of pressures to expand settlement onto indigenous land or to develop newly discovered resources within treaty territories. The famed struggle over the Black Hills is an excellent case in point. The land was assigned to the Sioux under the Treaty of Laramie of 1868. It was soon overrun by miners and developers anxious to exploit the rich goldfields in the region. The Sioux, led by the famed warrior Sitting Bull, resisted, with the conflict peaking at the Battle of the Little Big Horn in 1876. Although victorious, the Sioux were forced to flee north to Canada, where they stayed until the early 1880s. In 1877, the United States government confiscated treaty lands in the Black Hills. Similarly, the Treaty of Waitangi promised the bicultural development of the resource rich islands of New Zealand and seemed to assure the Maori of a critical role in the development of the area. British authorities and newly arrived settlers paid scant attention to the document; the bold promises in the Treaty (which read differently in English and Maori) proved to be illusory. Instead of purchasing Maori land, settlers and developers simply moved onto rich tracts. For almost three decades, from 1845 to the early 1870s, the colony of New Zealand found itself beset with a series of bitter conflicts, the first sparked by Hone Heke of the North Island. The struggles ended when British troops defeated the powerful Maori leader, Te Kooti, forcing him to flee into the King Country on the North Island. The end of the wars did not see a return to the principles of the Treaty of Waitangi. The clear commitments and assurances of the accord were virtually ignored – save by the Maori, who regularly reminded government of the treaty's existence – until it was resurrected in the 1970s.

Treaty-making with indigenous peoples began, in the first decades of contact, as accords between nations, designed largely to prevent conflict and to solidify alliances. Over the decades, treaties took on a new role, that of clearing the way for settlements and development and of formalizing the subordination of tribal peoples to the will of the colonial powers or nation-states. Once signed, and despite being assigned central importance by the indigenous leaders and communities, the treaties typically played little practical role. The British, for instance, signed a series of treaties with groups in Kenya, focusing on those occupying agricultural land, thus identifying areas available for British settlers and development. Indigenous groups that remained in the forests of Kenya and therefore on the margins were not offered treaties. National governments generally felt free to abrogate the terms of the treaty if a broader national or non-indigenous purpose had arisen. Indigenous leaders, as in the Canadian west, struggled in subsequent years to get the Canadian government even to acknowledge the existence of promises clearly made during the treaty negotiations. Even the terms of the accords were not always honored or implemented, raising serious doubts among the indigenous populations about the integrity of the governments and individuals who signed the documents. From a non-indigenous perspective, however, the treaties accomplished one clear and central goal: they provided tangible evidence that the question of land and resource ownership had been settled, opening indigenous lands for occupation and development. The treaties may have failed dramatically from an indigenous perspective, but to the degree that smoothing the path for settlement was a primary motivation for government involvement, the accords met the needs of the newcomer populations.

Government Relations Without Treaties

While treaties were, particularly within the British colonies, a primary point of contact between indigenous and newcomer authorities, numerous occupations of aboriginal territories occurred without formal accords. Instead, the demands of commerce and international diplomacy and the pressures of migrants resulted in governments proceeding without negotiated arrangements. Furthermore, most colonial authorities thought little of the political and international status of indigenous peoples; treaties were often more about demonstrating the legitimacy of their claim to new territories before the world community. Particularly in the early years of expansion, when the first Europeans ventured to the Americas, Africa, and Asia, colonial powers were obsessed with their relations with the complex hierarchical societies they encountered. They relaxed considerably when they were confronted by smaller, tribal populations, without the military power and internal organization necessary to prevent a long-term threat to their expansion plans. In such circumstances, treaties of convenience were negotiated or imposed on the aboriginal peoples. Even more commonly, indigenous lands were simply occupied by the newcomers, who used the assumed superiority of their civilization as a justification for imposing themselves on a new population.

The British faced a unique challenge in India, where a large and diverse population of indigenous peoples lived amidst, not a growing newcomer population, but rather a number of complex existing agricultural and industrial Indian societies. The indigenous peoples lived in the largely inaccessible mountain regions, and their territories attracted little attention until the establishment of British imperial administration. New roads, formal land registration systems, and an aggressive approach to economic development resulted in large-scale migrations into indigenous territories. The indigenous peoples fought back in a series of uprisings, including the Santhal Revolt of 1855, the Sardari conflict two years later, and a Bihar struggle in 1895. Fearing further unrest, the British authorities passed laws designed to protect the rights of indigenous peoples to their lands, protecting them from control by provincial legislatures. Dr. J. H. Hutton, of the Indian Civil Service, wrote of the government's effort:

> Far from being of immediate benefit to the primitive tribes, the establishment of British rule in Indian did most of them much more harm than good. It may be said that the early days of British administration did very great detriment to the economic position of the tribes through ignorance and neglect of their rights and customs ... . Many changes have been caused incidentally to the penetration of the tribal country, the opening up of communications, the protection of forests and the establishment of schools, to say nothing of the openings given in this way to Christian missionaries. Many of the results of these changes have caused acute discomfort to the tribes.[4]

Settler societies evolved slowly in many parts of the world. Initial occupations tended to involve traders and soldiers, seeking economic and political advantage. In many areas, for example, India, Indonesia, and China, the size, complexity and deeply entrenched nature of the local population, combined with the challenges of the climate and geography, made it virtually impossible for the colonizers to see a permanent place for large number of nationals in that corner of the new worlds. The early emphasis in regions as diverse as Southeast Asia, Africa, the Caribbean, Central and South America, and North America was on the assignment of economic rights to large chartered companies. The British East India Company, Hudson's Bay Company, Dutch East India Company, Russian America Company, and others, secured valuable commercial authority and were charged with maintaining or supporting the colonial presence in a specific zone. Where local conditions and commercial opportunities suited, the charter-holders or the colonial authorities granted large landholdings to friends and supporters. They believed that the importation of near-feudal economic structures would produce substantial profits and stabilize the colonial society. These arrangements, the colonizers discovered, worked best in areas with large domestic workforces; failing such a local resource, as in the Caribbean and the Americas, the landholders fell back on the slave trade as a source of abundant labor.

In treaty and non-treaty situations alike, settlers discovered that the imperatives of colonial expansion rested uneasily with the indigenous population. The rapid expansion of migrant populations threatened the stability of local ecosystems and drained available resources. The ideology of the new order, based on personal or government land ownership was imposed on indigenous territories. Indigenous peoples were quickly displaced by farms, ranches, plantations, town sites, commercial fishing developments, mines, or other intrusions of the new economic order. (The situation described here, presented in the context of sixteenth- to nineteenth-century developments, is very close to that currently underway in parts of the Amazon basin, Sarawak, and Irian Jaya.) The settlers themselves had been schooled in a view of the world which described indigenous peoples as savage, uncivilized brutes – ideas which provided ample justification for the confiscation of indigenous land and resources. They saw the indigenous peoples living around the colonial settlements in sharply negative terms. If they were not a military threat, they were viewed as diseased and impoverished. If they had economic potential, the colonizers believed that they could be incorporated into the new order as cheap labor. And if, as with most tribal peoples, they inhabited harsh, isolated, and non-agricultural lands, the simple fact of their continued existence was used as evidence of their primitive nature. In such circumstances, the intruders saw little risk and felt less guilt in occupying indigenous territories, even if it meant an accelerated assault on aboriginal societies and lands.

When settlers moved quickly onto indigenous territories, colonial authorities faced a very different task than that of negotiating treaties, maintaining military alliances, and otherwise working on a nation-to-nation basis with aboriginal peoples. Instead, intensive settlements required the marginalization and regulation of indigenous populations. They had to be removed from the path of settlement, so that agricultural and other developments could proceed. Indigenous communities had to be neutered militarily; it would not do to have powerful, armed aboriginal societies living amongst and around settler populations. Collectively, they had to be controled and managed so as to ensure that they did not interfere with the activities of the incoming colonial settlers.

Administering Indigenous Populations

In this phase of the occupation of indigenous territories, which might occur with or without a formal treaty in place, the newly dominant governments had to reconceptualize the aboriginal population. They could no longer be seen as allies or worthy adversaries. Instead, they had to be viewed as cultural works in process, uncivilized peoples capable, with effort, of being transformed into valuable, contributing members of the colonial order. The self-righteous Christians believed themselves free to impose their spiritual views, and the cultural baggage which accompanied them, on the original peoples. Indigenous communities, therefore, were deemed to be in urgent need of cultural, economic, and spiritual salvation. The incoming settler population had to be protected from the aboriginal people and vice versa. Government policy, therefore, was typically built around the contradictory motives of separating indigenous peoples from the settlers while simultaneously attempting to ensure that the aboriginal communities became increasingly like the new colonial societies.

These processes, best known in the context of Britain, the United States, and the settler Dominions, were not unique to European empires. Japan's advance toward the Ainu island of Ezochi showed many of the same elements. The area had been disrupted by armed conflict, epidemic diseases, and considerable trading activity before the mid-nineteenth century. Under the expansionist Meiji regime, the Japanese government redefined the Ainu homeland as Hokkaido, declared it to be vacant land and brushed aside any Ainu claims to ownership. The Ainu themselves were ethnically redefined as being Japanese and the promulgation of the Hokkaido Aborigine Protection Act (Kyu-Dojin) in 1899 launched an era of intense assimilationist activity. As in the British and European colonies, the government of Japan used national schools to undermine Ainu language and culture, encouraged intermarriage, and sought to integrate the Ainu into the agricultural economy. The Meiji era saw, on a very broad scale, the Japanese make a concerted attempt to join with the western industrial nations; perhaps it is not surprising, then, that the desire to perform like the West resulted in a virtual replication of British and colonial European indigenous policies. The image held of the Ainu by the national majority (called Shamo by the Ainu) was rife with condescension and paternalism, a sense of quaintness and interest in primitive peoples. And while the Ainu were not held in the same contempt as were the Burakumin or Koreans, they were seen as quaint remnants of a dead or dying culture.

Asserting political dominion over a population did not inevitably result in the disappearance of indigenous peoples as political communities. As governments sought to incorporate aboriginal societies, they often allowed the societal units to survive. In South and Central America, where government policies toward indigenous peoples were regressive and aggressive, the indigenous groups typically had no formal legal identity, but nonetheless remained together in small, poor, and marginal settlements. Across Siberia, the small peoples of the north remained largely separate from the Russian communities, using distance and isolation as a buffer against incursions, a circumstance which obtained in the Australian outback as well. The Russian management of the northern regions fit into three general periods. In the era of direct rule, 1580–1720, the Russians largely left the indigenous peoples alone, but collected taxes (*iasak*), often holding people hostage to secure payment. In the time of indirect rule, 1720–1822, local aboriginal leaders collected taxes for the government, and during the period of native rule, 1822–1900, sought to integrate native-run administrative units into the broader state apparatus.

Tribal peoples remained as distinct social entities, at least in part because of limited interaction with newcomers. The Maori, although they owned a significant percentage of New Zealand, were not granted large contiguous holdings for settlement purposes; most of the Maori, however, stayed away from larger, urban, and developed areas and remained in remote, Maori-dominated villages. In most nations, mixed-blood populations emerged in the early decades of conduct, as the newcomer males took indigenous women as short-term partners or wives. In most parts of the world, the children of these unions did not create a unique cultural group and did not survive as distinct political units. Only in Canada, where the Métis established a formidable military and political presence in the western districts, did people of mixed ancestry preserve and project a distinctive political community.

Managing indigenous affairs required, in most states, the creation of bureaucratic structures and legislative frameworks. In the United States, the Bureau of Indian Affairs was responsible for establishing and maintaining the numerous reservations set up across the country. For Canada, the Department of Indian Affairs, initially a branch of the Department of the Interior charged with settling the prairie west and later associated with northern development, managed aboriginal issues. A highly structured legal environment, centered on the Indian Act, codified indigenous rights and restrictions. Other countries offered similar systems, ranging from the National Indian Foundation in Brazil to the Bureau of Non-Christian Tribes in the Philippines, the Department of Orang Asli (Aboriginal Affairs) in Malaysia and the Hokkaido Aborigine Protection Act in Japan. In Australia, the federal government maintained responsibility for Aborigines in the Northern Territory and pursued an activist agenda in that jurisdiction. In the rest of the country, however, Aboriginal policy rested with state governments, most of which paid scant attention to indigenous issues. This changed only when a 1967 referendum granted Aborigines full citizenship rights and asserted a national role in responding to indigenous affairs. The creation of the Aboriginal and Torres Strait Islander Commission in 1990 was a major attempt to provide national direction on this important issue. (ATSIC was dismantled by the Howard government in 2004, with the politicians arguing that the Aborigine-led organization had failed to improve social and economic conditions.)

There is, in contrast, the policy of the Chinese government, which refuses to accept that any of its peoples are "indigenous" in the internationally understood context of that word; there are over fifty "national minorities" identified within the country, but no acceptance of indigenous rights or indigenous cultures. As Chinese official Long Xuequn said before the United Nations Commission on Human Rights in 1997,

> The indigenous issues are a product of special historical circumstances. By and large, they are the result of the colonialist policy carried out in modern history by European countries in other regions of the world, especially on the continents of America and Oceania. As in the case of other Asian countries, the Chinese people of all ethnic groups have lived on our own land for generations. We suffered from invasion and occupation of colonialists and foreign aggressors. Fortunately, after arduous struggles of all ethnic groups, we drove away those colonialists and aggressors. In China, there are no indigenous people and therefore no indigenous issues.[5]

Government land policy in certain countries reenforced the sense of indigenous identity within the nation-state. Catholic priests in California established an extensive mission system, beginning in the late eighteenth century which tied Native Americans to specific locations. Aboriginal groups were, in a manner similar to the treatment of the indigenous peoples of Brazil, tightly controled, denied the chance to move across their traditional lands, and more vulnerable to disease than before. Native American groups in the United States were assigned to small reservations, typically on unattractive and economically marginal lands. Problems persisted, however. In the case of the Shoshone of the Death Valley region, the establishment of a national park resulted in the removal of the people from their homelands, although they were subsequently allowed to return. Similarly, the Wanniyala-aetto of Sri Lanka had much of their traditional territory incorporated into the Maduru Oya National Park and subsequently lost control over their traditional livelihoods. In Canada, land allotments called reserves, usually small, uneconomic, and deliberately separated from other indigenous settlements and from newcomer populations, were allocated to both treaty and non-treaty Indians. The Miskito Indians of Nicaragua made a concerted effort to hold onto their autonomy. When foreign powers squabbled about control over the Miskito land in eastern Nicaragua in the mid-nineteenth century, the Amerindians insisted on local control. The British Administration in Nicaragua relented in 1860 and created a substantial reserve for exclusive Miskito use. Difficulties ensued, and the Miskito eventually accepted integration into Nicaragua, but with the assumption that they would continue to enjoy considerable freedom to manage their affairs. In northern Australia, at the urging of officials and anthropologists, a large tract of land in Arnhem Land, Northern Territory, was established in 1931 for exclusive Aborigine occupation.

There were other occasions when indigenous lands proved too attractive to leave in aboriginal hands. The famously painful Trail of Tears ("The Trail Where They Cried," is the Cherokee translation) march forced upon the Cherokee people by US President Andrew Jackson in the late 1830s was but one example of indigenous peoples being removed forcibly from their traditional territories and relocated to unattractive lands great distances away. As many as half the Cherokee may have died in the march. There were numerous such actions across North America. Canada routinely moved indigenous peoples around for administrative purposes, the most notable instance being the relocation of dozens of Inuit to the high Arctic Islands in the 1950s. In the Middle East, the government of Israel removed Bedouin tribes from their traditional territories and relocated them in a "closed security zone" in the early 1950s. These policies ensured that indigenous peoples remained within a group. They were often ordered to remain in a community or on a reserve/reservation unless they had official permission to leave. These policies helped retain the sense and reality of being a political community, however constrained and powerless, and also to reinforce among newcomer populations the separate and distinct identities of indigenous peoples.

Governments were not consistent in their motivations for placing indigenous peoples on tribal lands. The United States was comfortable with the idea that Native American governments would exercise considerable control – even calling it sovereignty – on tribal lands. New Metlakatla, established in Alaska in 1887 by a group of Tsimshian wishing to leave Canada, was granted a significant range of self-governing powers. The community enjoyed substantial freedom in subsequent decades. Similarly, the US granted the Navaho both a large block of land in their traditional territories and considerable authority to manage their affairs. British officials in what is now Bangladesh, in South Asia, passed the Chittagong Hill Tracts Regulation of 1900, seeking to protect the interests of the Chittagong Hill people, by endeavoring to keep outsiders at bay and to thereby ensure that local inhabitants retained access to traditional territories. Indigenous peoples in other settings, including Arnhem Land in Australia's Northern Territory and more contemporary efforts to set aside lands to protect indigenous peoples in the Amazon basin, lacked the self-government and autonomy elements; their primary objective was to keep development removed from the homelands of the tribal peoples.

Governments hoped that the indigenous people would soon abandon communitarian approaches to property ownership in favor of individual control of land. The Maori Land Courts and the Native Lands Act set up to protect Maori land rights and holdings, individualized what had been *iwi* (tribal) and family rights. The resulting administrative mess, in which individuals held rights to small percentages of specific parcels of the land, complicated Maori landholdings and sales dramatically, making it difficult for the Maori to get full value for their properties. In the United States, the 1887 Dawes Act reflected the American government's belief in the "civilizing power" of private property. The Act gave Native American tribes the authority to replace collective ownership with individual land rights. In operation, the Act resulted in the dispossession of thousands of Native Americans and hundreds of tribes; it proved an administrative disaster and as an effort at cultural transformation was a dismal failure. (Canada flirted with a similar plan in 1969, only to have aboriginal organizations mount an effective public campaign against the initiative.) In 1935, under reformer John Collier, the American government passed the Indian Reorganization Act, returning a substantial measure of sovereignty to the Native American nations and recognizing, belatedly, the shortcomings of the more aggressively assimilationist policies. It was more common, in fact, for national and colonial legislation to make it illegal for an indigenous person to own land. Under the Canadian Indian Act, a status Indian (a person deemed eligible under the Indian Act) had to surrender their claims to being aboriginal in order to be permitted to own real estate. Few indigenous peoples voluntarily took this option, which amounted to renouncing one's ethnicity; others were enfranchised automatically as a result of having enroled in a university, entered a profession, started a business, or otherwise demonstrated the capacity for integration.

Managing the activities of indigenous peoples was among the highest priority after ensuring that the government and the settlers had effective control of the land. Colonial administrations used a variety of approaches, ranging from the United States pattern of opening army posts in the middle of Native American territory to the Canadian tradition of using the North West Mounted Police (later and best known as the Royal Canadian Mounted Police) to assert sovereignty over widely dispersed indigenous populations. The Spanish and Portuguese worked largely through military units, generally small in number but armed with sufficient firepower to impose their will throughout the claimed territories. Pre-Soviet Russian authorities opened combined trading and military forts in locations as widely dispersed as Yakutia, Alaska, and California, hoping to assert domination over the indigenous peoples. In the Soviet era, Russia did not immediately impose order on the "small peoples" of the North, leaving them with considerable autonomy from the state and the freedom to remain on the land. Over time, however, this policy shifted. The Soviet state began to collectivize the reindeer herds in isolated corners of Siberia, including among the Chukchi, with the unanticipated result that reindeer harvests declined precipitously. The Soviets, though intrusive, were also more respectful than most societies to the traditional activities of indigenous peoples. They created mobile indigenous *soviets*, which were charged with protecting indigenous interests and representing aboriginal needs and concerns to higher-level authorities. The pattern paralleled that used by the Japanese when they expanded initially onto Ainu territory on the island of Hokkaido in the second half of the nineteenth century. In Australia, governments used roaming police units, typically reinforced by Aborigine guides, to impose order on mobile Aborigines. Tribal peoples in remote regions, small in number and moving across vast expanses, proved difficult to control and influence, if only because their movements meant that they had relatively little direct contact with the newcomers.

The presence of military, paramilitary, or police units had considerable impact on indigenous populations. Aboriginal communities found themselves encouraged, and eventually compelled, to adhere to a foreign code of laws and regulations. The forces protected land rights as spelled out in the legal structures of the colonial authorities; much more rarely did they seek to ensure adherence to the terms and conditions of treaties between foreign powers and indigenous peoples. Governments used their authority in a wide variety of ways: to compel residence on selected reserves or community sites, protect newcomers who ventured onto aboriginal lands, and force adherence to the legal system (civil and criminal codes) of the colony. The new legal structures often bore little resemblance to aboriginal constraints on personal and collective behavior. In some settings – the Canadian North being perhaps the best example – authorities were slow to impose the full rigor of the law and sought instead to bring the indigenous peoples gradually under the national legal umbrella. In other quarters – the United States and Australia, for instance – police and military authorities were not as forgiving and understanding. Indigenous peoples were supposed to understand, accept, and internalize the newcomer standards of legal conduct and comport themselves accordingly.

Most governments hoped that indigenous peoples would adapt to the new economic order, if only to reduce demands on the state for food and supplies to support displaced and hungry peoples. On many occasions, the expansion of settlement and development resulted in indigenous peoples being undermined in their traditional pursuits, such as harvesting and trading, but denied ready access to the new economy. A few groups, particularly the Maori in New Zealand who took to farming, whaling, and mining with alacrity, the whale-hunting and fur-trading Inuit in the Arctic and the Sami in Scandinavia who operated commercial reindeer-herding operations, made significant advances toward the more commercial and industrial order. Many others had few skills and less inclination to adapt to the unattractive and unreliable work opportunities provided by the newcomers. Only a tiny number – paragons of Christian and capitalist virtue held up by church, state, and business as examples of what was possible – made a personal transition from the indigenous economies. Many others who attempted the shift found their way blocked by discriminatory attitudes and restrictive hiring practices. Most indigenous peoples quickly found that, government policies aside, there was little place for them in the newcomer economy.

Discriminatory barriers did not stop governments from trying to encourage change. Indigenous economic activity was closely watched and often regulated, occasionally with a view to punishing or threatening the aboriginal peoples. Peasant farmers in Central America rarely enjoyed unfettered access to markets (a problem which persists to the present day), and often found themselves with spoiled crops they could not move to trading centers. First Nations in Canada had to secure government approval to sell their products, particularly beef and crops; more than a few times, the Indian agents withheld the necessary permission in order to ensure that local non-aboriginal farmers and ranchers did not face undue competition. In many locations – Brazil, Argentina, the Philippines, and temperate parts of Africa – indigenous peoples were pushed off arable land and forced onto unattractive territory where they struggled to maintain a living. Without the meager protections of the British legal and moral code, indigenous peoples in these areas had few protections against the development and commercial priorities of the colonial or national governments.

Education and the Assimilation of Indigenous Peoples

Education was the cornerstone of government efforts to transform indigenous peoples and communities. In almost all nations, authorities held out little hope for the adults. Raised on the land and tied to traditional lifestyles, these people were, in the minds of most authorities, largely lost to the emerging modern world. Children, on the other hand, had enormous potential. Government-run schools, often made more cost-efficient and more culturally intrusive through cooperation with missionaries, were established in countless indigenous communities. The schools included time-limited summer and day schools, operated only when missionaries or government teachers were available. Such schools had minimal impact, save for allowing the authorities to believe that they were doing something to civilize the aboriginal peoples. At the other extreme, several countries established residential schools, removing the children from the strong influences of family and community and placing them in intensive cultural and educational settings where they could be introduced to the knowledge and teachings of the colonial state.

Canadian and American governments took the lead in the establishment of residential schools. They operated from the mid-nineteenth century through to the 1960s, and served as the highly celebrated centerpiece of government efforts at acculturation. The children and graduates were routinely identified as the "promise" and the future of the aboriginal people. In remote regions, particularly in the Canadian North, children were removed from their homes, typically for the entire academic year and on occasion from the time of admission until graduation. These children grew up in awkward spaces. Separated from family and community, they were taught to abhor the values, customs, and lifeways of their parents and grandparents. The children were ostensibly trained in the ways of the new material and industrial order. Many of the schools were created as industrial training centers and the students often participated in agricultural and other activities designed to support the institutions. Upon graduation, however, they found themselves trapped between a world they did not fully understand – their home communities – and a society that did not accept them. Few aboriginal graduates found acceptance in the non-indigenous economy, even when they were properly trained, and most foundered between the indigenous and the non-aboriginal worlds.

Indigenous students complained about the experience of the industrial and boarding schools. They did not enjoy the military-type regimen and the harsh discipline masquerading as Christian love. Many criticized the food, the cramped dormitories, and the often long hours of work. They did not, as students, understand the full implications of being punished for speaking their language or being denied access to cultural and ceremonial activities. They would come to appreciate the cost of these intrusions in later life. The residential schools became, tragically, the site for physical and sexual abuse; many indigenous residents complained bitterly about their treatment at the hands of the teachers. Although, on balance, the residential schools caused enormous harm throughout the indigenous world, the experience was not entirely one-sided. Some students experienced considerable compassion and support from their instructors and monitors. The students were, as well, often radicalized by the experience, drawn together from various cultural groups, clearly treated differently simply because of their race, and yet armed with the skills and abilities necessary to take on the dominant society on their own terms. It is hardly surprising, therefore, than many prominent aboriginal leaders emerged, angry and determined, out of the residential schools.

Education of indigenous children figured prominently in many countries. In Siberia, the famed "Red Tents" followed the tribal peoples of the North on their annual journeys across the land. The Soviet-trained instructors sought to inculcate enthusiasm for the new order among indigenous communities, largely by focusing on the education of the youth. In Australia, the government paid relatively little attention to the Aboriginal children, but focused instead on half-caste children (those of mixed parentage). These children were often removed forcibly from their Aborigine mothers and placed in boarding schools or foster homes so that the non-indigenous part of their ancestry could be exploited to ensure a more prosperous future. In many countries and colonies, Catholic and Protestant missionaries worked consistently through the classroom to bring aboriginal children closer to the norms of the western world, attacking indigenous "superstition" while they taught reading, writing, and arithmetic.

Attacking Indigenous Culture and Social Activities

The era of administration witnessed, in many nations, a systematic assault on indigenous cultural activities. Many authorities believed that the continuation of age-old rituals – dances, singing, ceremonies, and other cultural endeavors – slowed the integration of aboriginal peoples into the emerging mainstream society. They saw in these activities convincing evidence of the barbarism and backwardness of the indigenous peoples and therefore felt compelled to eradicate them. Officials believed that many of the practices were, in fact, antithetical to the values and expectations of the emerging economic and social order. Some practices – cannibalism and human sacrifice – were generally agreed to be abhorrent and governments insisted that they be stopped. On others, like polygamy, they were more flexible, although the preferences of the external administrators were generally very clear. In general, if the traditional practices were deemed to be quaint and of marginal authority, they were tolerated. Activities which offended the newcomers' sensitivities and value systems, in contrast, were outlawed, suppressed, and otherwise undermined.

As a consequence, systematic attempts were made to eliminate the most provocative or disturbing activities. Missionaries and government officials along the Canadian west coast sought to eliminate the potlatch, the ceremonial and economic redistribution of personal effects. Traders had encouraged the gifting exercise, which other non-aboriginal peoples argued had gotten out of hand. Stringent laws forbidding the potlatch were introduced. Enforcement was quite rigorous, and several aboriginal people ended up in jail. Many communities found alternate strategies for continuing the potlatch, including holding the feasts in private and disguising the gift exchange as a Christmas event, an irony which the missionaries and government officials appear to have missed. The Sun Dance of the North American plains, an elaborate ritual associated with the empowerment of indigenous peoples, attracted hostile attention in both Canada and the United States, with systematic efforts made to wipe out the practice.

Governments were not altogether sure how to stop unwanted social, cultural, and spiritual activities. Australian officials disliked the many ritual activities of the Aborigines, ranging from initiation ceremonies for young men and women to large ceremonial gatherings, and attempted to break-up the social or cultural patterns. Canadian and American authorities jailed some indigenous peoples for participating in spiritual ceremonies, believing that their activities had to be stamped out. Colonial authorities throughout Asia, Africa, and South America took numerous steps – from attempting to eliminate public nudity to arresting spiritual leaders – to suppress elements of traditional cultures. They found, time and again, that it was easier to pass laws, regulations, or administrative rules than it was to enforce them, particularly when the indigenous peoples remained on the land. Mobile populations typically spent very little time in immediate proximity to the newcomers; when they were out of sight, they were effectively out of control.

Indigenous peoples found creative ways of keeping their most valued traditions alive. Throughout the indigenous world, outsiders made particular efforts to undermine spiritual beliefs, seeing them both as evidence of aboriginal lack of civilization and as barriers to the peoples' integration into the new social order. In parts of Central America, where the Catholic Church made vigorous and even violent efforts to suppress indigenous spirituality, the traditional beliefs resurfaced as soon as the authority of the church declined. Russian authorities had little time for the shamanistic traditions of the small peoples of the North and sought to remove them as authority figures within indigenous societies. Many indigenous communities which had been officially Christian for several generations nonetheless provided ample evidence that traditional spirituality continued. West Coast potlatch traditions survived concerted efforts to destroy them, as did a wide variety of initiation rituals, spiritual beliefs, and practices, and other central elements of the indigenous world-view. On other matters, polygamy being perhaps the best example, many indigenous groups quickly heeded the directions of church and state that they adopt monogamous relationships. That they did so, of course, revealed as much about the changing nature of the economy and harvesting activity as it did about changing social mores.

There was, curiously, considerable enthusiasm for selective public displays of indigenous culture. Even as the United States continued the occupation of aboriginal land and fought devastating wars with selected Native American groups, the country was warming to Wild West shows, complete with fearsome warriors. Sitting Bull, having returned to the US from exile in Canada, was put on public display, along with other noted Native American chiefs. The Maori *haka*, an aggressive chant associated with the commencement of battle, became a staple element in New Zealand ceremonial life. It became, in fact, the signature of the country's rugby team. In Canada, aboriginal peoples were invited to set up encampments, wear traditional dress and otherwise serve as an attraction at the agricultural fairs which figure prominently in western Canadian life. Australia proved much slower than other countries in turning to Aboriginal culture as a centerpiece of its ceremonial life, but by the 1980s didgeridoos (a musical instrument) and Aboriginal dances began to figure prominently in national affairs. The celebration of indigenous cultures had, by the last decades of the twentieth century, become commonplace in many nations, even if efforts to sustain and support aboriginal societies languished.

Government Aspirations for Indigenous Peoples

One further element of colonial aboriginal policies needs to be highlighted. Contemporary critics, indigenous and non-indigenous alike, have correctly identified the culturally destructive and paternalistic elements in national and colonial indigenous initiatives. Less attention has been given to the idealistic elements which ran through many of government policies directed at aboriginal peoples. Through the nineteenth and much of the twentieth century, national governments and colonial administrations had a strikingly critical perspective of the newcomer societies. They were well aware of the cultural and, some officials believed, genetic limitations of the lower orders within their midst. Church leaders, moralists, and government officials decried promiscuous behavior, abhorred the propensity to alcohol, worried about the intellectual quality of many members of the newcomer society, and routinely criticized the excesses of the male-dominated communities which characterized much of the early history of the colonial world.

Faced with the reality of what they viewed as abhorrent behavior by their own people, colonial officials did not actually hope that aboriginal people would become just like the newcomer mainstream. In fact, many government policies sought to restrict contact between indigenous and newcomer communities. First Nations people on reserves in the Canadian West operated under pass laws which allowed Indian agents to control personal movements. The Australian government declared it illegal for a non-Aboriginal to have sex with an Aboriginal. And in many of the British settler Dominions, it was illegal for indigenous people to possess, consume, or sell liquor. In other words, governments hoped that aboriginal communities would have little contact with the lower orders in newcomer societies and would abstain from alcohol. They also aspired to the creation of new indigenous societies which had been stripped of their primitive and pagan elements of the old ways and which avoided the excesses and shortcomings that were so evident in the colonial world. In yet another of the interesting twists which run through indigenous policies, government officials hoped to convert indigenous peoples into "proper" colonials while at the same time attempting to ensure that they did not pick up the least attractive characteristics of the soldiers, traders, miners, sailors, and others who represented the home country in the New World.

This effort failed, often miserably. Some of the initiatives designed to keep aboriginals and newcomers apart had the opposite effect. Prohibiting indigenous peoples from buying alcohol through normal channels, as the Canadian authorities attempted to do, forced aboriginal peoples wishing to purchase a drink to get their supplies from boot-leggers and petty criminals, the very individuals the government was trying to keep away from indigenous communities. Also, criminalizing a large number of aboriginal activities, from the Sun Dance in the United States, to the potlatch in Canada and initiation rituals in Australia only highlighted the unfairness and cultural specificity of national aboriginal legislation. Throwing indigenous people in jail for commonplace acts – such as possessing beer in a public place – served to discredit the legal system in the eyes of the aboriginal communities. Police and the courts were seen for what they clearly were: instruments of the colonial, non-indigenous society, with a strong bias against the equality and cultural rights of the aboriginal peoples.

It was equally clear that governments typically viewed indigenous peoples in harshly negative and pejorative terms, and saw little worth salvaging in their cultures and traditions. The colonial impulse was suf-fused with the "white man's burden," which involved bringing civiliza-tion to the heathen and pagan peoples of jungle, tundra, mountain, and desert. When European powers gathered at Berlin in 1884–85 to divide Africa into colonial bits, they pledged themselves to "elevating" the tribes to a "higher" plane of culture and civilization. Both the League of Nations, founded in 1922, and the United Nations, established in 1945, committed themselves to having the "advanced" countries assist other peoples with their economic, social, and political progress.

The intrusions of government into the lives of aboriginal people often went to considerable lengths. Many officials worried that children were not being looked after properly within aboriginal communities and were quick to remove them to either residential schools or, later, to put them up for adoption by non-indigenous families. Australia was among the most interventionist in this regard. The government banned interracial sexual and marital relations, legislative initiatives which had relatively little practical effect. Australian authorities, particularly in the Northern Territory where the national government had full constitutional authority, paid particular attention to half-caste or mixed-ancestry children. Believing that the children were, automatically, better off within non-Aborigine society, they removed thousands from their mothers and placed them in orphanages and foster homes. The process continued for generations, causing great pain and hardship within Aborigine families. Only in the 1980s and 1990s did the practice become the focus for public debate in the country, leading eventually to a national inquiry and the release of a major report, *Bringing Them Home*, on this now-controversial government policy.

Governments hoped, if for no other reason than fiscal prudence, that indigenous communities would take care of themselves economically. Authorities worried, from very early days, that the indigenous peoples would become an economic charge on the state. While there was some willingness to pay costs temporarily, the hope and expectation was that the aboriginal peoples would adapt to the new economy. Land was set aside for some communities, in the hope that they would take up agriculture. Across the Canadian and American Wests, concerted efforts were made to introduce indigenous peoples to commercial farming, albeit typically with insufficient financial backing or training, and with other intrusions that upset indigenous adaptations. Those indigenous peoples living in remote regions, where traditional economies remained substantially unchanged, were generally left to fend for themselves. Around major cities and in developed areas, governments provided basic welfare support, typically through the provision of food and basic necessities. In very few areas, however, did the non-aboriginal people and authorities make accommodations necessary to draw indigenous peoples into the regional economy. They were viewed, in most countries, as comparable to the peons, peasants, slaves or ex-slaves, and other peoples assigned to the lowest rungs of the economic ladder.

But the current analyses of government approaches toward indigenous peoples are often one-sided and, often, simplistic in their emphasis on colonialism and the politics of domination. Bad things happened along the line of encounter, but the relationships that unfolded were more complex and interactive than can be summarized by singular concepts of European imperialism. In a thoughtful and insightful study of British actions in the South Pacific, Jane Samson drew attention to the importance of adding the humanitarian impulse into the reading of British intentions and actions in the region. When the reality that the British – from a particularly cultural, economic, and political perspective – were earnestly seeking to do the right thing is added into the equation, a more nuanced and balanced understanding emerges. As Samson wrote:

> British benevolence in the Pacific Islands was based on the assumption that islanders had the same potential for "civilization" as any other human beings. The duties of Britain's naval representatives were, therefore, much more than "policing." Officers believed they had moral obligations, as members of a Christian and civilized society, to help primitive peoples improve themselves. Island leaders, especially in Polynesia and Fiji, could be useful catalysts for "reforming" island societies, something naval captains were determined to do without violence or coercion. In other areas, especially Melanesia, they believed the activities of British traders to be a greater threat than island "savagery."[6]

If pre-1960 interpretations of the actions of colonial administrators were too uncritical, more recent analysis has tended to be overly cynical. Recognizing that officials often intended to improve the lot of indigenous peoples, and that a humanitarian element often ran through government programming, helps provide a more balanced assessment of the nature of government–indigenous interaction.

Because government motivations were typically mixed, few official initiatives achieved the publicly declared objectives. With few exceptions in most countries, most indigenous peoples remained outside the mainstream economy, stood apart from the newcomer societies, and failed to measure up to the confused expectations of official policy-makers. Aboriginal peoples did not quickly absorb the languages, religions, and values of the new dominant societies. In most instances, traditional customs remained active, even if forced underground by government prohibitions and punishments. Aboriginals found few places in the mainstream economies – and then typically on a casual and low-wage basis, a situation which held in Siberia as much as it did in Arizona or New Zealand's North Island. Deeply entrenched racial discrimination and generations-old hostilities proved too broad a gulf for well-meaning but generally ineffectual government policies to bridge. Generally, government initiatives succeeded primarily in keeping indigenous peoples apart from non-aboriginal populations, at least until the post-World War II era. At that time, aboriginals by the tens of thousands began to leave their isolated, culturally separate communities to take up residence in and around cities, sparking a very different sent of crises and challenges for indigenous peoples.

Aboriginal societies responded differentially to the impositions of the age of administration, varying in large measure according to the speed, intensity, and imperatives behind the government measures. Indigenous peoples responded more favorably than is generally acknowledged to many initiatives, including agricultural development and education. Yet mobile aboriginal populations realized that the new order had undermined their way of life. Buffalo hunting ceased to be an option on the Great Plains of North America when the massive herds that sustained life for centuries were destroyed in the last third of the nineteenth century. Ranching and herding cut into traditional indigenous land use in broad areas of Argentina, Brazil, Australia, and many African colonies. Mining and forestry operations undercut the viability of harvesting activities in many parts of the world, and the expansion of commercial agriculture removed millions of acres of land from exclusive indigenous use. Faced with a cruel reality, indigenous leaders spoke to their communities about the need to adapt, to sign treaties, to learn the skills of the new order, to adapt to new economic systems. Where the opportunity existed, some aboriginal peoples withdrew from non-indigenous settlements and sought to survive in marginal lands away from the newcomers.

Evasion occurred in many forms. Cultural practices did not die out in the face of government regulation. Most often, they simply went underground. In some parts of Mexico, indigenous practices suppressed by the Catholic Church reemerged several centuries later when the church withdrew its priests from the region. Some spiritual and cultural activities were merged with Christian practices in order to make them more palatable to authorities. Indigenous peoples became adept, as well, at having ceremonial lives separate from their encounters with government officials and the dominant society. Indigenous languages, often singled out for attack by the authorities, survived under oppressive conditions, although there was a noticeable decline in use and fluency with each successive generation. Indigenous peoples clearly wanted their culture to live on, even if adaptations to the new order were required.

The processes of domination, incorporation, and administration, it needs to be emphasized, are still being played out. Until World War II (see Chapter 8), indigenous peoples in many remote districts retained considerable freedom and substantially unchallenged access to resources. Yanomami in the Amazon, Inuit in the High Arctic, Sami reindeer herders, !Kung Bushmen in Botswana, tribal peoples in Papua New Guinea, Irian Jaya, Sarawak, northern Thailand, and dozens of other hard-to-reach and economically marginal zones, lived with relatively little intervention by outsiders. Even across the Russian North, intrusion from outsiders remained relatively limited before World War II and the creation of national districts provided the Siberian indigenous peoples with considerable protection from development. The dynamics of ideological conflict, population growth, independence movements in the Third World, the Cold War, an increasingly globalized economy, adventure tourism, and late-twentieth-century altruism and paternalism brought developers, government officials, and the multiple traumas of incorporation to the remaining tribal peoples. Beginning in the 1940s and 1950s and continuing into the twenty-first century, these remote populations began to experience processes and dislocations strikingly similar to the intrusions associated with the earlier expansionary efforts of colonial powers. Put simply, the process of becoming "administered peoples" occurred at different times in different places, and continues through to the present.

Colonial powers and the fragment states which followed clearly thought little of the long-term viability of indigenous cultures and economies. For generations, it has been stated that the governments observed the striking demographic trends – falling populations, declining birth rates, and frequent epidemic and endemic illnesses – and concluded that the original peoples would soon die out. To the extent that this was true, government policy was like palliative care, designed to ease the pain of dying and to provide a measure of comfort during difficult years. After the Japanese imposed their authority on the Ainu in the late nineteenth century, they passed the Hokkaido Aborigine Protection Act (1899) and endeavored to encourage the integration of the Ainu into mainstream society. Officials were generally pessimistic about the prospects for change. They admitted, with chagrin, that the aboriginal problem would be around for many decades, if not centuries, and that subsequent governments would face comparable dilemmas in the future. They managed, in the process, to problematize an entire group of people, for the conception of tribal peoples varied little around the world. In country after country, colony after colony, it was assumed that the cultures of the indigenous peoples were unsustainable, primitive, and doomed to be displaced by the new industrial and material order.

There was, therefore, an incomparable irony in the fact that these same countries found so much to celebrate and to promote in the uniqueness of the indigenous cultures. Countries around the world idealized the very societies they sought to undermine and replace. Colonial exhibits at major expositions, like the famous 1851 Great Exhibition in London, celebrated the diversity of indigenous cultures. Colonies and, in later years, fragment states that had little otherwise to distinguish themselves from other nations displayed aboriginal artifacts. Their presentations, reflected in national, colonial, and regional museums, mirrored the contradictions in government policy toward indigenous peoples. While there was much gawking at ceremonial headdresses, elaborate carvings, and dances or other cultural activities, there were often also presentations of indigenous educational accomplishments. The juxtaposition of traditional and transitional cultures symbolized the difficulties colonial and national governments had in determining just where indigenous peoples stood within the newcomer societies. It was a dilemma few people resolved.

Once indigenous peoples had been dealt with as a military threat, and once strategic alliances were no longer essential to ensure peaceful settlement, governments faced a difficult challenge. It was hard to figure out where aboriginal communities stood in the evolving colonial and national order. Optimists believed that they could be incorporated into the mainstream through educational efforts and the transformation of cultures. The Japanese, for example, saw education as the cornerstone of their efforts to assimilate the Ainu, an effort that almost succeeded in undercutting the viability of their language. Pessimists believed that the indigenous peoples were doomed to die a slow and painful death. Both could agree that extended contact with the newly dominant, non-indigenous society was not in the interests of either group. Indigenous peoples became, as a consequence, administered and controlled by external agencies whose policies bore little evidence of being derived from consultation with the aboriginal communities. Governments knew best; there was virtually no questioning of this basic assumption. But governments were also wary of spending too much time and money on what some believed to be a hopeless cause. The resulting policies proved to be intrusive and, in many instances, culturally destructive.

Indigenous peoples resisted, where they could, but often to only limited effect. Scholars have demonstrated that indigenous groups exercised agency – they knew what they wanted, they found as many ways as possible to make their wishes known, and they developed sophisticated means of cultural persistence in the face of demands for change. But there were real, practical limits on what was possible. In the eyes of the authorities and their supporters in the churches, and in the non-indigenous societies at large, aboriginal cultures were doomed. Moving them into the mainstream was, therefore, an act of charity and compassion, not an exercise in aggression. For the indigenous peoples, ravaged by epidemic and endemic diseases, and suffering from dislocation from traditional activities and lands, falling into the grip of administrators brought wide-ranging and little-understood transformations. Many aboriginal parents supported schooling; they wanted their children to have the chance to participate in the new economic and social order and could not have anticipated the culturally and personally destructive experiences that many young people endured. The era of administration created, as well, the foundations for post-World War II cultures of dependency, as the national and regional systems brought indigenous peoples under the daily control of non-aboriginal authorities.

It is vital, finally, to understand the place and status of indigenous peoples in the context of evolving notions of nation and nationalism. Through the latter half of the nineteenth century, the nation-state emerged as a major political and constitutional entity. Before that time, even within the major imperial powers, most people had only vague allegiances to national governments. The grand nations of Britain, France, Germany, Spain, Russia, Japan, Italy, and Belgium existed more as cartographical descriptions than as shared or well-understood communities. This began to change in the nineteenth century, with German and Italian unification, the reconstruction of the United States after the Civil War, and efforts to create, through school systems and national government administration, a sense of belonging and citizenship. It is worth noting, in this context, that as late as World War I, the French army had difficulty managing its troops because they did not share a commonly understood language. This era, too, saw the emergence of new states – Canada, Australia, New Zealand, South Africa, Brazil, Argentina, Chile, and others – and the early growth of nationalistic and anti-colonial sentiments in major colonies like Indonesia, India, and China.

The development of nationalist sentiments and the coincidental emergence of new states in the former colonies created formidable challenges for indigenous peoples. Once a threat to development and settlement, they remained both that and a barrier to national integration. Their differentness and their unwillingness to conform automatically to the values, structures, and assumptions of the nation-state were seen by governments and colonial powers alike as a challenge to the integrity of the national unit. With a state-wide emphasis on conformity, through national schools, a common legal system, and shared political structures, the indigenous peoples were once again viewed as the "Other." The reaction of the nation-states was uniform: indigenous peoples were expected to change, to conform to national social codes and conventions, to participate in the national economy, and eventually, through processes of civilization, to become full citizens in the new entity.

Governments devoted considerable effort and money to the challenge of assimilating the indigenous peoples to the national norms, but enjoyed many fewer successes than they had anticipated. Through the coercive power of the state, governments forced most indigenous peoples to leave their traditional lands and to move onto managed reserves, reservations, or other indigenous settlements. In many regions, they undermined indigenous languages and challenged traditions and customs. The indigenous peoples were generally left marginalized and isolated socially, economically, and politically. But, to the dismay of numerous colonial powers and national governments, they did not surrender their indigenity. Their commitment to culture, community, and land remained strong, often in the face of grotesque indignities and physical force. Values, world-views, and spiritual understandings survived, though weakened and often seriously damaged by the intrusions of state education and missionary activities. The indigenous peoples around the world became, in a variety of different ways, administered communities, under the influence of governments and following the directives of the nation-state. They did not, as many had predicted, surrender their identity as indigenous peoples to the uncertain benefits of the nations and settler societies.

For political scientist Greg Poelzer, the evolution of the modern state was the single most important development in the transformation of indigenous–newcomer relations around the world. As he observed in his comparative study of aboriginal self-government in Canada and Russia:

Modern state-building forever changed aboriginal–state relations and, as a consequence, the course of aboriginal political development. The change in aboriginal-state relations reveals as much about the nature of modern states as it does about aboriginal political life. Colonial and absolutist regimes tolerated the coexistence of "other" political communities within the boundaries of the territories over which these political orders claimed domination. Under colonial British North America and absolutist Tsarist Russia, aboriginal peoples could exist on the political, cultural, and geographical frontiers of the state. From the perspective of the peoples of European descent, aboriginal peoples were always the "others." However, the Canadian and Soviet states were to transform frontiers, eliminating differences. The "others" were no longer to exist. This logic brought aboriginal peoples into inescapable conflict with the modern state. As a result, modern states and aboriginal people became political *enemies* in Schmitt's sense of term: the political enemy is "the other, the stranger; and it is sufficient for his nature that he is, in a specially intense way, existentially something different and alien, so that in the extreme case conflicts with him are possible." Modern state-building changed the politics of aboriginal-state relations from one of coexistence to one of "friend and enemy."[7]

For Poelzer, the state initially emerged for the purposes of waging war. The modern nation-state, in contrast, had primarily internal priorities and commitments, including: the assertion of sovereignty, the maintenance of borders, the establishment of a bureaucracy, universal citizenship, the creation of a sense of nationalism, centralization of political and administrative proceses, internal pacification of all "others," and the development of a universalizing ideology.

The transformation of the indigenous peoples from allies and military foes of the emerging states to the internal wards or residents within the rapidly developing nation-states of the industrial world had profound implications for indigenous populations. The new states, proud, confident and determined, believed that they were operating in the interests of the country at large. Their aggressive tactics, particularly in education and cultural control, were matched by paternalistic assumptions about how best and how fastest to convert indigenous peoples into "citizens." The transformation of administrative cultures associated with the emergence of the nation-state in the nineteenth and twentieth centuries was, as Poelzer argues, among the most important and influential changes in indigenous–newcomer relations in history.

8

FINAL INVASIONS: WAR, RESOURCE DEVELOPMENT, AND THE OCCUPATION OF TRIBAL TERRITORIES

The invasion of indigenous territories occurred in broad, sweeping waves, spread over hundreds of years. For sheer intensity, sweep, and impact, however, few generations in history have witnessed the dramatic transformations of the period between 1940 and 1970. In these thirty years, indigenous peoples insulated by distance, geography, and climate from outside populations faced unprecedented pressures and technological change. The combination of a truly global military conflict – one which reached from the frozen expanses of Siberia to the central desert of Australia, and from Greenland to hundreds of tiny islands in the Pacific – and a postwar development boom of massive proportions broke the final barriers between tribal peoples and surplus-producing populations.

General understanding of historical processes typically focuses on the distant past. As liberal democratic nations sought to understand better their impact on indigenous peoples they tended to look back into the nineteenth century or before. The crises facing tribal societies, these arguments went, rested in the aggressive moves of earlier generations, including the early explorers, missionaries, and armies of conquest. People rarely examined their own times with the same critical eye. The modern era, most believed, represented the improvement of humankind, particularly after the excesses and horrors of war had ended. Few realized that the generation shaped by wartime and the postwar era witnessed and oversaw one of the most rapid, destructive, and complex transformations of the indigenous world. The postwar era was not one of formal empires and conquering armies. The American empire was informal, wide-ranging, and culturally disruptive, but it lacked the focus of earlier periods of external domination. This was, instead, the age of multinational corporations – Alcoa, Exxon, Shell, Toyota, BHP, and dozens of others – and international financial institutions, such as the World Bank and the Asian Development Bank. Together, these powerful influences, rooted in the consumption-oriented, surplus societies of the western industrialized world, offered a strong ideological formula of commercial development, government-sponsored investments in infrastructure, and support for free(r) trade. The resulting expansion into tribal territories was perhaps unprecedented in the annals of history.

Tribal Societies at the Start of World War II

By the outbreak of global war in the late 1930s, the indigenous world had been divided into two major groups. In most temperate regions, where agricultural, mining, and forestry potential attracted thousands of outsiders, indigenous peoples had been forced off their traditional lands. As settlement pressures mounted, governments had stepped in to manage indigenous affairs and to isolate aboriginal populations from the rest of the people. In many other areas – high in the mountains, in deserts, on the tundra, on isolated and resource-poor islands – indigenous cultures remained largely beyond the reach of governments and the powerful forces of industrial change. Mining and resource development interfered in a few locations, but vast expanses of the world remained largely in the control of tribal peoples. In the African deserts, the Amazon basin, huge districts in the circumpolar North, and the seemingly impenetrable mountains of Papua New Guinea, geography protected aboriginal people from the intrusions of outsiders.

Newcomers continued their efforts to reach into these still largely unknown lands. Prospectors scoured the land in search of mineral deposits and other resources and miners and mining companies rushed in at the first sign of promising returns. Loggers, farmers, and ranchers clawed at the edges of the final frontiers, the latter two groups often deterred by climatic and soil conditions from proceeding further. Low resource prices and uncertain demand provided a further, often fatal, disincentive to development. In many countries, government agents and missionaries moved tentatively across these uncharted spaces, seeking to help the "disadvantaged" souls still living without the benefits of the industrial age. The nation-state sought, as well, to ensure that the mobile and largely unchecked indigenous peoples understood and respected the law and their legal responsibilities – but most governments avoided costly entanglements with communities which seemed uninterested in pursuing modern commercial opportunities. Tribal peoples remained curiosities, exotic societies of marginal consequence to the rest of the world.

Only a small number of indigenous societies in such truly isolated zones as the Amazon, Papua New Guinea, Andaman Islands, and a few other areas existed without regular contact with outsiders. Across Siberia, the small peoples of the far north faced regular intrusions by the Soviet state, largely in the form of efforts at political indoctrination. Government ships brought supplies annually into the most remote reaches of the Canadian Arctic. Military expeditions regularly made contact with indigenous peoples in many countries. The indigenous peoples generally knew a fair bit about the "other" societies but opted not to move into a closer relationship. For many tribal communities, retaining contact with traditional territories took precedence over integrating with the values and material complexity of the industrial world. Knowing about the world of consumption, sedentary lifestyles, and resource exploitation did not convince the tribal societies that they should make dramatic changes in their lives.

Non-aboriginal peoples, in contrast, saw little reason to make extensive contact with the indigenous peoples. To the extent that they were curiosities, they attracted occasional interest by cultural observers, who came as anthropologists, assigned to recording the details of the last tribal cultures, as missionaries determined to pave their way into heaven, as adventurers and journalists looking to describe and interpret little-known regions, or as government agents seeking to ensure that the societies represented no threat to the established order. Whatever their motivation, the outsiders sought to explain the mysterious existence of peoples who seemed determined to live outside the "modern" world. There was opportunity and fame to be found in interpreting these unique societies to the industrial world, but the public's interest was superficial, not deep. These peoples' lands, moreover, were too remote, too unattractive, too impenetrable, and too poor to attract much interest. The better lands had long since been taken up, leaving hardscrabble desert, thick jungle, rugged mountain valleys, and snow-covered tundra for the few hardy and adaptable souls able to survive on the seeming uninhabitable lands.

War and the Occupation of Remote Regions

The technology of modern warfare changed the nature of military conflict in the 1930s and, unexpectedly, resulted in the rapid development of vast expanses of remote regions, typically occupied largely by indigenous peoples. The global conflict of the 1930s and 1940s started slowly, with Japanese troops launching aggressive attacks into China. The gradual expansion of Nazi Germany to the east beginning in 1938 and, continuing rapidly thereafter, brought Central Europe into conflict with peoples in Eastern and Southeast Europe and Scandinavia. When the Japanese bombed Pearl Harbour, Hawaii, in December 1941, the conflict exploded into a truly global conflagration.

This war differed from earlier conflicts, in large measure, owing to the vastly improved technology of warfare. Airplanes – bombers, supply planes, surveillance and fighter aircraft – figured more prominently than ever in military plans. Efficiently run long-distance supply lines, serviced by ship, train, and truck, moved vast quantities of military material across enormous distances. New telecommunications technologies, particularly radio and radar, allowed military planners to coordinate far-flung armies, navies, and air forces. To all of this must be added the rapid increasing speed of military maneuvers, major improvements in the construction of wartime infrastructure, and the availability (particularly in the United States and, in the first years of the conflict, Japan and Germany) of enormous sums of money to invest in military projects. World War II was larger, more expansive, faster moving, more integrated, and therefore more dramatic than any war in history. It engulfed the entire planet, including vast lands hitherto left largely unscathed by the advance of the industrial world.

The contours of World War II are very well-known, with the Axis powers (Germany, Italy, and Japan) facing off against the Allies (particularly the United Kingdom, Canada, the United States, Australia, New Zealand, and India). In Europe, the Nazi advance to the west and southeast brought most of the continent under German control. What proved to be an ill-timed or ill-advised attack against Russia in 1941 brought the Nazi armed forces into a difficult multi-front war, which included a dramatic conflict across the desert terrain of North Africa. Japan pressed aggressively into Southeast Asia, capturing Hong Kong, Singapore, and the Philippines, and standing on the verge of attacking Australia. In the process, they occupied hundreds of small Pacific islands, gaining effective control of vast expanses of Asia and the Pacific.

Descriptions and analysis of the war have, understandably, focused on the primary battlefields and the massive build-up of Axis and Allied troops near major population centers. This emphasis, however, has meant a general neglect of a surprisingly dramatic period of occupation and dislocation of indigenous peoples within their traditional territories. There was only passing public interest in the construction of a highway in the Canadian northwest when thousands had died or been captured during a failed attempt to take the French port of Dieppe. The development of airfields in Greenland could hardly compete in terms of urgency or importance with the opening of defensive positions in Eastern Australia. In remarkably short order, however, Allied forces moved aggressively into sparsely settled territories, anxious to protect the lands from Axis invasion or to use the little-known areas as supply bases or as a launching pad for military activities.

The catalogue of major military projects on and through indigenous territories is a thick one. Across Australia, American and Australian authorities built dozens of airfields and supporting facilities. Throughout northern Queensland, the closest secure Allied territory to the Japanese-held islands of the South Pacific, the United States Army Corps of Engineers built a series of major staging areas. Similarly, the New Zealand government welcomed American troops onto their lands, and several major projects were constructed around Maori communities. The Americans occupied dozens of islands across the South Pacific, racing to protect them from Japanese invasion and then using them as bases for subsequent attacks on Japanese-held territories. American and Canadian civilian and military contractors constructed several military highways, dozens of airstrips and a major oil pipeline complex in northwest North America, swamping the local population. Similar construction projects were undertaken in the eastern Arctic, specifically to provide staging fields for planes and supplies being ferried to the United Kingdom. The Americans, the largest and most expansive of the Allied powers in this era, built other facilities in the Caribbean, South Asia, South America, Iceland, and other locations.

The United States was not alone in moving into indigenous territories. Russian developers, spurred by urgent military needs for resources and by a desire to protect the far east from potential Japanese attack, expanded operations across Siberia. Military bases, particularly airfields, smaller weather stations, and other facilities were constructed throughout the sparsely inhabited North. German armies entered Sami lands in Norway and Finland and established control over large stretches of tribal territory in North Africa. The Japanese, for their part, asserted authority over island populations in the Pacific, overran tribal peoples in Southeast Asia, and dominated indigenous peoples in the Philippines and other lands. They also occupied, temporarily, several of the Aleutian Islands of Alaska and, before being driven off by a combined Canadian and American force, relocated a significant number of the Aleuts to camps in Japan, where they remained until the end of the war.

By the end of World War II, vast stretches of land previously ignored by industrial nations and their related authorities had been brought into the ambit of the non-indigenous worlds. In most of these areas, the original inhabitants had generally been treated with benign neglect. Governments from Australia to Russia, Norway to Alaska, had general policies designed to assimilate or dominate indigenous peoples. But in most instances, the governments saw no particular value – and a great deal of cost – in attempting to bring indigenous populations formally under central control. There had been efforts, from the Soviet Red Tents in Siberia to mission-run schools in the Canadian North and government outposts in the Australian outback, to start the process of integration, but the forces of separation remained strong. In the absence of sizeable non-indigenous populations and the comparatively small amount of industrial or resource development, tribal peoples found themselves generally left to their own devices. Fiji might have lived under the yoke of British rule, and Vanuatu may have existed under the uneasy dominance of the British and French *condominium* government, but most of the tribal peoples operated much as they wanted to do and followed a substantially traditional lifestyle.

Conditions changed throughout the war, even in areas that did not fall victim to bombing attacks or direct invasion. The peoples of occupied Pacific islands, particularly those controlled by the Japanese, faced enormous dislocations and, in many instances, saw their island existence torn asunder by invasion and battle. Populations near newly opened resource projects, hastily constructed highways or airfields, or major infrastructure initiatives experienced rapid changes in local conditions. Around the world, peoples subjected to the effects of the influx of thousands of Axis or Allied troops saw their way of life subject to vast disruptions. Indigenous people across Siberia endured the removal of large numbers of reindeer to support the desperate USSR war effort against the Germans; even more disruptive was the imposition of national conscription and the enlistment of thousands of indigenous peoples for military service, which caused significant changes in the indigenous camps. Conditions varied from country to country, often depending on the state of armed conflict and the urgency the occupiers attached to asserting dominance over the area. In most instances, civil authorities exercised little power, leaving the management of local affairs to military officials.

Although the specific impacts varied substantially across space and time, indigenous peoples experienced very dramatic changes as a result of the wartime occupations and activities. Military developers paid little attention to the preservation of the ecosystem; the imperatives of war took precedence over the needs of local peoples and wildlife, and the well-armed soldiers were not averse to using their guns on the latter. The arrival of thousands of soldiers and construction workers, typically young men with money, time, and a willingness to assert their dominance, overturned local economies and disrupted social relations. The soldiers and construction workers often mixed with local populations. Sexual liaisons with local women, consensual or aggressive, were commonplace. Occasional opportunities to find work with the construction projects were typically offset by the disruptions of local economies, a reduction in harvestable resources, and competition for local food supplies. The availability of industrial products ranging from manufactured clothing to processed foods at the military bases often distorted local markets even further, providing attractive alternatives to local stores. Experiences varied depending on the origins of the occupying power – friendly invasions were far less disruptive than enemy attacks – and the precise nature of the projects being undertaken. On a global scale, and in rapid order, indigenous communities found their lives turned upside down, the victims of a military "invasion" undertaken, for the most part, by Allied forces.

In some instances, the military occupations passed quickly, as the armed forces moved on to more strategic areas; when this occurred, as it did in isolated outposts in the Canadian eastern Arctic and the Australian outback, indigenous peoples could for a time return to the old ways. In many other cases, in contrast, the military projects represented more than a transitory shift. Often the armies stayed, as they did in Alaska, Siberia, Greenland, and in portions of Southeast Asia. They were soon fixed in place by the rapid transformation of the global conflict into the "Cold War" stand-off between capitalist and communist powers.

The United States pulled back most of its troops at war's end, but did not abandon its overseas activities. For the expanding and confident American empire, the foothold established by the wartime occupations ended up becoming the foundation for postwar defence and vigilance against the new enemies in the Soviet Union and communist China. And so the United States maintained its presence in such isolated locations as the Inuit lands of Baffin Island and Greenland, in Iceland, on aboriginal territory in Alaska, and in many strategic locations in Southeast Asia. Huge US military bases in locations from Japan to the Philippines to Alaska, and specialized facilities at isolated sites around the capitalist-friendly world provided both tangible evidence of the American's determination to protect the democratic states and their allies and a continuing disruptive influence on local indigenous populations.

The communist powers, for their part, were determined to protect themselves against the threat of attack by the United States, and they too maintained their military presence in hitherto neglected hinterland areas. The Soviets, in particular, extended their commitments to traditional indigenous territories in Siberia, which they reinforced militarily and developed strategically, pouring vast sums of money into mines, logging operations, hydroelectric stations, and other such projects. China expanded its military and administrative control to the west and south; it was in this period that the communist state established effect control over Tibet and placed the smaller indigenous groups in the far west and south under communist influence.

In areas of rapidly declining military importance – the Pacific islands, Australia, the Canadian North, Newfoundland (not part of Canada until 1949), New Zealand, and elsewhere – the withdrawal of the United States and the collapse of Germany, Japan, and Italy provided an opportunity for the reassertion of national control. In these cases, the military construction projects, which usually involved some mix of roads, airfields, wharves, supply facilities, telephone lines, and other basic infrastructure, were either abandoned or shifted to civilian uses. The military facilities had been constructed with little attention to long-term value or suitability; the imperatives of war had shaped most of the decision-making processes. Around the world, hastily built airfields returned to weeds and forests. Ill-planned roads and railway lines soon fell into disuse, as did hundreds of warehouses, barracks, and other wartime undertakings. Some, of course, had been damaged or destroyed by war – the Japanese facilities on the Pacific islands and in Southeast Asia, in particular, had been bombed and torched into use-lessness – and had little productive value. Other military investments, however, were seized upon by local authorities and businesses when the armed forces pulled out. These many projects, built by the Axis and

Allied powers at considerable cost, provided a foundation for economic and administrative activities in hitherto neglected regions. And even if the military facilities were not up to proper civilian standards – highways built in the Australian outback and the Canadian Northwest fell far short of finished quality – they represented to regional non-indigenous populations and national governments a vast improvement over the paltry infrastructure of the prewar period.

Indigenous peoples played very little military role during the war, save to be battered by the residual damage of warfare and disrupted by the massive and rapid military preparations. No governments, domestic, allied, or invading, consulted them on the use of their lands and resources. At war's end, as businesses and governments rushed to capitalize on the leftover benefits of military occupation, concern for indigenous issues scarcely made a dent on national or international consciousness. That non-aboriginal people saw the wartime projects as a foundation for postwar economic development meant that war's end represented a continuation, not an end, of a period of intense transformation. In isolated lands around the world, indigenous peoples discovered that their hitherto largely unchallenged use of traditional territories and resources had fallen to the imperatives of war and international politics. Operating well below the geopolitical radar, aboriginal communities suffered as well from the social, cultural, and economic dislocations associated with the expansion of military activity and the complex implications of having soldiers, sailors, and aviators occupying traditional lands.

On a broader level, the extension of national interests in remote regions convinced governments to pay greater attention to these regions. At war's end, even as the Axis powers retreated and the Allied/American forces pulled back to a peacetime footing, the vast indigenous lands occupied in this brief, intense period remained under external control. Military planners recognized the long-term strategic importance of these areas and, in particular, their resources. Government officials and private developers realized that the resource wealth of these remote regions might well hold the key to postwar national prosperity; they were determined, too, not to repeat the errors of the prewar period and to leave these now-valuable lands available for foreign occupation. As well, the completion of a wide variety of infrastructure projects provided a unique foundation for subsequent developments. And even if the military roads, airfields, construction camps, wharves, and other facilities fell below private- and public-sector standards and were often located in inappropriate places for peacetime purposes, they nonetheless provided an attractive foundation for regional development. The war had opened up vast expanses todevelopers; national governments were determined not to retreat from these areas at war's end.

By 1945, vast expanses of lands occupied almost exclusively by indigenous peoples had been drawn more intensely into the political economy of the industrial world. The territories had, as recently as the 1930s, attracted little national attention, as governments struggled to find practical policies to cope with the unique realities of mobile harvesting peoples who continued to shun the attractions of the sedentary industrial–agricultural world. Distance, extremely harsh climates, difficult terrain, and isolation made it easy for colonial and national authorities to pay little attention to such areas as the Australian outback, the Canadian North, eastern Siberia, the highlands of Papua New Guinea and Southeast Asia, and vast expanses of Central Africa and South and Central America. During World War II, significant portions of these territories fell under the sway of armies, governments, and developers. Much of the remainder would be substantially lost to indigenous peoples in the quarter-century following the war.

Consumer Economies and the Demand for Raw Materials

Imperatives other than government concerns about indigenous populations helped shape the timing, direction, and extent of the occupation of aboriginal-dominated territories. Three major postwar developments – the continued military build-up associated with the Cold War, the discovery by western democratic nations of the fiscal enticements of Keynesian economies (deficit financing to support national economies through economic downturns), and the rapid expansion of consumer demand in the 1950s and beyond – provided a significant impetus for the development of remote regions. Fueling the military states, particularly the United States and Russia, required vast quantities of raw materials – and the imperatives of a world in a state of apprehended war meant that top priority rested on securing these resources within the nation or among allied states if at all possible. Governments in both the capitalist and communist worlds, as well as in satellite or colonial states, recognized the growing material expectations of their dominant societies. Demand held in check during the war years burst into the open at war's end. Private developers moved quickly to meet the seemingly insatiable desire for consumables, requiring in the process access to new and cheaper resources. Put simply, the world needed more resources – and the once remote regions of the world seemed to offer an enormous storehouse of untapped wealth. Fortuitously, it seemed, wartime construction projects provided unexpected access to these previously isolated regions.

With stunning speed and intensity, the industrial world unleashed a development boom on the remote regions that had, only a few short years before, felt the effects of military occupations. In the Soviet Union, large cities grew around major resource deposits, with the government effectively bribing workers from southern and western cities to venture north. Huge development projects – hydroelectric dams and transmission lines, oil and natural gas fields, base metal mines, large sawmills and pulp-and-paper operations – sprang up through the 1950s and 1960s throughout isolated regions in Australia, Scandinavia, Southeast Asia, Canada, Russia, and Brazil.

Hydroelectric projects had profound effects around the globe, as traditional lands were flooded and indigenous peoples forced off their territories. Large-scale Canadian projects in Quebec, Labrador, Manitoba, and British Columbia were particularly disruptive, requiring the relocation of communities and the undermining of harvesting activities. The Temenggor Dam in Malaysia had substantial impacts, as did the Bakun project on the Upper Balui in Sarawak, the Okavango Delta initiative in Botswana, the Tamandua dam in lands of the Macuxi and Wapixana in the northern Amazon, and several major undertakings in India. The Sami in Norway attempted, without success, to stop the development of the Alta-Kautokeino dam, which threatened their reindeer-herding activities. A Purari from Papua New Guinea warned his people about the false attractions of hydro development:

So when the Government finally agrees to build the hydroelectric dam I personally believe that we will be spoilt in many ways. The great civilization will really swallow our old ways of life. I must agree that this civilization will mean a lot of change in your life. Some of these changes will not make you altogether happy, but maybe you will feel a very happy person in this world. What will happen if, for example, this place becomes over-populated because of the development of industrial sites and cities? I am sorry, very sorry to say that you will lose your ancestral lands to land-hungry governments. You will realise that you have lost almost everything that goes with the land once created by the cassowary mother. As an old man who is ready for dying, I would like to say, my children, whatever you do, never, and I repeat never, lose your traditional rights over your ancestral lands.[1]

In countries like Colombia, a combination of demographic pressures and the demand for resources resulted in the occupation of indigenous lands and the displacement of the original peoples. Mineral, hydroelectric, oil and gas, and military developments across Siberia proceeded at a breakneck pace, outstripping western developments in intrusiveness and negative impact on the indigenous peoples. But even in the farthest northern regions of North America, major developments were underway. The discovery of oil and gas deposits on the North Slope of Alaska resulted in the development of the Prudhoe Bay oil fields and the Alyeska pipeline. Of equal importance, this discovery sparked additional oil and gas exploration in the high Arctic, particularly in Canada's Beaufort Sea. Prospectors scoured the most remote districts for new mineral deposits, spurred on by governments anxious for ever more economic opportunity and even greater security of supply. Thousands of workers followed the discoveries into the remote areas, capitalizing on the high wages and seemingly endless opportunity associated with the development of what governments affectionately labeled "the last frontier."

Given the rapacious appetite for minerals and raw materials and given, in the developing world, the political need to balance the needs of the impoverished majority against the desires of a tiny indigenous minority, it is hardly surprising that tribal wishes were rarely factored into the development equation. A regional politician in Brazil captured this sentiment in 1975 when he commented, "An area as rich as this, with gold, diamonds, and uranium, cannot afford the luxury of preserving half a dozen Indian tribes which are holding up development."[2] Throughout Central America, from revolutionary Nicaragua to Costa Rica, governments chipped away at indigenous landholdings, reducing their control of traditional territories and undermining their economic base in the process. In the Soviet North, dramatic dislocations followed the expansion of industrial activity in the region:

[The] peoples of the North were never indifferent to the fate of their land. Seeing how it was treated, they suffered and tried to save it. As a protest, they were using expressions like: "We are the last generation of the taiga peoples, the tundra is like the cover of an old chum." More and more often their voices are heard in defense of their rights, and their interests. The indigenous population is protesting against the building of Turukhansk hydroelectric station at Nizhnyi Tungusk, calling this project satanic! They are fighting against the building of an atomic energy station at the Evoron Lake and a fertiliser complex on the banks of the Amur River, and against other giant projects. The peoples of the North are not against the exploitation of the riches of the area in general, but against the destruction of the environment in their living areas.[3]

Serving these widely dispersed resource projects required even more investment and development. National governments contributed major roads, railway extensions, serviceable airfields (often to replace the hastily designed wartime facilities), pipelines, and urban amenities necessary to support and sustain the increasingly non-indigenous population in the regions. The influx of newcomers forced governments to extend, as appropriate, the institutions of civil society, in the form of stronger regional authorities and greater local decision-making, although neither typically involved indigenous peoples in this era. Governments celebrated these accomplishments as signs of assured national prosperity, and spurred developers and government agencies to plan for an even greater development boom.

In the developing world, demographic pressures focused government attention on the most basic of natural resources: land. Through Southeast Asia, for example, expanding populations brought more and more people into the outer islands of Indonesia, the highlands of Thailand, or other comparable locations. The Chittagong Hill region of Bangladesh provides a particularly graphic example. This area had been protected from migrants for much of the twentieth century. The newly independent Bangladesh, faced with massive population growth on the coastal plains, lifted the protections on indigenous lands in the mid-1970s and encouraged settlement. An angry report on the occupation of the hills commented:

> June 30, 1984, the new Bengali settlers came to forcibly reap the rice crop from the ripe paddy fields of the Chakma inhabitants at Buushanchara. This was instigated by the Bangladesh army troops who then hid themselves. When reaping was started, the Chakma inhabitants tried to stop it. Then and there the Bangladeshi soldiers emerged and aggressively fired directly on the Chakmas. They then attacked vast areas of Chota Harina, Bara Harina, Chedoa, Garjangtali, Soguri Ps and Maudong. More than three hundred unarmed innocent Chakmas were murdered. The captured tribals were divided into three groups – old and young men, elderly women, and young women. Men and old women were shot dead. The young women were raped freely, some of them were killed and some were converted to Islam.[4]

The resulting conflicts and dislocations caused great difficulties for the Chittagong Hill peoples, and generated considerable international protest, but the government saw little justification in defending the interests of a small number of people while tens of millions lived in grinding poverty near the coast.

Aboriginal peoples fought back against the transformation of their landscapes and the potential threat to their lifeways. The proposed construction of a major hydroelectric project in northern Quebec in the late 1960s and early 1970s resulted in the creation of the Grand Council of the Crees and the launch of a major court challenge to the initiative. The Canadian and Quebec governments responded to the legal controversy by negotiating a treaty with the James Bay Cree, which recognized indigenous harvesting rights and granted the Cree considerable powers of self-administration. Similarly, the planned development of the North Slope oil fields in Alaska generated sharp resistance from indigenous groups, and resulted eventually in the Alaska Native Claims Settlement Act of 1971. In Brazil, the Yanomami were even more direct. Faced with the occupation of their territories by outsiders in the early 1980s and suffering from severe outbreaks of malaria and other illnesses they moved on the interlopers, though stopping short of armed conflict.

Capitalist countries were not alone in imposing the development model on indigenous territories. The Soviet Union had the most extensive program for capitalizing on the resources in remote regions – and paid the least attention to questions of environmental protection and care of indigenous communities. China needed access to resources in the western territories, and paid little heed to the needs of the small and politically powerless indigenous populations in the area. Newly independent nations, including many African states, India, and Indonesia, also largely ignored the needs of isolated tribal peoples, such was the urgency to develop marketable resources and new lands. Countries like Brazil and Chile, shifting in and out of democratic control, moved quickly to identify and exploit development opportunities.

Because the transitions are relatively recent, it is easy to understate and underestimate the scale and intensity of this postwar occupation and incorporation of indigenous territories. The imperatives of the industrial world, which needed energy, minerals, wood, and pulp, regardless of political ideology or government structure, drove nations to move aggressively into remote regions. In very few instances – Scandinavian nations were given to more compassionate and culturally sensitive approaches than most other countries – did the national governments take the concerns and needs of indigenous peoples very seriously. Instead, the need for resources to meet strategic needs, feed an appetite for profit, or supply the growing needs of expanding urban and industrial populations, pushed nation after nation to develop remote regions, largely without reference to the indigenous peoples of the regions.

New Approaches to Indigenous Peoples in Remote Regions

National governments, confronted with the reality of the indigenous experience and the dislocations associated with the war, took new approaches to the governance of aboriginal territories. Wartime military considerations gained renewed poignancy by the terrifying prospects of nuclear conflagration as tensions built between the capitalist and communist worlds. Within each ideological camp, major investments were made in military infrastructure to prepare for the seemingly inevitable conflict between the USSR and the USA. World War II projects were expanded, upgraded or replaced. Radar stations, strategically located bomber and fighter bases, and the necessary supporting facilities continued to dot the landscape of the sparsely inhabited districts in the world. The development of the Distant Early Warning Line across the American and Canadian Norths brought the imperatives of the Cold War into aboriginal communities across the region, distorting local economies to the detriment of indigenous harvesting and, time has shown, causing considerable environmental damage as well. Along the Bering Strait, the sudden and unexpected imposition of the USSR–USA boundary after World War II closed off centuries-old contact and trade across the strait and separated family members for close to fifty years (the border reopened in 1989). In Tierra del Fuego, the militarization of the Chile–Argentinian border caused considerable dislocations for the local Yanama people. If indigenous peoples thought that the end of the war would bring a return to the old order, they were to be bitterly disappointed.

Governments had also discovered a new agenda during their forays into indigenous territories. Indigenous peoples in these isolated areas, following largely traditional harvesting lifestyles and eschewing the imperatives of the industrial age, represented something of an affront to national norms. Countries as diverse as Australia and the Soviet Union,

Norway and Canada, launched substantial initiatives designed to integrate these peoples into the nation-state. Aggressive schooling campaigns were launched in an attempt to provide proper educational opportunities for indigenous children. The Canadian government, building on a pattern well-established in southern districts, expanded residential schools across the North and removed indigenous children from their families and communities. There were comparable initiatives in Siberia, where the government attempted to draw the small peoples into the values and responsibilities of the Soviet system. In colonial territories in Africa, likewise, European authorities (the British being particularly fond of educational integration) extended schooling to indigenous peoples hitherto largely ignored by missionary and official education.

The USSR, having taken a hands-off approach in the early Soviet years, moved more aggressively after the 1940s. Across the Soviet North, the governments established economic collectives, moved mobile peoples into settlements, and provided a broad range of new services to the indigenous communities. The availability of education, health care, and government support in times of hardship proved attractive, much as did Family Allowance payments in northern Canada and the state welfare supports offered in other western countries. Of particular consequence in the Russian North, however, was the mass immigration of outsiders, enticed by high wages and opportunities to circumvent the rationing imposed on southern communities. Indigenous peoples across Siberia found themselves to be a steadily declining minority in their own homelands. The situation reversed in the years following the collapse of the Union of Soviet Socialist Republics and the subsequent "opening" of the Russian economy in the 1990s. The reduction in subsidies and the declining economic conditions created significant hardships. This era also saw the West's discovery of the staggering ecological disasters wrought across indigenous lands in the Russian North and the growing realization of the degree to which the northern landscape had been desecrated by rapid resource and military development.

Administrative initiatives, most notably in the western industrial nations, had a profound impact on indigenous peoples. In the main, their lifestyles and economies involved substantial movements across the land, typically tied to seasonal resource activities. Such movements did not mesh with administrative imperatives, such as the opening of schools, hospitals, and the provision of state welfare. Each of these, to a greater or lesser degree, required permanent residence. Faced with the uncertainties of harvesting activities, particularly in light of rapidly accelerating resource developments and the construction of roads, airfields, railways, hydroelectric dams, and military bases, it is hardly surprising that many indigenous peoples took advantage of the availability of government support. In some areas, the USSR and Canada being good examples, government agencies made such moves more or less compulsory. Across Siberia, as a consequence, traditional villages disappeared, to be replaced by large and incongruous state-constructed apartment blocks. Canadian and American authorities built new villages (often to southern standards, even in northern districts), and worked to encourage the indigenous peoples to leave the land in favor of permanent community life. In Australia, after failed attempts to impose western housing styles on the Aborigines, the government built more culturally suitable shelters and water stations at key sites. In Botswana, the development of bore holes provided a magnet for indigenous settlement and movements.

In the western liberal democracies this impulse has generally been ascribed to an onset of liberal guilt and to the realization that indigenous peoples were being left behind in the rapidly industrialization and increasingly middle-class postwar world. An ideology of equality and anti-racism (to be discussed in the next chapter) merged with a growing recognition that massive development had been, at the very best, a mixed blessing for indigenous peoples. Driven to accept their responsibility to "elevate" aboriginal communities to the level of the rest of the population, national, and regional governments scrambled to develop and implement policies aimed at integrating indigenous peoples, typically as individuals, into the national mainstream. If this meant, as it did, a deprecation of aboriginal languages and cultures, a sharp critique of mobile lifestyles, and a vast increase in government intervention in the lives of indigenous peoples in remote regions, then these were accepted as an inevitable consequence of progress and modernization. Driven by a combination of liberal guilt and social responsibilities, freed from dependence on the missionary orders by declining confidence in organized religion, and buttressed by the wealth of the postwar industrial world, nations moved aggressively to provide aboriginal peoples in the hinterland districts with access to all that the modern, urban, and industrial world had to offer.

It is important to note that non-western nations adopted similar procedures, believing strongly in the value of modernization, education, and health care as means of ameliorating the condition of indigenous peoples. The liberal democracies could spend more money and time on aboriginal communities, but others followed much the same path. The Malaysian government, for example, adopted a settlement and centralization program, called the Rancangan Pengumpulan Semula, in an attempt to jump-start the assimilation of indigenous peoples. Similar initiatives have been undertaken in Thailand, in part to offset the pernicious effects of the highland drug industry, in India, and throughout Africa. Botswana, one of the few reasonably stable states in Southern Africa, undertook aggressive agricultural development programs, many of which have improved the lives of the nation's citizens. The San, however, have had their traditional territories reduced, controled and regulated in such a way as to interfere with their lifestyle and pursuit of sustenance. In many of these cases, the efforts have been supported by foreign aid payments, provided by the First World governments which have had a long-term commitment to the economic and social transformation of indigenous peoples.

In some quarters, revolutionary movements involving Cold War combatants had destructive impacts on indigenous peoples. Throughout the Philippines, for example, small tribal populations found themselves ensnared in a decades-long guerrilla war between government and insurgency forces. Similarly, the Orang Asli tribes on Malaysia became entangled in a 1950s struggle between communists and the British colonial authorities. The Miskito Indians of Nicaragua encountered significant difficulties throughout the Sandinista revolution and the subsequent conflicts with Contra rebels. Throughout Africa, bitter proxy wars between government, rebel, and mercenary forces allied with the Soviet Union, China, Cuba, the United States, and others had unanticipated impacts on the typically apolitical indigenous population, who nonetheless found their traditional territories turned into battlegrounds.

Aboriginal Response

By the end of the 1950s, almost all of the tribal peoples of the world operated with direct and extended contact with newcomers. Only a small number of tribal peoples, buffered by the seemingly impenetrable jungles in the Amazon, Papua New Guinea, and parts of Central Africa, existed without fairly regular exposure to outsiders. The disruptions of war, Allied occupation, and postwar resource development, together with the expansion of government intervention, brought sweeping changes to societies that had been protected by distance and isolation from the full impact of the expansion of the industrial world. New technologies and the seemingly insatiable desire for additional resources resulted in the step-wise occupation of indigenous territories through the 1940s and 1950s. Indigenous peoples from the Chittagong Hills in Bangladesh to the northern reaches of Canada's Mackenzie River valley found themselves joined on their traditional territories by developers, prospectors, and other users of the land and resources. In the case of the Chittagong, they had survived years of British rule, maintaining considerable cultural autonomy and separation from the surrounding agricultural settlements. Beginning in the 1950s and 1960s, however, forest and hydroelectric projects intruded on the Hill Peoples' territory. More ominously, the rapidly escalating population of Bangladesh, and the regular destruction of farm lands in floods and other natural disasters, caused the government of the poor nation to cast covetous eyes on the underutilized lands in the hills. In subsequent decades, government-sponsored settlement schemes combined with armed intrusions and efforts to remove the traditional inhabitants, undermining the longstanding communities. Interventionist governments offered schools to Aborigines in the Australian outback, urban settlement plans in New Zealand, training programs in Norway, and apartment-style dwellings in the Soviet Union.

Thus, in a twenty-five year period beginning in the late 1930s, the tribal peoples who still experienced generally unchecked use of traditional territories underwent dramatic changes. Few could have anticipated the speed and intensity of the transitions. In the first decade, they faced the lightning-fast invasions, friendly or aggressive, during World War II. After the war, an era of government intervention commenced, built around the belief that social and economic policies could speed indigenous assimilation into national norms. For indigenous populations, this two-pronged process of incorporation, linked by the transition from the heat of World War II to the prolonged militarization of the Cold War, threatened the cultural isolation of tribal societies and brought them directly into the orbit of the industrial world.

Tribal peoples proved to be generally powerless in the face of the advance of thousands of soldiers, aviators, or sailors. Governments which had hitherto paid scant attention to indigenous needs and aspirations brushed aside what few qualms they had when having to respond to the prospect or reality of armed invasion. Aboriginal considerations, be they access to traditional territories or harvestable resources or freedom from discrimination, carried little weight in the midst of a life-and-death struggle against enemy forces. Most of these occupations of indigenous lands occurred in peripheral districts, far removed from centers of administrative or political power. In these circumstances, it was difficult for government officials to maintain extensive oversight over the fast-moving armed forces. Construction teams pressed quickly through indigenous lands; military personnel fought or practiced over vast expanses of tribal territories. Resources which had sustained indigenous life for decades were destroyed by the generally unintentional actions of the Allied or Axis military.

Aboriginal peoples adapted as best they could to the sudden occupations. Some of the tribal peoples participated, as did Aborigines in northern Australia and the Inuit in the Canadian North, in defense of their territories. Many others, from the islands of the South Pacific to the highlands of Southeast Asia, were overrun by first the Japanese and later Allied troops, largely Americans. Where supply and distribution centers commenced operations in once ignored lands, tribal peoples found occasional work. Along the Alaska Highway, for example, a small number of First Nations people worked as casual laborers, sold meat and handicrafts to soldiers and civilian workers, and acted as guides for the construction teams. The social consequences of the military activities varied widely, ranging from medical assistance and the provision of food to sexual contact with indigenous women, and the widespread distribution of alcohol. The tribal populations could do nothing to determine the timing, pace, and duration of the military occupations, and had little opportunity to mitigate the more destructive influences of wartime activities.

The postwar era of government intervention was accompanied by a very different aboriginal response and sharply different reactions from the non-indigenous populations, particularly in the western democracies. The burst of social intervention, based on the belief that government programs could ease tribal societies into the national mainstream, helped open tribal territories for resource development and major government investments in infrastructure. Indigenous peoples, whether in capitalist or non-capitalist countries, found themselves again facing a formidable array of forces. The tools were now government housing projects and economic development schemes rather than military construction activities and armed invasions. Armed aggression had been replaced by the gentler, but equally pernicious intrusions of the ideologies of assimilation and cultural suppression. New armies – of teachers, social service workers, medical professionals, economic development officers – made their way into the tribal territories, offering assured routes into the prosperity and security of life and property enjoyed by other members of the national society. These missionaries of the new order, whether capitalist advocates in Alaska, Soviet representatives in Siberia, social democrats in Scandinavia, European colonizers in Asia and Africa, or liberals in Canada and Australia, sought to "improve" the indigenous condition, even if it meant undermining traditional lifeways.

The dual onslaught of resource development (with military activity still a major factor in many regions) and government-mandated social policy generated a significant reaction by the indigenous peoples. Some, particularly in the Arctic, the Australian outback, and heavily forested areas in South America, Africa, and Asia found that distance and social isolation still provided a buffer against government intrusion. The insistence on challenging indigenous cultures had, in most countries, a cost ceiling; governments moved slowly in their efforts to incorporate aboriginal peoples in the most remote places on earth. Similarly, the postwar decolonization movements in Africa and Asia, in particular, focused their attention on more densely populated areas and on the imperatives of nation-building. The incorporation of tribal peoples would, in such situations, await the 1970–90 period. For one last generation, the barriers imposed by climate, geography, and outsiders' perceptions remained largely impenetrable.

Even these remote regions, however, faced a simple reality. Global ecological change caused dramatic transformations in many parts of the world. Some of the shifts – like the Arctic haze that is now so noticeable around the circumpolar region in morning and at night – are subtle and misunderstood. Global warming, which carries particular challenges for the peoples of the far North, is now having marked and appreciable impacts on the region. While scientists continue to debate the existence and magnitude of the change, northern residents know that they are seeing new bugs and plants, that weather patterns have been altered and that uncertainty is growing. On a different part of the planet, island peoples in the South Pacific are extremely nervous about the implications of increased temperatures, for there are already signs of dangerous changes in weather patterns and, more worrying, rising ocean levels which threaten the habitability of many low-lying islands. More specific damage has also been done. The Chernobyl nuclear disaster, for example, emitted a large radioactive cloud which spread across Scandinavia. The cloud passed over prime reindeer-herding territory, forcing the Sami to destroy thousands of animals and undercutting their markets for years.

In more accessible areas, including those districts with high demand resources, the indigenous peoples faced rapid change. Governments moved whole communities to more accessible locations, and hoped that they would adapt quickly to the new educational, social, and economic regimes. They constructed railroads and highways to open vast tracts for development. The construction of the Cuiabo to Porto Velho highway in Brazil, for example, cut through the territory of the Nambiquara. The societies had to respond, as well, to yet another influx of outsiders, made up largely of resource users and government officials, the latter charged with easing the transition of the tribal peoples. Rapid changes in telecommunications capabilities meant that the newcomers brought radio and even television into once remote outposts. The Otavalos of Ecuador responded to commercial opportunities in the textile industry, developing a vertically controlled system from production to distribution and export, and using their economic clout to earn a significant measure of political power. These developments, combined with improved air service and, largely using wartime roads, land access to more populated centers, meant that the cultural and social intrusions of the outside picked up in intensity and severity. Whereas aboriginal peoples had formerly been able to dodge the activities of a few miners and the occasional missionary or government official, they found themselves swamped by the sweeping intrusions of television, popular music, and the material paraphernalia of the modern age. They were faced, too, with confronting the ideological values of the dominant society, whether the enthusiastic consumerism of western capitalism, authoritarian democracies in the Philippines and South and Central America, the austerity of Soviet or Chinese-style communism, or the often boisterous and Marxist-influenced decolonization movements in many other jurisdictions.

Equally important, many of these occupations had a strong military – some commentators described them as genocidal – elements. The Chittagong Hill Peoples' resistance to dispossession was, for example, met with government force. Thousands of people died in the resulting fighting. On a smaller scale, the expansion of mining and forestry activity in the Amazon resulted in frequent battles between resource developers, often backed by government troops, and the indigenous peoples. Attacks on indigenous communities in Colombia, Peru, and Brazil, and a series of violent outbursts directed at the Ache of Paraguay throughout the post-World War II area provides perhaps the best evidence of the continued use of violence as a means of shouldering aboriginal residents aside.

In more settled districts, tribal peoples had long since felt the force and determination of newcomer societies. By the 1940s, only a small number of indigenous societies had not already felt the traumatic and dramatic influences of being dominated by external populations and swept up into the vortex of the industrializing world. By the 1970s, there were virtually none of these isolated societies left. In this thirty-year period, tribal peoples around the world, among the last to enjoy largely unfettered use of traditional territories, had been incorporated into their surrounding nation-state.

There had initially been hope that a parallel process of environmental awareness would result in the preservation of lands for indigenous use. Throughout the 1960–2000 period, national governments became increasingly interested in protecting pristine wilderness from the effects of development. Since these territories were often the homelands of indigenous peoples, many of them still living very close to the land, the national park/preservationist impulse seemed a perfect match for the desire to ensure indigenous peoples secured a higher level of certainty about their traditional territory. It did not work out as expected. Environmentalists often drew on indigenous imagery and alluded to indigenous passions for the land when promoting preservationist strategies. The alliance proved somewhat shaky in implementation. Environmentalists were generally concerned primarily with the ecosystem; traditional pursuits, like trapping, that interfered with the flora and fauna were criticized or even condemned. Consider, for example, the establishment of a national park in Sri Lanka, a decision which struck directly at the heart of Vedda traditional life. The indigenous peoples were ordered to leave the area, in order to protect wildlife habitat. As one observer commented:

> Their whole way of life has become a criminal offense overnight, as a result of this decision. No Vedda has the right to catch any animal, take honey, plants or roots etc., which happen to be their basic food substance. Any hunting is considered poaching, and personnel from the Wild Life Dept. have been station at the different villages since 1983 to supervise compliance with the law. Any "poacher" would see his prey confiscated, be arrested and put on trial. The Vedda are mistreated, even their children, while the controlers share the approp[r]iated meat or honey.[5]

The transition proved extremely difficult, even if government-sponsored programs occasionally resulted in improved health, greater material wealth, and improved access to the technologies and services that non-remote societies had come to expect. For these tribal peoples in transition, the wartime and postwar period brought removal from traditional territories and into government-sanctioned centers, a forced interruption of harvesting activities, the substantial degradation of harvestable resources, and greatly increased contact with non-indigenous peoples. These changes, in turn, typically resulted in challenges to traditional means of social control, attacks on systems of tribal governance, generational conflicts between land-based elders and more assimilated youngsters, a burst in internally directed protest, largely in the form of alcohol abuse and domestic violence, and little practical integration with the dominant society. The dreams of government officials, the secular missionaries of the postwar era, proved largely fanciful; non-indigenous societies were not, in general, anxious to make accommodations to include tribal peoples and were certainly not prepared to make sufficient concessions for traditional languages, customs, and lifeways to flourish alongside and among the dominant order.

At few points in human history have so many peoples faced such rapid and determined non-military efforts at cultural conquest and reorientation as did the indigenous peoples in the remaining truly remote regions of the world after the 1930s. In that decade, many of the indigenous peoples in the isolated zones of the world lived much as their ancestors had done. Thirty years later, most of these same peoples – regardless of the political regime under which they lived – had suffered through the dislocations of war and postwar militarization, the aggressively paternalistic hand of government, the residual effects of largely unplanned resource developments, massive environmental degradation of traditional territories, and a concerted attack on cultural values and linguistic abilities. Vast tracts of land from Siberia to Western Australia, and isolated territories in the highlands of Papua New Guinea and the western districts of China, had come under the sway of previously distant national governments and dominant populations. Rarely in history had so much of the Earth's land mass and so many different indigenous populations faced such dramatic and traumatic transformations.

This period has, ironically, typically been understood as a time of increasing concern for aboriginal peoples and communities, albeit expressed with a paternalistic and interventionist tinge. It is generally considered to be the era when non-aboriginal peoples and governments began to recognize their responsibilities to and for the original inhabitants of colonial territories. Instead, it is important that the era from the start of World War II through to the 1960s be seen for what it truly was, an era of unprecedented aggression in the occupation of indigenous lands and, backed by the equally unprecedented wealth and power of the industrial world, the systematic dislocation of thousands of indigenous peoples around the world.

It is generally assumed that the occupation and transformation of indigenous lands has not been accompanied by the direct military action and violence associated with the pre-twentieth-century expansion. This assumption is only partially correct. There has been a large amount of local violence directed against indigenous peoples, particularly in frontier areas in South America (especially the Amazon), Indonesia (Irian Jaya or Western Papua), Borneo and parts of South Asia. Indigenous peoples in the Philippines – the Igorots, Mangayan, and others – resisted efforts to develop their territories, including the construction of hydroelectric dams. The Tuareg, mobile, pastoral herders from Saharan Africa, faced a series of attacks from Niger and Mali authorities. In the 1990s, reports surfaced of massacres of the Tuareg, followed by international appeals for support and intervention. Referring to conflicts which occurred in the 1960s, the Tuareg declared that an agreement between the government of Mali and neighboring nations

> cut off our retreat toward the north and gave the Malian army free rein to crush us with a merciless repression. We faced daily summary and public executions, our camps were razed, our water holes mined and poisoned, and our herds machine-gunned. No one tried to stop the massacres or even claimed the honour of renouncing the genocide of a people who were struggling for survival.[6]

These conflicts often involve miners, farmers, ranchers, and other developers who wanted access to indigenous land; governments, through their police forces and occasionally through direct military engagement, have also moved in, typically justifying their efforts as attempts at pacification. Canadians, New Zealanders, Australians, and Americans recoil at the suggestion that their countries are engaged in similar tactics, but the Oka (Mohawk) stand-off in Canada in 1990, numerous blockades, protests, and other conflicts in other parts of Canada and the liberal democracies suggest that the image of non-violent confrontation is at least partially misplaced. Indigenous peoples also find themselves drawn in, typically as bystanders, into civil wars and regional conflicts. The murderous rampages of Rwanda in 1994 are believed to have resulted in the deaths of over 200,000 Batwa Pygmies, for example. Similarly, the Jul'hoansi of

Namibia became enmeshed in the conflict between SWAPO and the South African government, and the Agta of the Philippines have been trapped in the middle of civil-war conflicts in the region.

Aboriginal peoples did not simply accept the intrusions and intervention of governments and outsiders in their lives. The new developments, be it military, industrial, or administrative, however, proved to be formidable adversaries. There was little that the Chukchi could do to stall the centralizing initiatives of the USSR. Indigenous peoples from Australia to Africa to Canada faced efforts to draw them into government service centers. While some retained the option to flee or to stay away, by so doing they put their access to various government services at risk. And, in the age of the expanding welfare state, many peoples came to rely heavily on government services. On a broader scale, massive ecological change and the depredations of war ushered in rapid and largely unavoidable transformations. The rapid, wide-ranging, and destructive intrusions into indigenous space generated a sharp rebuke from aboriginal cultures, whose determination to survive yet another phase of development, dislocation, and destruction remains very strong. In keeping with the realities of an ever-changing world, indigenous groups have sought new means and tactics for coping with the threats to their survival as peoples.

This era, finally, appears to have seen the last contacts with "new" indigenous peoples. In areas such as South Asia, Borneo, and the Amazon, indigenous societies protected by geography, personal choice, and the absence of compelling government interest in their territories continued to operate with little direct contact with outsiders. In the Andaman Islands, for example, Indian government officials undertook gift-giving rituals with the local residents, in the interests of convincing the indigenous peoples of their peaceable nature. Throughout the Amazon, conflicts between settlers, developers and indigenous peoples harkened back to the nineteenth-century struggles across North America and Australia. And like those earlier invasions, the "final occupations" have proven disruptive and deadly. The Guarasug'we inhabit the border region between Bolivia and Brazil, and found themselves caught up in the militarization of the Bolivian state. This small group, numbering only a few hundred, came under attack from the authorities and scattered, fleeing to other groups in Brazil. It appears as though the culture has disappeared, yet another victim of militarization and state violence. As a community leader wrote in despair, "Yaneramai (the almightiest god of the Guarasug'we) does not want us to live with the whites ... When the end of the world comes, we do not want our souls to die ... You can see for yourself how small our tribe is now, and that our end is near .... .[W]e have to leave and go to live far away from the whites."[7] As another Yanomami leader said, "We are the ones who have the right to the land here. Whiteman does not have the right ... if we, the Indians, go onto White lands, they will not allow us there, it is the same with us – we will not allow them on our land."[8] The destruction and dislocation of indigenous cultures, so often seen as an artifact of the nineteenth century, remained a crucial and disheartening part of the late twentieth century and beyond.

9

CONTINUING THE STRUGGLE: INDIGENOUS PROTESTS, LEGAL AGENDAS, AND ABORIGINAL INTERNATIONALISM

Aboriginal people have protested incursions by outsiders for centuries. A 1973 confrontation between the United States government and the Sioux Indians of the Pine Ridge Reservation in South Dakota lifted the struggle to a new level. The location – Wounded Knee – was auspicious, for it was the site of a nineteenth-century massacre of the Sioux by the US army. The American Indian Movement had established itself as a strong national voice on aboriginal issues, and fitted in with the American protest culture of the 1960s. But the conflict took a nasty turn in the coming years. In 1975, a firefight between AIM members and the FBI resulted in the death of two FBI agents. Leonard Peltier, subsequently charged with murder and imprisoned for his role in the deaths, became an icon of the Native American struggle, although commentators have described him not as a major leader but rather as "a not particularly beloved AIM regular." Over time, the conflicts at Wounded Knee and Pine Ridge have been conflated and have emerged as international symbols of the contemporary oppression of indigenous peoples.[1] The American government looked to the world like an aggressor against its own people, and a new spirit emerged in the world of aboriginal protest. The AIM struggles proved to be a significant turning point in public understanding of the plight, aspirations, and determination of indigenous peoples in North America and, ultimately, around the world. More importantly, the AIM resurgence provided graphic illustrations of the frustrations, political power, and anger that festered within Native American communities across the United States.

As we have seen, tribal peoples had, in many quarters of the world, been profoundly affected by World War II, the Cold War, and the post-war development boom. Vast areas that had experienced limited or episodic attention from outsiders underwent enormous changes. The invasions, together with longstanding frustrations with outsider domination, also sparked a resurgence and refocusing of indigenous protest. The post-World War II period witnessed a radical repositioning of indigenous peoples around the world and the emergence of an influential global protest movement. In the half century following the end of the War, aboriginal issues and organizations moved from the distant shadows on national politics into the spotlight of international diplomacy. Only a short time before dismissed as irrelevant or, even more, doomed to imminent extinction, indigenous peoples discovered a global constituency for their rights, demands, and aspirations. The struggle which began with the arrival of outsiders continued, albeit in new directions and with new tactics. It would, as had also been the pattern, experience uneven results, with aboriginal groups in the industrial world garnering the greatest benefits from the new activism and indigenous peoples in the developing world continuing to struggle for recognition and results.

United Nations, Human Rights and the Emergence of Indigenous Rights

While it has been commonplace to explain the rise of the indigenous-rights movements in the context of aboriginal organizations and national politics, that emphasis is misplaced. First, indigenous peoples had long, and often effectively, protested their condition and their dispossession. It is not that aboriginal peoples discovered their voice in the 1950s and beyond. Rather, select groups of non-indigenous peoples and countries discovered how to hear the words and pleas that had so often been spoken. Equally, the major changes did not emerge in response to the situation of indigenous peoples. Instead, a broader reconsideration of the nature of human rights and the rights of ethnic minorities brought about, indirectly, significant shifts in the political power of aboriginal groups. There was, as well, a direct link between the rhetoric and politics of decolonization and the state of public understanding of the plight of indigenous peoples. These forces, more than the simple idea that aboriginal nations and peoples discovered the ability to articulate their visions and needs, are critical to understanding the transformation of international indigenous politics.

At the end of World War II, peoples around the world were forced to face up to the atrocities and hatreds of the past. The discovery of Nazi concentration camps and of the systematic execution of millions of European Jews dismissed facile notions of civilized and uncivilized worlds and gave pause to those who assumed the cultural and ethical ascendancy of Europe. The veritable race war between Japan and its enemies was rife with hostile, dehumanized stereotypes on both sides and by the vicious mistreatment of military prisoners and civilian populations. The horrifying mass death associated with the dropping of atom bombs on Hiroshima and Nagasaki, plus the devastation caused by battles for Stalingrad and Moscow, the fire-bombing of Dresden and Tokyo, and civilian losses associated with Japanese attacks on Nanking and China, and the German bombing of Britain put the world's politicians in an unusually reflective spirit. Rhetoric about the "war to end all wars" flowed freely at the end of World War I, but the political will to address the root causes of conflict proved elusive. Not so following World War II.

In a series of dazzling and highly symbolic moves, the world community (led by the Allied nations of the United States, Great Britain, France, Canada, Australia, and Russia) agreed to the creation of the United Nations. While sceptics argued that this new institution would be as toothless and ineffective as its predecessor, the League of Nations, proponents asserted that the world could not, in the face of the development of atomic weapons, afford another military conflagration. The political structure proved to be only one piece of the puzzle. Shortly after the establishment of the United Nations, that body approved the United Nations Declaration on Human Rights. This seminal document challenged the cultural assumptions of the past – particularly the assertion that one culture, race, or ethnicity was superior to another – and stated boldly that all human beings shared the same basic and fundamental rights. In the same spirit, and driven on by international horror about the German death camps, the United Nations passed a declaration which defined and outlawed genocide – the deliberate attempt to eradicate a specific group of people. These initiatives, widely applauded in their day, transformed the basic ethno-cultural political landscape around the world. For the first time, the global community was put on notice that attempts to destroy societies and peoples faced the criticism and animus of the world and that international mechanisms had been developed to define, explain, and defend the fundamental human rights of all peoples.

The discussions leading to the establishment of the United Nations and the passage of declarations relating to human rights and genocide proceeded with virtually no reference to indigenous peoples. Aboriginal organizations were not represented at the founding meetings or subsequent gatherings. Indigenous issues were low enough on the political agenda that few national or international leaders saw the concerns of tribal people as figuring very prominently in future discussions. The United Nations was, after all, an assemblage of duly constituted nation-states – the very institutions and authorities which stood accused by indigenous peoples of ignoring their rights and engaging, in various overt and subtle ways, in cultural genocide. In fact, there is little evidence that political observers and analysts of that day had so much as an inkling of the long-term implications on indigenous peoples of these crucial political steps.

At the time of the founding of the United Nations, the issues were much broader. Racism and its associated patterns of institutionalized discrimination had been widely accepted parts of the political and social cultures of nations in the industrialized world. Few had thought that religious and race hatred could result in such horrifying acts as those witnessed during the War, including the stripping of rights and privileges from people of Japanese descent in Canada and the United States. The world's political leaders saw the attack on discrimination and attending violations of basic human rights as being the centerpiece of the new international agenda.

Tied to this, and once again widely supported, was the realization that European colonialism had run its course. As the industrial nations surveyed the world that they had created, they acknowledged a fundamental imbalance in power, opportunity, and wealth. The fault line lay, with few exceptions, between the industrialized world dominated by the United States and the rebuilding nations of Europe and their colonies and former colonies in the developing world. Decolonization movements, spurred on by major political successes in Indonesia against the Japanese and Dutch, and Vietnam against the French, and by the political ideas of Mahatma Ghandi, Ho Chi Minh, Sukarno, the Algerian psychiatrist Franz Fanon, Ché Guevera, and others, quickly emerged at the forefront of political unrest. Dominated peoples, controled by European elites and denied the opportunity for self-rule and self-determination, resisted post-World War II attempts to reassert colonial regimes. Across Asia, Africa, Latin America, and the Middle East, oppressed peoples rose up in protest and anger, demanding that the colonial powers retreat and that the local population be permitted self-rule. For their part, strongly influenced by the antiracism and pro-self-determination currents emanating from the United Nations, the colonial powers generally acceded to the demands for local control. Where they refused to do so, as in Vietnam, they found themselves embroiled in costly, unpopular, and politically unsustainable conflicts. Although the process varied widely around the globe, colonial powers pulled out of most of their international entanglements, leaving in their wake dozens of newly independent nations, each struggling to throw off the vestiges of colonial rule and, though typically locked inside imposed and artificial colonial boundaries, establish internal control and opportunity.

At the national level, growing concern with the rights of individual citizens merged with government willingness to invest in a wide variety of social and economic programs designed to reduce inequalities within the country. Governments recognized the need to provide financial support, educational assistance, health programs, and the like to those citizens on the lowest rungs of the national hierarchy. Although the definition of poverty reflected industrial norms – income levels became a surrogate for quality of life – governments in the industrial world rushed to provide assistance to poor citizens. With the enthusiasm of post-World War II social engineers, they endeavored to ensure tribal peoples had equal access to the middle class through compulsory education, health-care systems, and a variety of other supports. Rife with paternalism and suffused with commitment to the lifestyle of the industrial world, these programs proved extremely disruptive to tribal peoples, often adding to their grievances and sense of distress.

Indigenous rights emerged slowly out of the political fog of international and domestic politics. For most of the industrialized nations, the focus on the internal status of tribal peoples developed with direct reference to the global process of decolonization. Selected western countries, notably the United States, Canada, Australia, and New Zealand, were harshly critical of other nations, particularly Britain and France, that moved too slowly in response to the demands for decolonization. Attacks on South Africa, which refused to abandon its apartheid regime in favor of a more democratic and equitable system, were particularly loud. Indigenous groups and their supporters within this moralizing group of nations pointed out that the internal affairs of these countries were far from being in order. How could these nation-states, the critics asked, pontificate about self-discrimination, racism, and the need to end colonialism when tribal peoples within their borders lived with these realities every day? Tribal peoples learned, as well, that the rhetoric and international attention attached to decolonization struggles worldwide could readily be connected to the politics and activism of internal colonization. In media terms, the Maori struggle for self-determination in the Waikato was as marketable as the battle against French rule in West Africa.

The first major indication that indigenous rights had emerged as an international issue of note came in 1957, through the UN-affiliated International Labour Organization. The ILO had started working on indigenous issues when it operated under the aegis of the League of Nations, but it was unable to attract much attention. Only after World War II was it able to gain sufficient support from participating governments to develop a draft protocol. At a meeting of its General Congress in Geneva, the ILO agreed to ILO Convention 107. This declaration began:

> Considering that the Declaration of Philadelphia affirms that all human beings have the right to pursue both their material well-being and their spiritual development in conditions of freedom and dignity, of economic security and equal opportunity, and

> Considering that there exist in various independent countries indigenous and other tribal and semi-tribal populations which are not yet integrated into the national community and whose social, economic or cultural situation hinders them from benefiting fully from the rights and advantages enjoyed by other elements of the population, and

> Considering it desirable both for humanitarian reasons and in the interest of the countries concerned to promote continued action to improve the living and working conditions of these populations by simultaneous action in respect of all the factors which have hitherto prevented them from sharing fully in the progress of the national community of which they form part ...

The ILO Convention 107 then proceeded to offer strong directives to governments responsible for dealing with indigenous populations. In keeping with the mentality of the 1950s, considerable emphasis was placed on encouraging national governments to provide educational, training, health, and other forms of social assistance to groups known to experience markedly lower standards of living. The fundamental aspiration of the document was integration into the nation-state, not the establishment of tribal autonomy. On the critical question of access to traditional territories, the convention indicated (Articles 11 and 12) that "The right of ownership, collective or individual, of the members of the populations concerned over the lands which these populations traditionally occupy shall be recognized." Further: "The populations concerned shall not be removed without their free consent from their habitual territories except in accordance with national laws and regulations for reasons relating to national security, or in the interest of national economic development or of the health of the said populations." Finally:

> When in such cases removal of these populations is necessary as an exceptional measure, they shall be provided with lands of quality at least equal to that of the lands previously occupied by them, suitable to provide for their present needs and future development. In cases where chances of alternative employment exist and where the populations concerned prefer to have compensation in money or in kind, they shall be so compensated under appropriate guarantees.

International conventions, via the United Nations or subordinate agencies such as the International Labour Organisation, carried moral but not legal weight. Indigenous organizations took great delight in having a major international organization lend its authority to their aspirations and claims. ILO Convention 107 remained (and in many ways remains) the only significant international accord on indigenous rights. By the end of the century, it had been signed by only a handful of nation-states, principally those without significant populations of indigenous or tribal peoples within their borders. And among the signatories are several nations – Bangladesh and El Salvador – which subsequently paid little attention to the words and conditions in Convention 107. It was, caveats and shortcomings notwithstanding, the first international document which sought to respond to the aspirations of indigenous peoples. That it remained, more than forty years later, the only document of its sort to make it through the delicate processes of international politics suggests something of the resistance among nation-states and majority populations to the idea of sharing authority with or recognizing the autonomy of tribal peoples.

The recognition of the rights and aspirations of tribal societies did not emerge in a vacuum after World War II. The complaints of indigenous peoples were not new, nor was their desire to gain the attention of national governments. What changed – and this is profoundly important – was the international standing of ethnic minorities and the emergence of a fairly uniform condemnation of the philosophical underpinnings of colonization. The post-World War II preoccupation with human rights, decolonization, and self-determination created a new political atmosphere, one sensitive to the rights of identifiable groups and more respectful of different cultures, values, and traditions. The change was not immediate and remained far from complete. Old assumptions, in the politics of ethnicity as much as anywhere, die slowly, and nowhere is this more evident that in the complex world of indigenous rights. By creating a larger and more receptive audience for the political aspirations of tribal peoples, the new international politics of ethnic and human rights made it possible for aboriginal organizations to make new headway at the local and national level. Indigenous words and visions would, after many years absence, find their way back onto the world political stage.

Aboriginal Organizational Reaction to Colonial and Government Domination

Aboriginal political organizations had been common in most industrial nations through the early part of the twentieth century, although their effectiveness ranged only from minimal to non-existent. National governments and dominant societies in the democratic/industrial world paid only passing attention to the statements and requests of indigenous groups. They received sympathy from small segments of the middle class, but little substantial support. In non-democratic nations, aboriginal organizations failed to flourish and played virtually no role in the establishment of national policy. By the 1960s and 1970s, the situation had changed dramatically. Most countries had regional and national indigenous political movements. Dozens of organizations sprang up, some moderate in their approach to government and international agencies and others radical, sovereigntist in nature, enough to attract the attention of police and national security services. That anyone noticed the noisy, rambunctious, and often disturbing commentaries of the aboriginal political leaders after decades of neglect and ignorance speaks volumes about the impact of the international human rights and self-determination agenda around the world. That the organizations themselves sprang into existence and assumed the aggressive and often combative stance that they did in turn says much about the power of the decolonization movement and the passionate politics of the disenfranchised in the 1960s and after.

The rise of indigenous activism was not restricted to European nations and their fragment societies in the New World. India, for example, struggled with the challenges of managing indigenous affairs in the decades after World War II. The new nation sought to raise the national standard of living and to respect the cultural differences within the multi-cultural country. The government established a variety of measures designed to protect indigenous land and cultural rights and endeavored to offset indigenous autonomy with the need to improve social, economic, and health conditions. The considerable authority resting with the state governments has left many indigenous groups vulnerable to the demands of ethnic majorities, just as the overarching commitment to alleviating poverty has ensured that attending to the rights of indigenous peoples and communities is often accorded low priority. New economic development initiatives, ranging from hydroelectric projects and forest developments to road and railway construction, have encroached on indigenous territories, often despite indigenous efforts to block major initiatives. Internationally, India's indigenous peoples have attracted little attention, perhaps because it is difficult to differentiate the poor, ill-served indigenous peoples from the millions of impoverished and politically marginal non-indigenous peoples in the country.

The radicalism of the 1960s, of which indigenous protest formed a significant part, emerged in the wake of the devastation of World War II and the frightening nuclear and ideological instability of the Cold War. The social turmoil emerged first in the western industrial nations, communicated widely by expansive television and radio coverage. Protests ranged from aggressive campaigns against the American presence in Vietnam to demands for respect for women's rights. It included a new cult of sexual freedom, the birth of the environmental movement, and demands for civil rights and greater respect for ethnic minorities. It was the age of sex, drugs, and rock and roll, sparked by the unprecedented assertiveness of young people in the West and to a much lesser extent in other industrial nations, like Japan. At its most radical and violent edge, the protest culture sparked the Black Power movement in the United States, Irish nationalist movements, the anarchistic outbursts of the Baader–Meinhof terrorist group in Germany and the Japanese Red Army, and aggressive environmental organizations that sought to disrupt industrial and resource developments. The 1960s awakened the world to the demands of youth and the aspirations of the dispossessed and disenfranchised. It forced many nations, including those behind the Iron Curtain, which experienced the backwash of western radicalism, to recognize fundamental social tensions and inequalities. If most countries reacted defensively and conservatively to many of the demands, they could not ultimately ignore the imperative of addressing the major social ills and challenges within.

New and aggressive aboriginal organizations emerged within and around the social movements of the 1960s. The old guard indigenous groups, most operating within industrial nations, were deeply intertwined with the national status quo and often worked closely with government agencies. The older generation of aboriginal leaders, for the most part, looked askance at the tactics and assertiveness of the new radicals. Led by the American Indian Movement in the United States, the most articulate and well-organized of the indigenous organizations, the new groups offered blunt assessments of the impact of European colonialism and cultural genocide. Tactics expanded from negotiations and political statements to blockades, inflammatory speeches, sit-ins, attacks on symbols of newcomer society, and, on rare occasions, guerrilla attacks and armed conflict with authorities. A dramatic new rhetoric emerged, one immersed in the language of decolonization and antiracism. The Nishnawbe-Aski of central Canada declared to the government of Ontario in 1977:

> We agreed to share. We lived up to the terms of our agreement. We kept the peace, paid honour to the European sovereign, allowed the white man to settle and live according to his laws, and permitted his religions and cultures to be introduced to our people. You agreed to share. You said our rights would never be lost. You did not live up to the agreement. You took most of our land, outlawed our religious beliefs and practices, destroyed much of our animal life and forest, restricted our movements, stopped us from using our languages, and tried to convince us that our music, dances and arts were barbaric. Despite these overwhelming odds, we have survived the elements of conquest. Your cultural genocide is about to end.[2]

Most of the resistance was passive or designed to generate public awareness. Indigenous peoples knew only too well that their small size compared to the resources available to the nation-state made armed resistance futile.

One of the most dramatic transformations of the place of indigenous peoples within a national order occurred in New Zealand. The Maori had long been more integrated into the economy and society than most indigenous societies, but they remained well outside the mainstream through to the end of World War II. Improvements in health care, housing, and economic conditions resulted in a rapid expansion of Maori population in the twentieth century, pushing the people back into public view. The advent of Native Schools provided more supportive environments for children and helped rebuild confidence and assertiveness. They migrated into the cities in large numbers, drawn initially by wartime opportunities but equally pushed by population growth in rural areas. Maori men and women worked their way into the labor force and, more dramatically, into New Zealand's political life. They challenged the assimilationist culture of the Department of Native (later Maori) Affairs and assumed a much more active place in national politics. New organizations, like Nga Tamatoa, followed, as did a growing number of public protests, highlighted by the Land March (Hokoi) of 1975, the occupation of Bastion Point, in 1978 and of Moutoa Gardens in 1995. The government, with some reluctance, agreed to investigate breaches in the Treaty of Waitangi, opening up a legal hornet's nest that resulted in and reflected a rethinking of the core of the country's history. Maori played an active role in national politics, capitalizing on the opportunities created by the introduction of proportional representation to greatly expand their authority within parliament. Perhaps even more dramatic was the development of *kohanga reo* (Maori language preschools) and the rebuilding of cultural pride through language, ceremony, and greater adherence to tradition. At the end of World War II, the Maori had a significant but marginal place in New Zealand society; by the end of the century, Maori issues dominated public affairs on numerous occasions and the prospect of a bicultural nation promised in the Treaty of Waitangi no longer seemed to be a pipe dream.

In most cases, the new organizations emerged out of local and regional protests. Indigenous peoples are, by definition, intensely local in their attachment to traditional territories and resources. As a consequence, protests initially focused on immediate issues: access to traditional lands, harvesting rights, national treaty obligations (or the failure to provide such legal protection), housing, schooling, or economic commitments. In Australia, a 1966 cattleworker's strike at Wave Hill, Northern Territory, awakened Aboriginal peoples and the country to the frustrations of the Aborigine population and started a new debate about indigenous rights in the country. The Inupiat from Northern Alaska protested, in the early 1960s, the arrest of several hunters who shot ducks out of season. They challenged the authorities to arrest a larger group of hunters. When the government backed down, the Inupiat and other Alaskan Natives had learned the potential for political organizing. Battles with Australian authorities over proposed mining projects, particularly in the Kimberley district of Western Australia, brought Aborigines together to protest government actions. The "Tent City" protest by aboriginal peoples brought the regional angers to Canberra, the nation's capital, and ensured widespread publicity for the cause. In 1972, Native Americans undertook an ambitious Trail of Broken Treaties Caravan, traveling from Minnesota to Washington, DC to protest against anti-indigenous legislation and administrative actions. Proposed pipeline projects in the far North radicalized a generation of indigenous leaders in Canada and the United States. In a development of considerable international importance, the Canadian government appointed Justice Thomas Berger to investigate plans for a natural- gas pipeline along the Mackenzie River Valley. His 1977 report, which recommended that the project be delayed until the indigenous communities favored the proposal and benefited from it, provided a major spark for aboriginal rights in North America. Efforts to stop hydroelectric dams sparked Sami protests in Sweden and Norway and an intense conflict over a golf course helped galvanize Maori in New Zealand. The Penan burst onto the international stage through a series of well-coordinated protests about logging in their territories. These were, in many ways, contemporary manifestations of age-old struggles and tactics. In an age of mass media and nightly television coverage, the conflicts attracted nationwide attention. This, in turn, alerted aboriginal leaders and peoples to the reality of shared experiences and made it possible to mobilize protesters beyond the immediate district. Local groups discovered the power that lay in numbers and careful organization, and were soon able to transform largely invisible local disputes into issues of national concern.

Indigenous protests gained in two ways from the broadening of aboriginal activism. On a practical level, connections with other groups provided extra human resources, access to additional money, and assistance with publicizing otherwise local conflicts. Small, isolated communities – the vast majority of the indigenous settlements around the world – gained substantially from the simple logistical support provided through the growing national and international networks. On a broader scale, the radicalization of the indigenous movement offered an intellectual context within which communities could situate their struggle. Standing alone, the struggle of a tribal village was little more than a tiny, largely inconsequential protest in which the indigenous people sought to gain some measure of justice from local or national authorities. The intellectual leaders of the indigenous-rights movement, many drawing on the inspiring ideas of the global decolonization effort, painted a different picture. Indigenous battles over land were a reaction to a pattern of dispossession. In 1971, for example, Aborigines in Australia petitioned the United Nations to take action against a pattern of genocide in the country, demanding that their land and resource rights be addressed. For liberal democracies, international "shaming" was and is a powerful motivator. Conflicts over treaty rights revealed a lengthy history of broken promises. Efforts to mitigate the impact of major resource developments revealed the culturally aggressive and socially destructive imperatives of capitalism and its political allies.

While the international political activities of indigenous peoples attracted the greatest amount of publicity, aboriginal groups were also active on lower-profile matters. There was, in particular, considerable attention given to education. The operations of church and/or state schools had been credited, in many countries, with speeding the processes of linguistic and cultural decay. Aggressive education tactics, particularly in boarding schools, attacked indigenous parenting and cultural practices and sought to transform the children into members of the newcomer societies. In the social and political ferment of the 1960s, indigenous groups demanded control over educational systems. The Arhuaco of Colombia, for example, insisted in 1975 that their language be used in classes, that studies focus on the natural world, and that the school emphasize, not undercut, traditional values. Chuner Taksami, speaking at the inaugural meeting of the Association of the Small Peoples of the North in 1998, highlighted the importance of language:

> Comrades! It is particularly important to say something about the languages of the peoples of the North. The loss of any of them may lead to the extinction of the said people and its unique culture. All the peoples of the North without exception, have realized this fact. It is no coincidence that the question of preserving the languages was raised at every meeting, conference, or congress, where regional and national associates were formed ... .The critical language situation arose as a result of the playing down of the roles of the indigenous languages in society and politics. The sphere of use was getting constantly narrower. The almost total exclusion of indigenous languages from the Northern school-system led to a loss of prestige of the mother tongue and to a sharp reduction of its social function. At school, children were even

prohibited from speaking in their mother tongue. Among many peoples a whole generation grew up without knowing their mother tongue.[3]

Comparable concerns and demands emerged the world over. Indigenous radicalism provided broad explanations which helped make sense of the nuances and complexities of local historical circumstances. In an address to the United Nations, the Adivasi (Indigenous Tribal People) of India said:

> The system of education has domesticated and alienated Adivasi youth from their own culture and has destroyed the languages of the indigenous tribal peoples of our country. Under the above circumstances, territorial integrity, social and cultural identify of the Adivasis are being shattered and thereby all their social and cultural values: equality between men and women, dignity of labour, community ownership of means of production and distribution for common good, consensus in decision-making, education for life and facing life with songs and dance are being eroded very rapidly.[4]

It helped to discover that one's problems were part of an international pattern, that other indigenous peoples faced similar challenges, and that the broad effects of western industrialization and capitalism had marginalized the traditional owners of the land. Hearing descriptions of the historical origins and power of institutionalized racism and anti-indigenous sentiment provided a welcome explanation for problems with local newcomers. And while it was disturbing to learn of acts of genocide perpetrated against indigenous groups around the world, such information was ultimately empowering.

Aboriginal protest helped weave thousands of local struggles into a series of national, regional, and ultimately international organizations. And the new indigenous protests had shifted from local and practical struggles, focused on securing a response to a specific grievance, into historically and culturally rooted conflicts with the dominant society, fueled by an increasingly comprehensive understanding of the historical, political, and economic context of indigenous marginalization. The agenda shifted from relatively small demands for compensation, support, or ongoing assistance to insistence upon the honoring of decades-old treaties or the negotiation of new agreements before any new mines, oil fields, highways, or hydroelectric projects could be developed. Governments of all stripes were appalled at the discovery that their wards, children-like dependants of the nation-state, were heeding the advice of Ché Guevara and Franz Fanon and that indigenous leaders were offering their communities a portrait of historical and contemporary developments sharply at odds with the official government line.

The emergence of a global Fourth World movement out of thousands of local conflicts and defensive initiatives parallels the expansion of the international organizations in such areas as environmentalism, women's rights, and anti-capitalist and anti-poverty protests. Like the indigenous-rights movement, these global phenomena emerged when local activists discovered common cause with others in different parts of the globe. In some instances, a core or central organization undertook protest evangelization, spreading information about the cause and seeking adherents. In the indigenous field, much of this work was undertaken by the American Indian Movement, which made substantial inroads in English-speaking countries including Canada, Australia, and New Zealand. AIM brought its particular brand of assertive sovereignty to groups in many different countries, and quickly found adherents for its approach to national governments. Increasing contact between indigenous organizers and political leaders brought increasing awareness of the sameness of aboriginal protests and needs. With much of the impetus coming from the western industrial nations, particularly Canada, the United States, Australia, and New Zealand, indigenous organizations began to share information and ideas. As they traveled in each other's countries, they forged personal friendship and identified common cause. By the mid-1970s, cooperation was sufficiently advanced for aboriginal groups to contemplate the establishment of international organizations.

One of the most important of these initiatives came together in Port Alberni, British Columbia, in 1975, involving indigenous groups from across North and South America, Australia, New Zealand, and Scandinavia. Organized by Chief George Manuel, the meeting resulted in the establishment of the World Council of Indigenous Peoples. The meeting ended with a declaration of unity:

> We the Indigenous Peoples of the world, united in this corner of our Mother the Earth in a great assembly of men of wisdom, declare to all nations:
>
> > We glory in our proud past:
> > When the earth was our nurturing mother,
> > When the night sky formed our common roof,
> > When Sun and Moon were our parents,
> > When all were brothers and sisters,
> > When our great civilizations grew under the sun,

When our chiefs and elders were great leaders.
When justice ruled the Law and its execution ... .

Then other peoples arrived:
     Thirsting for blood, for gold, for land and all its wealth,
     Carrying the cross and the sword, one in each hand,
     Without knowing or waiting to learn the ways of our worlds,
     They considered us to be lower than the animals,
     They stole our lands from us and took us from our lands,
     They made slaves of the Sons of the sun.

However, they have never been able to eliminate us,
     Nor to erase our memories of what we were,
     Because we are the culture of the earth and the sky ,
     We are of ancient descent and we are millions,
     And although our whole universe may be ravaged,
     Our people will live on
     For longer than even the kingdom of death.

Now, we come from the four corners of the earth,
     We protest before the concert of nations
     That "we are the Indigenous Peoples, we who
     Have a consciousness of culture and peoplehood
     On the edge of each country's borders and
     Marginal to each country's citizenship."

And rising up after centuries of oppression,
     Evoking the greatness of our ancestors,
     In the memory of our Indigenous martyrs,
     And in homage to the counsel of our wise elders:

We vow to control again our own destiny and
     Recover our complete humanity and
     Pride in being Indigenous People.[5]

Manuel remained as president of the organization for six years, traveling
widely to strengthen the World Council and to educate himself about the
challenges facing indigenous peoples in different parts of the world. The
Council argued strongly for the preparation of a Declaration of the Rights
of Indigenous Peoples, a call ultimately picked up by the United Nations.

An organization like the World Council of Indigenous Peoples had
limited practical political clout. Their authority rested on the ability to
mobilize indigenous peoples around the world in support of a specific
campaign or protest and on the moral power that came from representing indigenous organizations throughout the world. In practical terms,

the World Council and associated regional and continental associations, such as the Indian Treaty Association centered in the United States, raised the profile of indigenous issues and tried to convince national governments that their actions and policies were being monitored worldwide. Over time, new international indigenous organizations have emerged, such as the powerful and extremely able Inuit Circumpolar Conference, perhaps the most effective indigenous lobby group in the world. The ICC represents groups from Alaska, Canada, Greenland, and Chukotka (Russia) and coordinates political, cultural, environmental, and economic initiatives throughout the circumpolar world. The Association of the Numerically Small Peoples of the North emerged to represent the complementary interests of the indigenous peoples across the former USSR. A comparable organization, the United Tribes of Palawan, represents indigenous interests in part of the Philippines.

In Africa, the Working Group of Indigenous Minorities in Southern Africa has sought to bring a regional perspective to aboriginal claims and initiatives. The many economic and political challenges of that continent, however, have interfered with efforts to improve conditions and resolve outstanding issues. There is, as well, a World Rainforest Movement, created in 1986 with a mandate of working "to secure the lands and livelihoods of forest peoples" and supporting "their efforts to defend the forests from commercial logging, dams, mining, plantations, shrimp farms colonisation and settlement and other projects that threaten them."[6] The Consejo Indio Sud America was created to publicize indigenous concerns on that continent. These organizations drew together indigenous and non-indigenous peoples, environmentalists, human rights activists, promoters of cooperatives, and other economic approaches, and seek to provide a higher profile for aboriginal issues.

Advocates and Saviours: Newcomer Supporters and Support Groups

Opponents of aboriginal demands found it easy to attribute aboriginal activism to the word of "outsiders," particularly Left-leaning, non-indigenous radicals, who, officials claimed, capitalized on aboriginal naiveté and misunderstanding to rally young people, in particular, to the cause. There was some accuracy in this assertion. Non-aboriginal activists were drawn to the indigenous cause in large numbers. The attraction lay in several directions: sympathy for the plight of indigenous communities, a desire to learn more about aboriginal values and traditions, and an opportunity to strike back at what they viewed as oppressive and authoritarian nation-states. Others were drawn by what they saw as the natural environmentalist tendencies of indigenous peoples and believed that the future of the globe rested on reinvigorating aboriginal societies with their ecologically sound principles. Many of these activists provided invaluable professional and logistical assistance, often with little thought for personal benefit. Others, a smaller number, imposed their ideas on unsuspecting communities and seemed more intent on implementing a political agenda than in responding to the needs of the indigenous people.

Whatever the presence and impact of outsiders, the indigenous protest movement did not begin or flourish because of the work of non-aboriginal advisors. Indigenous communities produced hundreds of talented and politically astute leaders, many of whom quickly grew into regional and national prominence. Most tribal groups took care in selecting their advisors and supporters and worked only with outsiders whose values and imperatives meshed with theirs. The energy, passion, and determination of the indigenous-rights movement came from the communities, and from a long history of struggle with newcomers.

Other outsiders, working through various support and advocacy groups, likewise provided assistance to indigenous protests. Much of the help came through organizations established for other purposes. Amnesty International, for example, established a watching brief on numerous indigenous prisoners, attempting to ensure that national governments treated protesters with fairness and due process. Environmental groups made common cause with indigenous protesters over major development projects and it appeared, for a time, as though the two groups would represent a formidable international force. A major falling out, particularly with Greenpeace's European and British arms, over the maintenance of the North American commercial fur trade exposed serious divisions between the organizations. In a similar vein, indigenous whalers from the Arctic (Inuit) and Northwest Coast (Makah Indians) took exception to efforts by the International Whaling Commission to clamp down on all whaling activity, representing yet another conflict between indigenous and environmentalist groups. When the Makah decided to exercise their declared right to harvest whales for local purposes, the resulting activity became a media sideshow, attracting enormous attention and considerable disagreement with the Makah's decision to proceed. Issue by issue, indigenous peoples and organizations found supporters among trade unions and among political parties (particularly those of the Left). Churches, many of which had devoted generations to the acculturation of indigenous peoples, shed some of their cultural imperialism and turned their attention to the support of aboriginal communities in their struggles with dominant societies. Celebrities weighed in on certain critical issues, such as the rock musician Sting's intervention on behalf of the Yanomami. As the political savvy of the indigenous groups improved, they became increasingly adept at pulling in supportive organizations and individuals, cause by cause and crisis by crisis, to assist with their struggle.

Perhaps the most critical organizations were those established specifically to promote and defend indigenous rights. In the nineteenth and early twentieth centuries, a group of pro-assimilationist non-aboriginal organizations intervened in defence of indigenous peoples. They shared many of the imperatives of church and state, and believed strongly in integration into the societal mainstream. As it became increasingly obvious that the paternalistic approaches had caused great harm among aboriginal peoples, these organizations faded into inactivity. In their place emerged new groups, such as the International Work Group for Indigenous Affairs (1968), Survival International (1969), Society for Threatened Peoples (1970) and Cultural Survival International (1972). The IWGIA is perhaps the most effective and active of the organizations. Based in Denmark and funded by the European Union and Scandinavian governments, it researched and publicized the plight of indigenous peoples and sought to alert both the general government and nation-states involved to the needs and demands of aboriginal communities. It has a well-deserved reputation for responsible and prompt reaction, based largely on strong cooperative relations with indigenous groups. Survival International, a more active and partisan organization, was established in 1969 in response to widespread outrage about the massacre of tribal peoples in the Amazon district of Brazil. It quickly established a reputation for aggressive campaigning on behalf of indigenous peoples, raising money, assisting with media coverage, and otherwise drawing international attention to the urgent plight of tribal peoples facing imminent danger.

Organizations like Survival International and IWGIA – and there are dozens operating at the national level – provide invaluable assistance to indigenous peoples in their struggles against national governments, development projects, attacks on their legal rights, and socio-cultural discrimination. Whereas earlier organizations assumed, paternalistically, that they knew best for aboriginal communities, the new groups take their lead from the tribal peoples. Their primary role is to provide assistance – financial, logistical, organizational, legal, and promotional – to small-scale communities that would otherwise have great difficulty gaining media and political attention. They emerged, over time, as the public shock troops for international indigenous rights, proving particularly adept at gaining access to the media on matters relating to aboriginal peoples.

Modern Treaty Processes

Aboriginal people succeeded in gaining the attention of governments, particularly in the liberal democracies. A series of favorable court rulings in the USA, Canada, and Australia raised the profile of indigenous rights and gave heart to aboriginal people who had lost confidence in the ability of the political and legal system to provide a measure of justice. Faced with the possibility that indigenous communities would win injunctions, stop development, or gain direct recognition of land and resource rights, national governments in selected countries began to negotiate concessionary arrangements. The offer of new treaties did not meet the aspirations of those leaders who argued that the indigenous peoples retained sovereignty over their territories, but they did attract the interest of pragmatists who worried more about jobs, housing conditions, and future socioeconomic conditions than lofty constitutional principles.

The process started in earnest with the Alaska Native Claims Settlement Act (1971), which provided the indigenous people of the newest American state with land, cash, and Native-run corporations. The initiative did not work as expected, as the imposition of the corporate model did not suit the needs of many communities. A major adjustment was made in the provisions of the Act twenty years after it was passed. In Canada, the James Bay Agreement of 1975 represented a calculated response to the fact that the Cree secured an injunction stopping the construction of a major hydroelectric project in northern Quebec. This sweeping agreement proved to be somewhat ineffectual and generated decades of legal proceedings and political wrangling. A series of other agreements across northern Canada, including the Inuvialuit Accord of 1984, the Council for Yukon First Nations agreements of 1993, and the Inuit Tapirisat/Nunavut Agreement of 1999, which resulted in the creation of the first indigenous-dominated political jurisdiction in North America, provided extensive powers of self-government, revenue sharing, sizable land allocations, cash, and resource rights.

Most of these treaties, including major settlements in the outback regions of Australia, represented on the part of national governments a curious and often contradictory mixture of liberal guilt, social conscience, genuine concern for the viability of indigenous cultures, and a desire to remove impediments to resource development. Contemporary governments have accepted dramatic changes in the legal, cultural, and social position of indigenous peoples living under treaty. The Navajo in the western USA, for example, enjoy sweeping powers of self-government and self-administration. The resolution of the century-old Nisga'a claim in Canada included the establishment of a constitutionally protected "third order" of government, based on Nisga'a traditional values and government structures, which assured the First Nation control over crucial services and decisions. In Australia, new approaches to the resolution of Aboriginal land claims include very powerful sacred-sites legislation, the Land Rights Act of 1976, which places an extremely high priority on protecting culturally significant pieces of land. The recognition in New Zealand of the legal authority of the Treaty of Waitangi resulted, as part of a major settlement, in the allocation of a large fishing company, the Sealord Corporation, to the Maori people. And in many jurisdictions, including Scandinavia, Canada, and the USA, national governments have stepped back from using education as a means of assimilation and have, instead, encouraged aboriginal control over elementary, secondary, and tertiary institutions.

Emphasizing International Law

Indigenous groups became, in the post-World War II era, increasingly frustrated by their failure to convince national governments to move quickly and decisively on their issues. Even in a time when politicians mouthed platitudes about respecting minority cultures and seeking just solutions to historical grievances, progress came slowly and without assurance of lasting success. Governments stumbled, prevaricated, changed their minds, and generally delayed their responses to indigenous demands which themselves changed significantly. Inside the various countries, including the western industrial democracies which spoke so eloquently about the need for increased social justice and equity, change occurred at a glacial pace. Given that the cost of delays weighed much more heavily on the tribal peoples than on the dominant societies, the sense of urgency in indigenous communities far outstripped that in the national government. The social turmoil and growing internationalism of the postwar period presented indigenous communities and organizations with another alternative. International law, long a philosophical rather than a practical field, assumed greater importance. Through the United Nations, the World Court, and other international agencies, minority groups had new opportunities to present their cause to non-partisan arbiters and to seek support for a fair and just resolution of their demands. The reality was that international legal tribunals carried more moral than practical weight, and that even the lofty conventions and declarations of the United Nations operated through moral suasion rather than enforceable codes of national conduct. The establishment of the period 1995 to 2004 as the United Nations' Decade of the World's Indigenous Peoples helped raise their international profile for a time, and was particularly useful for drawing attention to conditions among aboriginal communities in non-western countries. For indigenous peoples, however, international courts and tribunals represented something of a "last cannon shot," a final, public, non-partisan venue for appeal. Because these international courts and assemblies were not controled by a single national government, tribal peoples believed that they had an opportunity for a fair hearing. If successful, they would gain consider able moral weight for their cause, even if the judgements could not be made formally binding on the governments, companies, and other agencies involved in the actions.

For tribal peoples the world over, international law provided a critical opportunity and indigenous organizations and their supporters moved to get the international organizations behind their cause. Efforts undertaken even before World War II to gain the attention of international organizations fell flat. Even after the establishment of the United Nations and the passage of conventions on international human rights, indigenous peoples found themselves excluded from discussions. Their demands and aspirations went unanswered. The United Nations, after all, is an organization of sovereign nation-states. One of its key principles is that the UN focuses on conflict between nations and generally leaves internal matters to the member governments. This obviously has the effect of freezing out internal minorities, including indigenous peoples. The International Labour Organisation, as discussed earlier, was the first agency to develop specific guidelines, passed in 1957. They carried little formal authority, however, and very few countries ratified Convention No. 107, stripping even this integrationist/assimilationist document of much of its potential power.

The United Nations commitment to self-determination, only solidified after intense debate through the 1960s, seemed to offer a philosophical and political foundation for indigenous aspirations. Member states again, however, emphasized that self-determination referred only to long-lasting colonial relationships and not to the situation of indigenous peoples within nations. Although the aspirations of tribal peoples bore a great deal of resemblance to those of colonized peoples – certainly the cultural, economic, and social impacts were much the same – this valuable political avenue was effectively blocked. Within the scope of the United Nations, viewed as the most promising venue for indigenous internationalism, the best opportunity rested with the UN's commitment to protect minority rights and overcome discrimination. The Conference on Indigenous Peoples of the Americas coordinated in 1977 by the International Non-Governmental Organization helped raise the profile of aboriginal rights. The United Nations Human Rights Center in Geneva became the focal point for debate about bringing indigenous issues within the realm of the United Nations. The Sub-Commission on Prevention of Discrimination and Protection of Minority Rights agreed in the 1970s to tackle the issue, commissioning a study by José Martinez Cobo on the suitability of addressing discrimination against indigenous peoples under the auspices of the United Nations.

Support inside the United Nations merged with the activities of North American indigenous organizations and advocacy groups (particularly those concerned about developments in South America) to keep the issue on the global agenda. Slowly, western governments joined the chorus in support of the international approach. In 1982, after decades of agitation, a working group under the Commission on Prevention of Discrimination and Protection of Minorities was established. The UN Working Group on Indigenous Populations represented the first major international recognition of the legitimacy of indigenous aspirations. Although Asian indigenous populations were not initially included in the deliberations – their governments rejecting the argument that, as tribal peoples, they warranted special attention – there was fairly comprehensive representation by tribal peoples in the initial deliberations.

The UN Working Group on Indigenous Population tackled two formidable challenges: developing a workable definition of "indigenous" so that political lines could be more clearly delineated and developing a summary of the legitimate rights and responsibilities of indigenous peoples within the nation-state. The first task proved elusive. Preparing a workable and globally acceptable definition of "indigenous peoples" foundered on special cases and the vastly different agendas of tribal peoples and national governments. In addition, as the political potency of the "indigenous" label improved over time, communities and peoples searching for international political attention sought to adhere themselves to the expanding global movement. This, in turn, created odd and difficult situations, such as when Boers from South Africa (architects of the infamous apartheid regime in that country) and Orkney Islanders from the United Kingdom sought inclusion.

The Working Group focused its effort on the second agenda item and began to prepare a "Draft Declaration on the Rights of Indigenous Peoples." The effort attracted a great deal of international attention from indigenous peoples and has been cited, even as a draft, numerous times by tribal communities seeking political attention. The Draft remains, as of 2004, a work in progress and has yet to be ratified by the Working Group. Furthermore, the document has taken on strongly sovereigntist tones and has clearly gained the support of most indigenous organizations around the world. At the same time, the nature of the document has encouraged most national governments to step back from the process. While politically unable to abandon the global discussions, most United Nations member states are extremely wary of what they see as the pro-indigenous nature of the Draft Declaration. It is highly improbable that the document would be ratified by more than a handful of national governments – and then largely those without sizable indigenous populations within their borders.

The preamble to the Draft Declaration provides a good indication of the supportive tone of the document:

Affirming that indigenous peoples are equal in dignity and rights to all other peoples, while recognizing the rights of all peoples to be different, to consider themselves different, and to be respected as such,

Affirming also that all peoples contribute to the diversity and richness of all civilizations and cultures, which constitute a common heritage of humankind,

Affirming further that all doctrines, polices and practices based on or advocating superiority of peoples or individuals on the basis of national origin, racial, religious, ethnic or cultural differences are racist, scientifically false, legally invalid, morally condemnable and socially unjust,

Reaffirming also that indigenous peoples, in the exercise of their rights, should be free from discrimination of any kind,

Concerned that indigenous peoples have been deprived of their human rights and fundamental freedoms, resulting, inter alia, in their colonization and the dispossession of their lands, territories and resources, thus preventing them from exercising, in particular, their right to development in accordance with their own needs and interests,

Recognizing the urgent need to respect and promote the rights and characteristics of indigenous peoples, especially their rights to their lands, territories and resources, which derive from their political, economic and social structures and from their cultures, spiritual traditions, histories and philosophies,

Welcoming the fact that indigenous peoples are organizing themselves for political, economic, and social and cultural enhancement and in order to bring an end to all forms of discrimination and oppression wherever they occur,

Convinced that control by indigenous peoples over developments affecting them and their lands, territories and resources will enable them to maintain and strengthen their institutions, cultures and traditions, and to promote their development in accordance with their aspirations and needs,

Recognizing also that respect for indigenous knowledge, cultures and traditional practices contributes to sustainable and equitable development and proper management of the environment,

Emphasizing the need for demilitarization of the lands and territories of indigenous peoples, which will contribute to peace, economic and social progress and development, understanding and friendly relations among nations and peoples of the world,

Recognizing in particular the right of indigenous families and communities to retain shared responsibility for the upbringing, training, education and well-being of their children,

Recognizing also that indigenous peoples have the right freely to determine their relationships with States in a spirit of coexistence, mutual benefit and full respect,

Considering that treaties, agreements and other arrangements between States and indigenous peoples are properly matters of international concern and responsibility,

Acknowledging that the Charter of United Nations, the International Covenant on Economic, Social and Cultural Rights and the International Covenant on Civil and Political Rights affirm the fundamental importance of the right of self-determination of all peoples, by virtue of which they freely determine their political status and freely pursue their economic, social and cultural development,

Bearing in mind that nothing in this Declaration may be used to deny any peoples their right of self-determination,

Encouraging States to comply with and effectively implement all international instruments, in particular those relating to human rights, as they apply to indigenous peoples, in consultation and cooperation with the people concerned,

Emphasizing that the United Nations has an important and continuing role to play in promoting and protecting the rights of indigenous peoples,

Believing that this Declaration is a further important step forward for the recognition, promotion and protection of the rights and freedoms of indigenous peoples and in the development of relevant activities of the United Nations system in this field,

Solemnly proclaims the following United Nations Declaration on the Rights of Indigenous Peoples: ... .

The Draft Declaration does not exist formally in international law and has no official standing before any legal tribunal at a national or international level – save as a clear statement of the aspirations and expectations of indigenous peoples around the world. Indigenous groups the world over cite the document, which runs for forty-five articles, each of which clearly articulates longstanding and crucial tribal aspirations. The Declaration addresses such wide-ranging topics as political power and land tenure, access to resources and education, and clearly seeks to situate indigenous rights within both the realm of minority rights and the self-determination debate. It is, in draft form, a powerful statement and a strong indication of the political organization of indigenous peoples over the past thirty years and their increasingly assertive stance on the international stage.The Draft Declaration is also at an impasse. National governments are loath to tackle the document and its proponents publicly. It is unseemly, in the extreme, particularly for governments of western industrial nations to be seen criticizing the aspirations of indigenous peoples. Developing nations have fewer qualms and recognize that there is virtually no chance that they will agree to the dramatic and sweeping conditions of the Draft Declarations. Indigenous politicians, for their part, appear unwilling to compromise (or to agree on a working definition of "indigenous," an essential element in any lasting accord on the rights of indigenous peoples) and continue to pressure both the United Nations and member states to accede to their demands. Meetings intended to continue the dialogue sparked walk-outs by indigenous organizations, silence from critical national representatives, and a growing unease about the viability of the international process. Further, it is clear that many indigenous organizations attach a great deal of importance to the Declaration, believing that it will provide their people with the moral and legal authority necessary to achieve substantial change within their countries. The historic experience of UN regulations, conventions, and declarations is such, however, that the optimism of indigenous peoples is likely misplaced.

The emphasis placed by indigenous organizations and politicians on legal means of resolving their problems and issues reflects, in the main, the failure of the political process. Over the past thirty years, most national governments have resisted major concessions on tribal demands. Where significant steps have been taken – Australia, Canada, New Zealand, the United States, and the Scandinavian nations standing out in this regard – new issues and problems have emerged. Tribal peoples, facing imminent threats to their culture, language, and traditions, often find the stalling and uncertain tactics of national politics creates an unfavorable forum for resolving disputes. Where possible – and again, western industrial nations have provided the best venue – they have turned to the courts. Major legal challenges have recast the very foundations of indigenous rights in specific nations and, since lawyers in the countries involved often rely on international precedent, on a global scale as well. Protests by the Ainu in Japan including bombings (often attributed to left-wing radicals) and organized pressure campaigns on government resulted in the passage of Ainu Shinpo in 1997, an act which recognized for the first time in a century the very existence of the Ainu people, but which did little to ensure them of significant legal status. The Ainu made contact with other indigenous groups and gained a growing sense of international connectedness and cultural pride. The Director of the Hokkaido Ainu Association said of the movement "At least some of our people have got to the point where they can say with pride – I am an Ainu. But it took us years to reach even this point. The next step is to preserve our culture."[7] The Ainu have not shared a common approach to their relationship with Japan. Some favor integration through the development of a "double identity" as Ainu and Japanese. A second group favor retaining a distinctive Ainu identity but working with the Japanese to improve living conditions. The most radical group of Ainu reject cooperation with the government and call for greater

Ainu activism. In other countries, including Australia and Canada, legal actions have been crucial in forcing national governments to act. The Eddie Mabo case in 1992 (the decision came down after his death) forced the Australian government to recognize unresolved Aboriginal claims to traditional lands. As popular t-shirts in Queensland declared, "Captain Cook Stole Our Land – Koiki Mabo Got It Back." A series of Canadian cases – Sparrow, Guerin, Delgamuukw, Marshall, and others – defined and refined indigenous harvesting rights and provided greatly expanded access to critical food and commercial resources. The Delgamuukw case, brought by the Gitxsan-Wetsuwit'en of British Columbia, involved almost 400 court days and resulted in an initial decision which damned indigenous cultures and rebuffed most of their claims. Appeals resulted in several significant legal decisions in favor of the group's cause. A lengthy series of court victories in the United States, like the 1974 Boldt decision on salmon rights off the northwest coast, paved the way for recognition of tribal sovereignty and provided a foundation for the establishment of autonomous tribal governments in the country.

The law, therefore, has emerged as the cornerstone of indigenous protest and activism, particularly in countries with western legal traditions. The enormous effort devoted to the Draft Declaration on the Rights of Indigenous Peoples provides further evidence of the importance that tribal peoples attach to securing state and international recognition of their unique and specific rights. This commitment to the definition and recognition of rights has required an enormous amount of energy and resources over the past thirty years, and has attracted much of the time of the indigenous leadership around the world. There is little evidence as yet that the initiative has borne fruit, and the stalwart resistance of national governments to the Draft Declaration suggests that meaningful change remains a distant dream. In the postwar era of international recognition of human rights, self-determination, and decolonization, however, indigenous leaders concluded that they had no choice but to ensure that their issues and perspectives were on the global agenda.

Tactics of International Indigenous Mobilization

For many tribal communities, the time required to address the niceties of international politics and law is simply not available. Faced with the destruction of traditional territories by loggers, miners, or hydroelectric developers, and often blocked by the use of the courts in a quick and effective manner, indigenous peoples have had to find other ways of securing support for their cause. Military encroachment on tribal lands, an increasingly common reality over the past generation, is not something that can be easily slowed through representations to national governments. In Labrador, Canada, for example, the North Atlantic Treaty Organization began low-level flight testing over Innu lands in the mid-1980s. The Innu responded with a variety of protests, petitions, blockades, and other attempts to influence international opinion. In other instances, discriminatory economic and social policies cause enormous hardship for tribal peoples – and there are few if any legal recourses available. The imminent disappearance of a centuries-old language is not a matter for nuanced discussion at a negotiating table. The culture of self-abuse, suicide, and internal violence that has come to plague the dispossessed tribal peoples is not something reducible to carefully crafted legal documents. Nor, as the richest nations have discovered, can these problems be addressed even through sizable financial allocations or minor self-administration initiatives. Indigenous leaders clearly hope that, in the long run, the legal agitation and international political moves will provide the authority and legal clout necessary to protect their people. In the short term, more immediate measures are required.

Since the 1960s, and beginning with startling revelations by Norman Lewis and others about the destruction of tribal peoples in the Amazon, indigenous communities and politicians have discovered the power of the media in promoting their cause. National governments that reject out of hand indigenous requests for negotiations and legal rights have been seen to buckle in the face of international protest, boycotts, and public disapproval. As a consequence, a formidable network of indigenous activists, non-aboriginal supporters, and political/advocacy organizations have emerged around the world. They have drawn, in part, on the experience of organizations like Amnesty International and Greenpeace, which developed similar tactics for fighting different and occasionally overlapping battles. Aided by the development of the Internet, which has improved response time and permitted a rapid expansion of the protest, aboriginal organizations have learned how to put their case before the media and use public debate to pressure national and regional governments into action.

Tactics vary according to the situation, but typically involve mass writing and mailing campaigns. Survival International is particularly effective at securing names on petitions, letters to government officials, and front-page news-stories. IWGIA provides journalists and supporters with background research and endeavors to place specific causes in broader context. The more anarchistic world of email and the Internet allows groups to spread news of dangers and crises around the globe within minutes, thus mobilizing public protests in ways unimaginable a few years ago. Sympathetic columnists and journalists in television, radio, and newspaper newsrooms around the world are fed a steady flow of information about emerging and active conflicts. Organized lecture tours, typically highlighting a tribal leader in full traditional dress, have capitalized on this longstanding means of garnering public support and mobilizing local groups to back the specific protest movement.

Governments are acutely aware of the effectiveness of the international indigenous network and, particularly in the West, seek to manage their affairs accordingly. Governments of liberal democratic nations are often incensed when their policies or commitments are dragged onto the world stage, and argue that indigenous groups and their supports spread inaccuracies and one-sided perspectives. Tribal peoples, for their part, make few apologies for courting international public opinion, having discovered that authorities are otherwise unlikely to take much notice of what is, in national terms, a relatively minor issue. Liberal governments abhor being embarrassed on the international stage, particularly when these same governments are often prominent in criticizing other nations for abuses of human and civil rights. The same sense of embarrassment, however, makes these countries prime candidates for public activism and organized protest. Put simply, it is much easier to force Canada, Sweden, or Australia to act in response to international pressure than it is to convince China, Myanmar, or Zimbabwe to react to unfavorable editorial comment in London and New York and to CNN broadcasts about crises facing indigenous peoples within their borders.

Indigenous issues, presented from a tribal perspective and typically relying on indigenous leaders to explain the nuances of the case, now appear regularly in the international press. Tribal peoples in Papua New Guinea, the Amazon basin, the highlands of Bangladesh, and the forest districts of Indonesia and Malaysia have relied on media campaigns to draw attention to their plight. The Zapatista movement in Mexico, fighting for recognition of indigenous rights, has been one of the most effective users of email and Internet communications to generate international understanding and support. A substance-abuse crisis among the Innu at Davis Inlet, Labrador, attracted global attention when Survival International launched a public campaign to shame Canada into action.

There have, likewise, been initiatives in support of indigenous rights in Russia, China, Japan, and many other countries. At a minimum, these efforts have convinced tribal peoples that they are not alone and that there are thousands of supporters, indigenous and non-indigenous, standing with them. More commonly, effective international campaigns have forced governments to react, often reluctantly and claiming that they are not, in fact, responding to global pressure. In ways unimaginable a half century ago, however, indigenous issues now have a regular and even prominent place on the international political agenda. There is an increasing understanding of the basic issues and, although it ebbs and flows with changes at the domestic level, a substantial body of public support for the urgent needs and aspirations of tribal peoples.

The general assumption has long been that capitalism and its political manifestations (colonial powers and nation-states) are largely responsible for the dislocation of indigenous peoples. It is quite clear that, in the postcolonial world, newly independent nations from Indonesia to Bangladesh and Botswana have wrestled with aboriginal issues and have often been as harsh and aggressive in their treatment of indigenous peoples – or more so. The USSR and the Peoples' Republic of China, likewise, did not deviate significantly from the practice followed by their capitalist enemies in placing the material and economic interests of the majority ahead of the needs and aspirations of aboriginal minorities. The dislocation and relocations endured by the Small Peoples of the Russian North caused substantial cultural and social pain. The assumption of power in the late 1970s by the radical Sandinista party in Nicaragua raised expectations for better treatment, if only because the rhetoric of the revolution spoke so favorably about fairness and equity. The Miskito Indians subsequently encountered considerable difficulties in their dealings with the new administration, which rejected demands for autonomy as incompatible with state policy.

The primary consequence of a generation of legal and political struggles has been official acknowledgement of the land and resource rights of indigenous peoples and some recognition of the need to attend to their political aspirations. International pressure has been particularly important in identifying traditional lands and resources for protection, although the security of the land and safety of the culture remain much in doubt in most countries. Repeated incursions into the Cuiva lands in Colombia, combined with negative international publicity, convinced the government to protect indigenous territories. The government of Botswana reacted to threats to the San people by establishing a Remote

Area Development program in 1974, hoping to shore up a threatened mobile harvesting lifestyle. Land-and-resource legal decisions and negotiations in Canada and Australia have solidified indigenous rights and landholdings. But the underlying problem and issues remain. Tribal politicians and organizations sparked a revolution in international politics. From a very small base before World War II, and capitalizing on global interest in human rights, self-determination, and decolonization, indigenous communities have forged international networks. They worked their way into the operations of the United Nations and now represent a potent political force, able to mobilize international opposition to hitherto localized issues. In country after country, they launched important legal challenges to existing government policy and, particularly in the liberal democracies, won impressive victories. Energized by these developments, and aware of growing public sympathy toward indigenous aspirations, tribal peoples launched a coordinated campaign through the United Nations to establish internationally accepted principles for the treatment of indigenous peoples.

These various initiatives have experienced uneven success. Legal victories on the home front have changed government policy and resulted in the return of land and resources to some indigenous groups. Several of the efforts to shame national governments on the international stage have been successful, although primarily among the western industrial nations and not the countries in the developing world. The much-lauded effort to prepare a Declaration on the Rights of Indigenous Peoples has foundered on internal and international politics and remains a long way from becoming a viable and substantial instrument of international law. Work done to date, however, has improved the morale of tribal peoples around the world and has provided a focal point for the articulation of indigenous aspirations.

It is instructive to note that the most creative and meaningful efforts to address indigenous aspirations and rights appear to be coming from outlying, frontier districts. No country has yet found a means of reconciling historic injustices with settlement and development of prime areas by non-indigenous peoples, although New Zealand continues to make significant strides in this direction. In the sparsely settled lands, however, governments often have economic, social, and constitutional space to operate. As a consequence, the rights of indigenous peoples in settled areas of Brazil go largely ignored, while substantial tracts of land are set aside for Amazonian populations. In Australia, the thinly settled Northern Territory has an aggressive Aborigines' rights policy, particularly through the Aboriginal Land Rights (Northern Territory) Act of 1976, while Aborigines whose traditional lands overlap with prime agricultural or urban lands struggle for attention. So it is in Canada, where major northern land-claims deals have accepted significant indigenous demands for land, money, and autonomy while only a few urban groups have had much satisfaction in their dealings with government.

Not since the mid-nineteenth century, when news of conflicts with tribal peoples from the American West to New Zealand and from Africa to Central America routinely made the front pages of major newspapers, have indigenous peoples experienced such global attention. In the earlier era, the dominant image was of "backward" peoples standing in the way of "progress" and prosperity. Now, the world view has shifted. Tribal peoples are generally seen as "victims" of unchecked expansionism and of industrial colonialism. News reports generate sympathy and public support where they once created fear and anger. By developing greater skill in influencing the media, pressuring national governments, and orchestrating actions through the United Nations and other international bodies, tribal peoples have established a reputation as savvy and talented political operatives. For indigenous communities, however, the struggle is more than a simple contest for political advantage. At stake, instead, is the future of tribal societies and the ability of these peoples to control their destinies.

There is no mistaking the pain, anger, disappointment, optimism, and commitment which runs through the indigenous struggle in the post-World War II period. Aboriginal groups have come to believe (too much, one fears) in the sanctity and power of international law. Indigenous groups have retained their commitment to historic lifeways, but recognized how much had been lost through colonization, dispossession, and the other newcomer influences. The legal struggles, however polite the interventions to government and international bodies, were suffused with anger. At the Survival Gathering held in South Dakota, USA, in 1980, John Trudell of the American Indian Movement offered a succinct description of the issues at hand:

> We must not become confused. We must not become confused and deceived by their illusions. There is no such thing as military power; there is only military terrorism. There is no such thing as economic power; there is only economic exploitation. That is all that it is. They try to program our minds and fool us with these illusions so that we will believe that they hold the power in their hands, but they do not. All know how to do is to act in a repressive, brutal way.

We are a natural part of the Earth. We are an Extension of the Earth; we are not separate from it. We are a part of it. The Earth is our Mother. The Earth is a spirit, and we are an extension of that Spirit. We are Spirit. We are Power. They want us to believe that we have to believe in them and depend upon them, and we have to assume these consumer identities, and these political identities, these religious identities, and these racial identities. They want to separate us from our Power. They want to separate us from who we are – genocide.

As the Indigenous People, I don't know how you all relate. But the Indigenous people, understanding Power, we are Spirit. We are a natural part of the Earth. And All Our Ancestors, All Our Relations who went to the Spirit World, they are here with us. They have power. They will help us. They will help us to see if we are willing to look. We are not separate from them because there is no place to go. This is our place, the Earth. This is our Mother. We will not go away from our Mother. No matter what they do to us – no matter how they ever strike at us ... everytime they do it, we must never become reactionary. The one thing that has always bothered me about revolution, everytime I have seen the revolutionaries, they have reacted out of hatred for the oppressor. We must do this for the Love of our People. No matter what they ever do to us, we must always react with the Love of Our People, and the Earth. We must never react out of hatred against those who have no sense.[8]

10

UNCERTAINTIES: THE FUTURE OF INDIGENOUS SOCIETIES

The indigenous struggle to survive and to adapt to continually changing worlds continues across the globe, but the battleground has shifted. From an over-heated and crowded office on the outskirts of Moscow, the staff of Riapon (the Russsian Association of Indigenous Peoples) struggle with the complexities of developing economic development training courses, seek ways to ensure indigenous participation in the expanding Russian electoral process, support political and legislative reforms necessary to protect traditional cultures, and network with aboriginal organizations from around the world. Modern administrative offices in the Nass Valley of northern British Columbia, supported by a multi-million-dollar land-claims settlement signed by the Nisga'a people, provide visual evidence of the pride and professionalism of First Nations negotiators and government officials. Penan forest dwellers show up in traditional dress on university campuses, trying to generate outrage about commercial logging practices in Southeast Asia. United Nations gatherings – from South Africa and Geneva to the Canadian North – regularly devote a considerable amount of time to grappling with indigenous issues, with indigenous politicians sharing podiums with the sophisticated diplomats of one of the world's most important organizations. Scholars who previously studied indigenous peoples with academic detachment and paternalism now work closely and cooperatively with elders and spiritual leaders to understand the complexities of indigenous world view.

At no time in the past two centuries have indigenous peoples had as many non-aboriginal people and organizations committed to their survival. Indigenous "support" groups a century ago sought assimilation, not cultural survival. And most non-indigenous observers saw aboriginal societies as impediments to economic growth and societal development. It is ironic, then, that at few times in human history have indigenous peoples faced such dire threats. Language use declines, mass culture works like a cancer on centuries-old traditions. Elders struggle for the attentions of youth, and degradations of traditional territories and life-giving resources appear to suck the vitality out of harvesting communities. Governments respond with cautious and unimpressive attention. They recognize selected and limited legal rights, typically involving land and access to resources and the dominant societies in even the richest nations move only reluctantly beyond limited measures aimed at alleviating poverty.

These are, it seems, the worst of times. A review of the global history of indigenous peoples demonstrates that clouds of human sadness have often spread across the aboriginal world. In the first decades after initial contact with Europeans, deadly epidemics swept through indigenous communities, killing high proportions of the local population. Those not killed by disease saw their territories transformed by the introduction of new plants and animals. They were attacked by armies, dislocated by settlements and rapacious resource development, or controled and herded onto marginal lands by government officials. Other challenges followed: the complex intrusions of Christian missionaries and western schoolteachers, incorporation and marginalization within a surplus-based economic order, and the subtle changes associated with intermarriage and social contact with the newcomer population. Seen in the context of hundreds of years of contact, challenge, and change, the contemporary situation takes on a different hue.

There are many, among both supporters and the unconcerned, who forecast the imminent demise of the world's remaining indigenous societies. Organizations struggle to preserve, with some degree of ecological and cultural integrity, tracts of land for indigenous occupation. Others work to preserve and record dying indigenous languages. Still others contend that the future lies in more culturally sensitive incorporation into mainstream societies. Expectations of cultural death, spoken countless times over the centuries, remain premature, exaggerated, and unconvincing. Indigenous societies will do as they have for centuries. They will struggle, often against seemingly insurmountable odds, and they will survive. But determination remains. As the Taos of New Mexico say, "We have lived upon this land from days beyond history's records, far past any living memory deep into the time of legend. The story of my people and the story of this place are one single story. No man can think of us without also thinking of this place."[1] These peoples and communities will not persist in pristine, pre-contact condition, as some supporters hope. Rather, like all human societies, they will adapt to new realities. Some changes will be incorporated voluntarily; others will continue to be imposed on them. The resulting societies will be indigenous and aboriginal, but they will not be precisely the same as those that first emerged in their traditional lands.

There are some reasons for optimism, particularly in the liberal democratic countries, where concern or guilt about the challenges facing indigenous peoples has attracted both sympathy and government action. Scandinavian governments appear genuinely interested in supporting Sami culture and language. The establishment of the new territory of Nunavut by the Canadian government, on 1 April 1999, gave the Inuit of the eastern Arctic political control over a huge territory and a high level of self-government and southern subsidization. Denmark's acceptance of Greenland's autonomy has, likewise, empowered the Inuit in this land. The 'Pakeha' (newcomer) people of New Zealand seem strongly committed to revisiting the terms and commitments of the Treaty of Waitangi. The proliferation of Native American-run and -owned casinos across the United States provides evidence of the country's willingness to open the economy a crack for aboriginal participation. The fact that the Japanese government has finally recognized the cultural existence of the Ainu provides, for the first time in a century, an opportunity to address separately the concerns and aspirations of this group. And international pressure is encouraging countries in the developing world to take into account indigenous concerns and priorities when undertaking major economic and infrastructure projects.

Explaining the global patterns of the occupation of indigenous lands and the transformation of aboriginal societies is not a simple task. Fairly straightforward explanations have been advanced by many indigenous leaders. Colonialism, particularly the expansion of European powers, is offered as the primary explanation. The colonial powers, the argument goes, came armed with the confidence, arrogance, and racism of Europe in the age of expansion and quickly ran rough-shod over small tribal populations. This explanation has proven convenient and consistent with contemporary legal and political challenges. Emphasizing European responsibility has played nicely on liberal guilt in Europe and the European fragment nations, convincing the wealthier nations to invest heavily in programs of amelioration. The forces at play, however, extend beyond the interaction of Europeans and indigenous peoples, although these contact experiences were a crucial element in a complex, global process.

Eurocentric explanations, particularly those focusing on the advance on overseas empires, are not sufficient. Other colonial and expansionary powers occupied indigenous territories, typically in areas contiguous to the lands of the dominant societies. In Scandinavia, European peoples pushed the Sami further north, just as the Russians did in the north and east. Indian administrations marginalized the small tribal societies on the culturally complex sub-continent. Aztec and Inca empires imposed control on indigenous peoples, as did dominant populations in Africa. The Japanese expanded north into Ainu territory on Hokkaido. Throughout Southeast and East Asia, external and imperial powers formed over the centuries and found ways of imposing their will on marginal peoples. Throughout vast regions, hill tribes, island peoples, and isolated communities wrestled with the challenges of adapting to non-European intrusions.

Current, largely Eurocentric assumptions about the experience of indigenous peoples over the past centuries accommodate the aboriginal societies of Brazil (especially the Amazon), but pay little attention to indigenous cultures in Chile and Argentina. They speak to the very different realities of the Inuit in Greenland and the Aborigines in the Cape York region of Australia, but largely ignore the hill tribes of Thailand and Vietnam. An overtly European focus fails to incorporate the historical experience of aboriginal peoples in the western regions of China, the mountainous areas of Bangladesh, and the desert districts of southern Africa; and yet, the dislocations endured by these tribal societies bear a striking resemblance in nature, intensity, and impact to the transformations associated with the expansion of European imperial powers.

The western media and academic critique of the experience of indigenous peoples has also linked the assault on aboriginal societies to the imperatives of capitalism. There is obviously considerable merit in this analysis, for there was clearly a pattern of intensive resource demands, aggressive exploitation of labour, and the environmental destruction associated with European expansion. But the experience of other nations and socioeconomic systems followed a similar path. Nineteenth-century Japan approached the Ainu much as Britain and France dealt with the indigenous peoples of northern North America. The Soviet Union imposed educational, cultural, economic, and social constraints on the small peoples of the North that looked strikingly similar to what the United States did in Alaska. Post-independence Malaysia, Indonesia, and India proved as dismissive of indigenous rights as were Canada, Australia, and South Africa in earlier decades. Even overtly revolutionary regimes, like the Sandinista government of Nicaragua, failed to match the highly principled rhetoric of its constitutions and laws with practical programs that supported indigenous populations.

The correlation between capitalist ideology and the struggles of tribal societies is nowhere near as strong or complete as critics of western society would have it. There have been a few indigenous populations which have experienced less dislocation and dealt with more benign dominant societies. These few aboriginal peoples – the Sami, the Maori, the Inuit of Greenland (but not of the Canadian or Alaskan Norths) – lived under the colonial of European, capitalist powers, which on a global basis had a more destructive track record. The point is not that European and capitalist states were gentle, understanding, and flexible in their dealings with tribal peoples, for on balance the evidence shows that they were not. Instead, the critical element is that many different cultures, from pre-revolutionary China to post-Soviet Russia, from the Raj of India to the multicultural nationalism of Suharto's Indonesia, imposed economic, social, and political structures on indigenous peoples, largely overrode their linguistic and cultural independence, and subordinated their land and resource needs to those of a larger collectivity.

If the critical element was not European ethnicity or capitalist ideology, as analysts have often implied, the question remains as to the root cause of the difficulties indigenous peoples have experienced with other societies. Although the global pattern is complex and multifaceted, the fundamental divide appears to be between surplus and subsistence societies. Although they differed greatly from the primary European empires, the expansionary states of Japan, China, the Soviet Union, and post-independence Asian nations shared a belief in the efficacy of work specialization, the production of agricultural and material surpluses, the reliance on trade in both raw and finished products and, eventually, in industrial processes. Whether the organizing sociopolitical structure was capitalist/democratic, communist, Confucian, imperial, social democratic, or a dictatorship, these societies emphasized the production of surpluses and consequently placed far greater demands on the land and resources than did indigenous peoples.

In terms of determining the impact of an expansionist people on indigenous societies, having a political system which spoke directly to equality of opportunity, equality of condition, the special privileges of an elite few, or any other economic assumptions at their core ultimately mattered less than did the nature of land and resource use. In the age before expansion, most societies in the world worked largely within the constraints of known and readily accessible resources. Navigation and technology opened the world's oceans and land masses to exploration and development. Human societies subsequently divided into two fundamentally different groups: those who continued to live within ecological constraints and those who altered basic ecological, cultural, spiritual, and other assumptions about land and resources, asserting human primacy over the animal, plant, and inanimate world. The global tensions between indigenous and expansionist powers can be traced to this fundamental dichotomy, which continues to define and shape the struggle of aboriginal peoples.

Over the past forty years, enormous energies have been devoted to identifying avenues for the protection and survival of indigenous peoples. Efforts have ranged, as described earlier, from the setting aside of large tracts (generally of commercially unattractive land) to self-government agreements, treaties, and efforts to develop a code of indigenous rights. While these political and media activities have enjoyed some successes, most notably in wealthy, liberal nations, the net effect has been limited. Cultures remain under attack, intergenerational difficulties expand, and the struggle continues to preserve cultural activities and values in the face of enormous pressures to change. Virtually none of these efforts have involved a systematic attempt to address the fundamental dichotomy outlined above. Indigenous societies have historically been based on a sustainable approach to land use, where expansionary powers are founded on the production and redistribution of surplus, either for personal profit or collective empowerment. Much more energy has been expended on convincing indigenous peoples to adopt the imperatives of the surplus economy than on examining ways in which indigenous concepts of work, wealth, land, and resource use can be supported alongside more consumption-oriented approaches.

Since so little attention has been paid to the root cause of the indigenous–newcomer divide, it is hardly surprising that the prognosis is that the future will hold more of the same. In a consumption-rich world, where poor farmers and peasants are increasingly joining an ever-expanding urban, industrial workforce, there are precious few constraints on the increased exploitation of resources and continued expansion onto undeveloped or underdeveloped lands. Many of these areas yet to be exploited for surplus purposes continue to be inhabited by indigenous peoples, ensuring that the now centuries-old struggle between newcomers and aboriginal societies will continue into the future. There is an ever-dwindling supply of undeveloped territories, now mostly in the harsh lands of the deserts, in Arctic regions, and in the dense jungles of Africa and Asia. There is every reason to anticipate that the disruptions visited upon the indigenous occupants of other lands will soon be experienced in these few remaining areas.

Those indigenous people hoping to be able to continue exercising control over their lands might wish that no meaningful, exploitable resources are found within their territories and, equally important, that the nation-state expanding into their area is one of the handful of wealthy, liberal (and somewhat guilt-driven) countries that is open to more flexible approaches to the management of indigenous affairs. The experience in Scandinavia, Greenland, and the North American North shows the value of the alignment of these imperatives. If, in contrast, the resources are promising and the government and dominant society is either disinterested or preoccupied with other struggles, more ominous threats emerge. In numerous countries in South and Central America and in South and Southeast Asia and Africa, these conditions apply, raising very serious questions about the trajectory of indigenous–newcomer relations and about the capacity of indigenous peoples to retain effective use of traditional territories. The challenge is formidable. The industrial world's demand for resources is seemingly unlimited. There is little evidence that, even in the medium term, indigenous considerations will stop major resource projects from proceeding. At a very fundamental level, patterns of human consumption – some would say greed – that underlie the contemporary world are pressing the limits of the globe's resources and challenging traditional uses of the land in ways that are all too familiar.

The expansion of non-indigenous peoples over the past centuries continues to exact a considerable cultural toll. In many parts of the world, traditional language use has fallen dramatically. Hundreds of indigenous languages are at risk of disappearing within a generation or two, and only a few are truly vibrant. There have been some notable successes, perhaps the best being the efforts to support Sami language use in Scandinavia and Maori language in New Zealand. In most countries, the language of the dominant societies continue to shoulder aside indigenous dialects, which are rarely taught in schools, receive little government support, and are used by a steadily declining number of native speakers. There is considerable academic interest in the languages and in the knowledge and world view imbedded within the linguistic conventions of indigenous societies, but the urgent effort to document the language and cultural information seems, at times, to heighten the sense of desperation and fear.

The grudging acceptance of indigenous culture and tradition as a critical part of the legal, intellectual, and informational base of western societies is no assurance of long-term integration of aboriginal knowledge. A particularly troubling case in Australia involved a proposal to build a bridge to Hindmarsh Island. The local aboriginal people, the Ngarrindjeri, stopped the project when a group of women told the court about a secret tradition, part of *women's business*, that forecast a great calamity if a bridge was built. Australian authorities had earlier accepted aboriginal testimony as justification for stopping the Coronation Hill Gold Mine project in the Northern Territory. After the court decision in favor of abandoning the project, other Ngarrindjeri women challenged the "secret" tradition and argued that it was false. After further review, the Australia courts and politicians accepted the argument that the island story was not convincing and authorized the construction of the bridge, which was duly built. This episode reveals the difficulties inherit in working across cultural divides, and in particular of using indigenous knowledge within a western legal tradition. It is but one example of a worldwide struggle to understand and reconcile knowledge, beliefs, and priorities between indigenous and non-indigenous peoples.

The story is not altogether one-sided. In the wealthiest countries – Canada, the USA, Australia, New Zealand, Greenland/Denmark, Sweden, Norway, and Finland – respecting the rights and aspirations of indigenous peoples has become politically acceptable, if not politically necessary. Cynics will point out that this renders indigenous rights a luxury available only to the richest nations and indicate that poorer nations, like Bangladesh, Sri Lanka, Vietnam, Russia, and others have neither the time nor the money to indulge in the sizable transfers of wealth and power that have become characteristic of the First World governments. In the richer nations, at least, indigenous peoples are securing greater legal and constitutional recognition, have secured autonomy or self-governing arrangements, have received compensation for past injustices, and have otherwise been allowed to participate more equitably in resource development. There is a very long way to go, and the Penan in Sarawak, !Kung in Botswana, the Chittagong Hill People in Bangladesh and the Yanomami in the Amazon share few of the legal and financial opportunities of the Dene in the Mackenzie Valley of Canada, the Navaho in the western United States, or the Aborigines in Australia's Northern Territory.

Even these gains, slight as they may be, come with a cost. Through the 1960s and 1970s, indigenous peoples were able to draw on a well of liberal "guilt" in the industrialized nations, capitalizing on the dominant societies' recognition of the injustices of the past. As aboriginal groups have secured significant political concessions or, even more significantly, enjoyed major legal successes, a strong and often bitter backlash has emerged. In Australia, the now-weakened One Nation Party tapped into rural and working-class anger about the "entitlements" of Aborigines. Continuing criticism of the Aboriginal "industry" in the country and of the failure of costly government programs to ameliorate social and economic conditions resulted in the 2004 decision of the Howard administration to eliminate the Aboriginal and Torres Strait Islanders Commission, the primary Aboriginal body charged with attending to indigenous needs in Australia. Legal victories in the United States touched off strong protests from resource users who saw themselves losing out to indigenous rights holders, particularly as regards fishing in the Pacific Northwest and hunting in Alaska. Across Canada, a series of major concessions on resource rights by the federal government and Supreme Court of Canada decisions in favor of aboriginal peoples generated hostile reactions from non-indigenous peoples, many of whom argued for a "one law for all" approach in the country. According to polls conducted in 2003, a majority of Canadians now oppose the continued extension of indigenous and treaty rights. Similarly, the revitalization of the Treaty of Waitangi in New Zealand sparked angry outbursts from Pakeha spokespeople who opposed the creation of "special" status for Maori people. The reaction against the re-empowerment, limited though it may be, of indigenous peoples is not likely to dissipate and may grow as aboriginal groups become more insistent, secure additional gains, or increase their protests and acts of civil disobedience.

Indigenous peoples in countries around the globe share a common concern about the future. In nation after nation, community after community, they debate the relative merits and dangers of greater integration with the mainstream economy or of encouraging separation from the dominant society. They discuss the best ways to sustain traditional values and customs in the face of the integrating influences of popular culture and the intrusions of resource developers, settlers, government officials, missionaries, and other agents of change. Indigenous leaders generate discussion about legal or illegal means of protest, and work with support groups and international indigenous organizations to secure greater attention to their cause. They consider a wide variety of constitutional and political relationships, rarely emerging from indigenous traditions, that might provide greater protection for their communities. And they watch the steady encroachment of the surplus societies, with their considerable appetites for resources and land.

Indigenous societies and cultures are not unchanging or unchangeable, despite the desire of some outsiders who wish for the maintenance of traditional ways. Indigenous peoples respond to changes in their environment, just as all other societies do. The responses are sometimes creative and sometimes conservative. Some of the reactions support longstanding values and lifeways; others challenge the very core assumptions of the society. The introduction of new animals and plants, germs, land tenure systems, political structures, different social assumptions, alternate spiritual beliefs, non-indigenous settlers, mass communications, and new technologies affect any society, not just those based on indigenous traditions and customary ways. The fairly common assumption of the newcomer societies is that indigenous peoples cease to be indigenous if they adapt to the new ways, a major falsehood that reflects a fundamental misunderstanding of the core values and commitments of indigenous peoples.

Non-indigenous peoples have found numerous ways of demonstrating their interest in and support for the struggles and determination of the aboriginal populations. In addition to backing indigenous protests and supporting indigenous demands for government action, non-indigenous peoples celebrate their artistic expression. Significant markets have emerged for indigenous literature and celebratory movies about indigenous historical and contemporary crises, ranging from *Black Robe*'s depiction of the devastation of Great Lakes peoples to the controversial *Rabbit Proof Fence* from Australia and two extremely popular New Zealand movies, the gripping and disturbing *Once Were Warriors* and the more poetic *Whale Rider*. This interest has created large and sustainable markets for aboriginal art such as Inuit soapstone carvings and prints, Aborigine dot paintings, Coast Salish masks, and Northern footwear and coats. The very aggressiveness of newcomer interest has, in turn, proved troublesome. In Siberia, for example, folk-art collectors have been purchasing and removing from the region sacred items, spiritual objects, historically important material, and numerous drawings, paintings, and pieces of clothing, reproducing a pattern which earlier affected indigenous peoples in other areas.

As contact experiences unfold – and some of the indigenous–newcomer relationships are now many centuries old – all partners in the exchange are affected. Non-indigenous societies have long learned from the traditional owners of the land, and the indigenous peoples have gained and lost from the newcomers. In some parts of the world, social relationships have encouraged a stronger, deeper, and more complex interrelationship. The pattern of intermarriage in New Zealand, across the United States, in parts of Canada, among the Ainu and Japanese, in Siberia, and other locations has drawn indigenous and newcomer societies together. The social and cultural implications of this pattern of intermarriage vary widely, from the intense understanding of each other's culture that can accompany such relationships to a potentially sharp decline in the number of women and men available for marriage within an indigenous society. In many quarters, intermarriage is viewed as harming the stability of indigenous communities and hastening assimilation. In others, New Zealand being perhaps the strongest example, the practice of intermarriage is often viewed as encouraging greater interaction between indigenous and newcomer peoples. Intermarriage, of course, is not a new phenomenon, and the understanding of the full implications of their personal and social relationships lies, in part, in a great awareness of the comparative impact of these marriages involving indigenous peoples around the world.

This book began with a very simple premise: that the examination of indigenous history in global perspective would reveal important commonalities and differences in the transformation of aboriginal societies. There is growing evidence of the degree to which indigenous peoples see their struggles and their survival in global terms. While efforts to comprehend their experiences are often framed in local, regional, or national terms, the aboriginal peoples and organizations are discovering vital connections and support networks around the world. There is, as well, a distressing congruence of experience. Indigenous peoples, regardless of whether they live in a liberal democracy, an authoritarian state, or a developing nation, face comparable challenges. The Innu of Labrador face conditions of unemployment, cultural change, and dislocation that appear strikingly, even distressingly, familiar to the Itenm'i of Kamchatka, the Yamana of southern South America, the Aborigines of Cape York, the Tsimshian of the west coast of Canada, or the Penan of Borneo. The degradation of indigenous lands continues apace, as do state efforts to regulate, control, or support aboriginal cultures. Indigenous peoples in liberal democracies do better, financially, than those in the developing world, but the pattern of economic, social, and cultural marginalization is much the same. There is, to put it simply, an indigenous reality around the world, one that is reflected in the history of indigenous–newcomer interactions and has been conditioned by that same history. Efforts to come to terms with contemporary realities and future prospects for the indigenous peoples of the world must, it seems, be balanced by an understanding and acceptance of the importance of historical relationships and experiences.

The lifestyles and harvesting activities which sustained indigenous cultures for centuries have, in large measure, been undermined by development, settlement, or government policy. Compared to two centuries ago, relatively few people continue to hunt, trap, and fish for subsistence. Those who struggle for sustenance have often been moved to government centers or have been induced to accept a more agricultural and sedentary existence. Estimates suggest that there are between 375 and 400 million indigenous people worldwide (with the numbers depending largely on the definition of "indigenous"). Of these, only a small percentage continue to live off the results of their harvests. Only a few groups, mostly in the liberal democracies, have access to significant amounts of capital and employment. The vast majority of the world's indigenous peoples live at or below acceptable national and international standard-of-living levels. They are almost always among the poorest peoples, in material and financial terms, within their countries. While there are increasing organizational and logistical efforts directed at these peoples and communities, the efforts are small in comparison to the need. Legal rights remain the focus for court challenge and political negotiations. Only a few observers have recognized that legal rights rarely translate into a substantial and lasting change in material and cultural conditions. Around the world, and at a pace that is almost unprecedented in human history, indigenous peoples struggle to respond to changing realities and shifting economic and social conditions. To label this era as one of uncertainty is to state the obvious and to understate the scale and nature of the challenges which lie ahead.

A significant level of uncertainty also permeates scholarship on indigenous history and the history of indigenous–newcomer encounter. The effort to explain the history of encroachment, occupation, conquest, and domination has typically been fueled by anger and frustration, drawing much inspiration from the difficult if not tragic situation of contemporary indigenous populations. John Bodley, one of the most important analysts of indigenous-newcomer encounter framed his seminal study, *Victims of Progress*, in a pessimistic manner:

Industrial civilization is now completing the process of transformation and absorption or extermination of the world's tribal peoples and cultures that politically organized states have been carrying out for 6,000 years. According to many authorities within industrial civilization, this disappearance or drastic modification of these cultures is necessary for the "progress" of civilization and is inevitable, natural, and, in the long run, beneficial for the people involved. However, ironically, now that we foresee the imminent possibility of the total disappearance of free tribal peoples, we are just beginning to realize the staggering worldwide costs of industrialization.[2]

The subsequent resistance scholarship, of which Bodley's work is a leading example, has emphasized two main elements: the dominance and aggressiveness of the colonial powers and the ultimate inability of the indigenous peoples to stand in the way of the newcomers' advance. This scholarship, which is global in reach and wide-ranging in its analysis and contribution, has played a crucial role in awakening the scholarly world and the general public to the depredations of history. Only forty years ago, both the academic community and western industrial societies at large paid very little attention to the historic experiences and contemporary struggles of indigenous peoples. To the degree that there was administrative, political, or societal awareness of the indigenous situations, the difficulties were ascribed to the failures and shortcomings of the aboriginal population and to their inability to capitalize on the myriad opportunities presented by the modern world. Resistance scholarship has corrected these impressions. But the studies have also tended to be one-dimensional, focusing largely on the actions of the outsiders and on the evils and consequences of European colonization.

There are emerging signs of a more nuanced scholarship emerging, one which builds on the resistance studies of the past and which seeks to explore the complexities of the encounter experience. Consider Zaheer Baber's observations about Indian scholarship: "[A] word of caution is necessary against the tendency all too common among contemporary academics of invoking 'colonialism' as the sole explanatory device in accounting for almost every aspect of society and politics in contemporary India."[3] Akeel Bilgrami pushed this concern further, when he deplored the intellectuals' "neurotic obsession with the Western and colonial determination of their present condition." He argued that "it will prove a final victory for imperialism that after all the other humiliations it has visited ... it has lingered in our psyches in the form of genuine self-understanding to make self-criticism and free, unreactive agency impossible."[4] David Abernathy critiqued the contemporary approach to encounter studies:

> But chronicles of resistance, far from accounting for European imperialism, only deepen the mystery as to why invaders could have been so successful when confronted by determined local opposition. Resistance studies imply that imperialists were more powerful than their apologists imagined or more cleverly diabolic than their more fervent detractors asserted or both. But a theory of imperialism that treats Europeans as giants or moral monsters fails for lack of credibility. Europeans can be restored to a status at once merely and fully human by acknowledging that people in other continents respond to their initiatives in many ways, some of which had the effect of facilitating empire. Resistance was clearly an important part of this story, being at times decisive in delaying or halting conquest. But the willingness of indigenous peoples to collaborate was also frequently decisive in providing the territorial footholds and social leverage Europeans needed to start carrying out expansionist designs. Non-Europeans contributed in important measure to their eventual colonization, even if they did not foresee or intend it.[5]

It is easy to understand the anger deeply embedded in much scholarship by and about indigenous peoples. Peoples living with the negative consequences of encounter situations and having comparatively little power in contemporary times, understandably see history as the root of current dilemmas. They have, through the history and culture of resistance and dispossession, come to understand the degree to which outside powers imposed on and assailed traditional structures, values, and lifeways. To a substantial degree, however, Bilgrami's comment about Indian commentators applies to the global indigenous situation, in that the indictment of colonial authorities and colonialism has become the centerpoint for analysis of the history of indigenous–newcomer relations. There are signs that the analysis is moving into more nuanced and, ultimately, inclusive perspectives. The increasing emphasis on community-based scholarship is allowing indigenous peoples to document more fully the internal dynamics of social, economic, and political change. Revisionist scholars, like Keith Windschuttle in Australia and political scientist Tom Flanagan in Canada, are attacking some of the fundamental assumptions of the resistance analysis, challenging scholars to reconsider or defend their understanding of the past.

Jiro Sasamura, leader of the Ainu Association of Hokkaido, responded enthusiastically to the passage of the Ainu Shinpo in 1997, offering some important comments on the place of history in Ainu priorities: "Protecting culture is the most important thing. During the Meiji period, the Ainu people were discriminated against. But we have to keep an eye out for our future and not stick to repeating stories about our past."[6] Other indigenous leaders, Ainu among them, argue that forcing the government and the dominant society to take full responsibility for a long history of injustice is the most important objective, and insist on proper compensation for the seizure of lands, destruction of resources and attacks on indigenous cultures. Among the indigenous communities of the world, debate over how to attend to the inequities of the past remains a crucial topic.

There is a long, complex, and fascinating history of indigenous–newcomer encounter that remains substantially untold. It is, as I have attempted to outline here, an account of conquest and resistance, demographic collapse, and spiritual collision. The pattern of encounter includes collaboration and cooperation, flight from the newcomers, and vicious mistreatment of the indigenous inhabitants of valued lands. The history speaks to fundamental ideological differences between indigenous peoples and outsiders, and to radically different conceptions of the place and role of human beings on earth. The story is one of treaties signed, ignored, broken, and, occasionally, rediscovered. It is one where the liberal democracies have revisited their past and accepted some responsibility for undoing historic wrongs and where countries in the developing world argue that they have neither the time, the money, nor the inclination to privilege the concerns of small indigenous tribes over millions of impoverished citizens. The history is one, increasingly, of legal and diplomatic dispute and negotiation, involving national governments, the United Nations, and, very often, the international media. It is one marked, as well, by the declining use of indigenous languages, continued cultural struggles, and a systematic search for the recognition of basic rights and resources. The indigenous world is, at once, angry at the past and determined to preserve and protect the values, traditions, and knowledge that are embedded within their society. The future for indigenous peoples, as for all societies, is uncertain. Understanding the past, in its full complexity and comparative dimensions, is an important part of coming to terms with contemporary challenges and of preparing

models for indigenous–newcomer relations which enable, empower, and
sustain indigenous cultures.

It is useful, finally, to reflect on the lingering influence of history and
historical knowledge on the peoples who have been subjected to the
kinds of experiences, struggles, and battles documented here. Stephen
Jay Gould offers a telling and poignant assessment of the psychological
impact of being oppressed:

> We only get to go through this world once, as far as we know, and if our lives
> are thwarted, if our hopes are derailed, if our dreams are made impossible
> by limitations imposed from without, but falsely identified as residing within
> us, then in a way that's the greatest human tragedy one can imagine. And
> millions – hundreds of millions – of human lives have been so blighted.[7]

Eric Wolf once famously referred to peasant and indigenous populations
as being "people without history," by which he meant that they had been
excluded from the nationalist and imperial annals of history. It is clear,
in fact, that the opposite is the case. Indigenous peoples, colonized peoples, oppressed peoples share a common heritage of living with their
histories, being suppressed and overwhelmed by it, and having to struggle to overcome the burdens of the past. Given that this is demonstrably
so – far more so than for the wealthy, industrialized populations which
have often moved beyond historical crises and transitions and whose
historical knowledge and self-awareness has declined dramatically in
recent generations – it is imperative that there be a greater understanding of the history of indigenous peoples, and greater awareness of both
their struggles and survival.

This account ends, as perhaps it should, with a recognition of how little
has changed. Struggles continue, and the indigenous peoples survive.
But the conflicts that accompanied the expansion of surplus societies and
nation-states into indigenous territories continue, albeit with a variety of
new twists. National governments now struggle to balance the desire to
protect indigenous cultures and their land and resource rights with the
need to encourage economic growth. The international media is drawn
to conflicts between traditional occupants and developers, and have no
difficulty finding zones of tension. And so, it is hardly surprising that in
the early weeks of 2004, the indigenous peoples of the upper Amazon
basin found themselves locked in a major struggle with developers and
the non-indigenous population. The Brazilian government, responding
to indigenous demands, proposed the establishment of the Raposa/Serra

do Sol, a 1.7-million-hectare reservation in a hotly contested area of water, forest, and mineral resources. The tense social environment of the State of Roraima has brought the indigenous communities and would-be developers to the edge of conflict. The federal government's plans angered miners, loggers, farmers, and non-indigenous developers, whose aspirations for economic growth clashed with the idea of setting aside large tracts of land for a small number of indigenous people. But, reflecting the growing complexity of the indigenous–newcomer relations, indigenous groups like Arikom reject the paternalism inherent in the "living zone" assumptions of the reserve. Many indigenous, advocates like Gilberto Makuxi assert, want a chance to prosper economically, not live locked into a traditional lifestyle. There are rarely simple indigenous–newcomer conflicts as in the distant past. Instead, debates over the future of indigenous peoples and their traditional lands typically end up, as in Roraima, Brazil, with indigenous and newcomer elements on both sides of the debate. The struggle to survive, and the definition of what form that survival should take, will clearly continue throughout the indigenous world.

NOTES

Introduction

1. "Chile: A History of Dispossession and Discrimination," *IWGIA Newsletter* (June 1985), 56–7.
2. Sharad Kulkarni, "India: Indigenous communities in the sub-continent," *IWGIA Newsletter* (October/December 1988), 31–48.
3. Julian Burger, *Report from the Frontier: the State of the World's Indigenous Peoples* (London, Zed Books, 1987), p. 12.
4. http://www.nciv.net/millenium/definitions/some-indigenous-peoples-english.htm.
5. Brian Goehring, *Indigenous Peoples of the World: an Introduction to Their Past, Present and Future* (Saskatoon: Purich, 1993), p. 7.
6. There is a sizable literature on this subject. See Tapan Bose, "Definition and Delimination of the Indigenous Peoples of Asia," International Working Group on Indigenous Affairs at www.iwgia.org. See also Douglas Sanders, "The United Nations Working Group on Indigenous Populations," *Human Rights Quarterly*, 11 (1989), 406–33.
7. Survival International website, www.survival-international.org.
8. IWGIA introduction folder (www.iwgia.org/sw617.asp)
9. Franz Boas, "Some Traits of Primitive Culture," *Journal of American Folklore*, vol. 17, no. 67 (1904), 243–54.

1 People the Earth: The Greatest Migration

1. There are numerous accounts of the creation stories of specific indigenous peoples. For a quick overview of a series of creation stories from around the world, see www.indigenouspeople.net.
2. These stories were recounted in Carl Etter, *Ainu Folklore: Traditions and Culture of the Vanishing Aborigines of Japan* (Toronto: Wilcox and Follett, 1949).
3. Colin Calloway, *The World Turned Upside Down: Indian Voices from Early America* (Boston: Bedford Books, 1994), p. 23.
4. Knud Fladmark, "Routes: Alternate Migration Corridors for Early Man in North America," *American Antiquity*, vol. 44, no. 1 (1979), 55–69.
5. There is a lengthy debate in North America about the proper names for indigenous peoples. In the United States, the phrase 'Native Americans' has generally replaced the long-standing 'Indian'. In Canada, 'First Nations' is more commonly used than 'Indian' in academic and political discussions.

'Amerindians' is becoming more common when referring to the indigenous peoples of Central America.
6. Felipe Fernández–Armesto, *The Americas: a Hemispheric History* (New York: Modern Library, 2003), p. 26.

3 Mutual Discovery: Tribal Peoples and the First Wave of Globalization

1. John Hemming, *Red Gold: the Conquest of the Brazilian Indians* (Cambridge, MA: Harvard University, 1978).
2. John Parry and Robert Keith, eds., *New Iberian World: Volume III: Central America and Mexico* (London: Times Books, 1984), pp. 268–9.
3. Hemming, *Red Gold*, pp.13–14.
4. Irving Leonard, ed., *Colonial Travelers in Latin America* (New York: Alfred Knopf, 1972), p. 48.
5. J.M. Moziño, *Noticias de Nutka: an Account of Nootka Sound in 1792*, ed. and trans. Iris Wilson Engstrand (Vancouver: Douglas & McIntyre, 1991), pp. 9–16.
6. H.K. Kaul, ed., *Travellers' India: an Anthology* (Delhi: Oxford University Press, 1979), pp. 109–10.
7. Hemming, *Red Gold*, pp. 11–13.
8. Ronald Wright, *Stolen Continents: the New World Through Indian Eyes Since 1492* (Toronto: Viking, 1991), p. 12.
9. John Brown, *Old Frontiers: the Story of the Cherokee Indians from Earliest Times* (New York: Arno Press, 1971), pp. 44–5.
10. Parry and Keith, eds., *New Iberian World: Volume III*, p. 197.
11. Anne Salmond, *Between Worlds: Early Exchanges Between Maori and Europeans, 1773–1815* (Honolulu: University of Hawai'i Press, 1997).
12. Colin Calloway, ed., *The World Turned Upside Down: Indian Voices from Early America* (Boston: Bedford Books, 1994), p. 35.
13. Colin Calloway, ed., *The World Turned Upside Down*, pp. 50–2.
14. Cornelius Jaenan, "Amerindian Views of French Culture in the Seventeenth Century," in Ken Coates and Robin Fisher, eds., *Out of the Background: Readings on Canadian Native History* (Toronto: Copp Clark Pitman, 1988), pp. 119–20.
15. John Hemming, *Red Gold*, p. 10.
16. Cornelius Jaenan, "Amerindian Views of French Culture," p. 112.

4 Resistance and Adaptation: Indigenous Reaction to Newcomer Occupations

1. B. de Las Casas, *The Devastation of the Indies: a Brief Account*, trans. Herma Briffault (Baltimore: Johns Hopkins University Press, 1992), pp. 33–4.
2. John Parry and Robert Keith, eds., *New Iberian World: Volume III: Central America and Mexico* (London: Times Books, 1984), pp. 297–8.
3. Francis Jennings, *The Invasion of America: Indians, Colonialism, and the Cant of Conquest* (New York: W.W. Norton, 1976), pp. 164–5.

4. Quoted in Russell Thornton, *American Indian Holocaust and Survival: a Population History Since 1492* (Norman: University of Oklahoma Press, 1987), p. 69.
5. Roger Moody, ed., *The Indigenous Voices* (London: Zed Books, 1988), vol. 1, p. 55.
6. Takarura Shinichiro, "The Ainu of Northern Japan: a Study in Conquest and Acculturation," *Transactions of the American Philosophical Society*, New Series, vol. 50, part 4 (1960), 44.
7. Shinichiro, "The Ainu of Northern Japan,", 28.
8. Ronald Wright, *Stolen Continents: the New World Through Indian Eyes Since 1492* (Toronto: Viking, 1991), p. 159.
9. Sarah Carter, *Capturing Women: the Manipulation of Cultural Imagery in Canada's Prairie West* (Montreal: McGill-Queen's University Press, 1997), p. 187.
10. John Pape, "Black and White: the 'Perils of Sex' in Colonial Zimbabwe," *Journal of Southern Africa Studies*, vol. 16, no. 4 (December 1990), 710.
11. Pape, "Black and White", 700.
12. James Belich, *Making Peoples: a History of the New Zealanders* (Honolulu: University of Hawai'i Press, 1996), 152.

5 Biological Changes: Ecological Imperialism and the Transformation of Tribal Worlds

1. Martin, Paul, "Prehistoric Extinctions: In the Shadow of Man," in Charles Kay and R.T. Simmons, eds., *Wilderness and Political Ecology: Aboriginal Influences and the Orignial State of Nature* (Salt Lake City: University of Utah Press, 2002).
2. Kirkpatrick Sale, *The Conquest of Paradise: Christopher Colombus and the Columbian Legacy* (New York: Penguin, 1990), p. 84.
3. Felipe Fernández–Armesto, *The Americas: a Hemispheric History* (New York: Modern Library, 2003), p. 32.
4. Russell Thornton, *American Indian Holocaust and Survival* (Norman: University of Oklahoma Press, 1987), p. 60.
5. James Belich, *Making Peoples: A History of the New Zealanders* (Honolulu: University of Hawai'i Press, 1996), p. 147.
6. Alfred Crosby, *The Columbian Exchange: Biological and Cultural Consequences of 1492* (Westport: Greenwood, 1972), p. 36.
7. Bernardino de Sashagún, *Conquest of New Spain* (1585 revision), trans. Howard Cline (Salt Lake City: University of Utah Press, 1989), p. 103.
8. Crosby, *The Columbian Exchange*, pp. 40–1.
9. Crosby, *The Columbian Exchange*, p. 56.
10. Colin Calloway, *New Worlds for All: Indians, Europeans and the Remaking of Early America* (Baltimore: Johns Hopkins University Press, 1997), p. 35.
11. Ronald Wright, *Stolen Continents: the New World Through Indian Eyes Since 1492* (Toronto: Viking, 1991), p. 136.
12. David Abernethy, *The Dynamics of Global Dominance: European Overseas Empires, 1415–1980* (New Haven: Yale University Press, 2000), p. 229.

6   Spiritual Contests: Missionaries, Christianity, and Indigenous Societies

1. Roger Moody, ed., *The Indigenous Voices* (London: Zed Books, 1988), vol. 1, 257.
2. Larry Poston, *Islamic Da'wah in the West: Muslin Missionary Activity and the Dynamics of Conversion to Islam* (New York: Oxford University Press, 1992), 16.
3. Felipe Fernández–Armesto, *The Americas: a Hemispheric History* (New York: Modern Library, 2003), 67.
4. Colin Calloway, *New Worlds for All: Indians, Europeans and the Remaking of Early America* (Baltimore: Johns Hopkins University Press, 1997), 71.
5. Calloway, *New Worlds for All*, pp. 71, 73 and 76.
6. Moody, ed., *The Indigenous Voices*, vol. 1, p. 249.
7. Norman Lewis, *The Missionaries: God Against the Indians* (London: Arrow, 1988), p. 114.
8. Lewis, *The Missionaries*, p. 156.
9. *Indigenous Peoples of the Soviet North* (Copenhagen: IWGIA, 1990), p. 27.

7   Administered Peoples: Indigenous Nations and Regulated Societies

1. John Parry and Robert Keith, eds., *New Iberian World: Volume III: Central America and Mexico* (London: Times Books, 1984), p. 79.
2. Ronald Wright, *Stolen Continents: the New World Through Indian Eyes Since 1492* (Toronto: Viking, 1991), p. 204.
3. Colin Calloway, ed., *The World Turned Upside Down: Indian Voices from Early America* (Boston: Bedford Books, 1994), p. 92.
4. Sharad Kulkarni, "India: Indigenous communities in the sub–continent," *IWGIA Newsletter* (October/December 1988), 36.
5. "China Concerned with the Protection of Indigenous Peoples' Rights," 1 April 1997, at http://www.china–embassy.ch/eng/11985.html.
6. Jane Samson, *Imperial Benevolence: Making British Authority in the Pacific Islands* (Honolulu: University of Hawai'i Press, 1998), p. 174.
7. Greg Poelzer, "Aboriginal Self–Government in Canada and Russia," draft manuscript. The Schmitt quotation comes from *The Concept of the Political*, trans. George Schwab (New Jersey: Rutgers University Press, 1976), p. 27.

8   Final Invasions: War, Resource Development, and the Occupation of Tribal Territories

1. Roger Moody, ed., *The Indigenous Voices* (London: Zed Books, 1988), vol. 1, p. 195.
2. Julian Burger, *Report from the Frontier: the State of the World's Indigenous Peoples* (London: Zed Books, 1987), p. 3.

3. "Bangladesh: Oppression Continues," *Indigenous Peoples of the Soviet North* (Copenhagen: IWGIA, 1990), 29–30.
4. *IWGIA Newsletter* (June 1985), 15.
5. "Sri Lanka: the Veddas – a People Under Threat," *IWGIA Newsletter* (June 1985), 175.
6. "We, the Tuaregs," *IWGI, Newsletter* (December 1990), 137.
7. Moody, *The Indigenous Voices*, vol. 1, p. 69.
8. "Brazil: Calha Note project and mining prospecting – two aspects of the same invasion," *IWGA Newsletter* (October/December 1988), 17.

9 Continuing the Struggle: Indigenous Protests, Legal Agendas, and Aboriginal Internationalism

1. Paul Chaat Smith and Robert Allen, *Warrior, Like a Hurricane: the Indian Movement from Alcatraz to Wounded Knee* (New York: New Press, 1996), pp. 218–77.
2. "Declaration of the Nishnawbe–Aski," in Roger Moody, ed., *The Indigenous Voices* (London: Zed Books, 1988), vol. 2, p. 57.
3. *Indigenous Peoples of the Soviet North* (Copenhagen: IWGIA, 1990), p. 35.
4. "We are the indigenous peoples of Indian," *IWGIA Newsletter* (October/ December 1987), 47.
5. Douglas Sanders, "The Formation of the World Council of Indigenous Peoples," *IWGIA Newsletter*, no. 29, 1977.
6. online at: http://www.wrm.org.uy/.
7. *Japan's Minorities: Burakumin, Koreans, Aino Okinawans* (London: Minority Rights Group, 1983).
8. John Trudell, "We Are Power," in Roger Moody, ed., *The Indigenous Voices* (London: Zed Books, 1988), vol. 2, pp. 299–306.

10 Future Uncertainties

1. Colin Calloway, *New Worlds for All: Indians, Europeans and the Remaking of Early America* (Baltimore: Johns Hopkins University Press, 1997), p. 9.
2. John Bodley, *Victims of Progress*, 3rd edition (Mountain View, CA: Mayfield, 1990), p. 1.
3. Zaheer Baber, *The Science of Empire: Scientific Knowledge, Civilization and Colonial Rule in India*, p. 253.
4. Quoted in Baber, *The Science of Empire*, p. 254.
5. David Abernethy, *The Dynamics of Global Dominance: European Overseas Empires, 1415–1980* (New Haven: Yale University Press), p. 255.
6. "Diet to pass law on Ainu culture," *Asahi Evening News*, 8 May 1997.
7. Stephen Jay Gould, quoted in David Abernethy, *The Dynamics of Global Dominance*, p. 375.

SELECTED BIBLIOGRAPHY

There is a vast and complex literature relating to the history of indigenous peoples. Much of the work – including a variety of superb studies – are local-level monographs detailing the specific experiences of individual indigenous groups. There is, as well, a very large amount of scholarly writing on government policies and legal aspects of indigenous affairs. The reading list provided below offers a sample of some of the better works on the subject, with an effort made to provide examples from around the world. For those interested in more contemporary accounts of the experiences of specific indigenous groups, the publications of the International Work Group on Indigenous Affairs are very useful.

Abernethy, David, *The Dynamics of Global Dominance: European Overseas Empires, 1415–1980*. New Haven: Yale University Press, 2000.

Baber, Zaheer, *The Science of Empire: Scientific Knowledge, Civilization, and Colonial Rule in India*. Albany: State University of New York, 1996.

Balzer, Marjorie Mandelstam, *The Tenacity of Ethnicity: a Siberian Saga in Global Perspective*. Princeton: Princeton University Press, 1999.

Barkan, Elazar, *The Guilt of Nations: Restitution and Negotiating Historical Injustices*. New York: W.W. Norton, 2000.

Barnard, Alan, *Hunters and Herders of Southern Africa: a Comparative Ethnography of the Khoisan Peoples*. New York: Cambridge, 1992.

Barnes, R.H., Andrew Gray and Benedict Kingsbury, eds., *Indigenous Peoples of Asia*. Ann Arbor: Association for Asian Studies, 1995.

Battiste, Marie, ed., *Reclaiming Indigenous Voice and Vision*. Vancouver: UBC Press, 2002.

Belich, James, *Making Peoples: a History of the New Zealanders*. Honolulu: University of Hawai'i Press, 1996.

Benson, Linda and Ingvar Svanberg, *China's Last Nomads: the History and Culture of China's Kazaks*. London: M.E. Sharpe, 1998.

Berger, Thomas, *A Long and Terrible Shadow: White Values, Native Rights in the Americas, 1492–1992*. Vancouver: Douglas and McIntyre, 1991.

Berkhofer, Robert, *The White Man's Indian: Images of the American Indian from Columbus to the Present*. New York: Vintage, 1979.

Berndt, R.N. and C.H., *The World of the First Australians*. Sydney: Smith, 1977.

Boas, Franz, "Some Traits of Primitive Culture," *Journal of American Folklore*, vol. 17, no. 67, (1904), 243–54.

Bodley, John, *Cultural Anthropology: Tribes, States, and the Global System*. Mountain View, CA: Mayfield, 1989.

Bodley, John, *Tribal Peoples and Development Issues: a Global Overview*. Mountain View, CA: Mayfield, 1988.

Bodley, John, *Victims of Progress*. Mountain View, CA: Mayfield, 1990.

Bordewich, Fergus, *Killing the White Man's Indian: the Reinvention of Native Americans at the End of the 20th Century*. New York: Doubleday, 1996.

Bowden, Henry, *American Indians and Christian Mission*. Chicago: University of Chicago Press, 1981.

Brody, Hugh, *The Other Side of Eden: Hunters, Farmers and the Shaping of the World*. Vancouver: Douglas and McIntyre, 2000.

Brow, James, *Vedda Villages of Anuradhapura: the Historical Anthropology of a Community in Sri Lanka*. Seattle: University of Washington, 1978.

Brown, John, *Old Frontiers: the Story of the Cherokee Indians from Earliest Times*. New York: Arno Press, 1971.

Brysk, Alison, *From Tribal Village to Global Village: Indian Rights and International Relations in Latin America*. Stanford: Stanford University Press, 2000.

Burger, Julian, *Report from the Frontier: the State of the World's Indigenous Peoples*. London: Zed Books, 1987.

Burger, Julian, *The Gaia Atlas of First Peoples: a Future for the Indigenous World*. New York: Doubleday, 1990.

Calloway, Colin, *New Worlds For All: Indians, Europeans and the Remaking of Early America*. Baltimore: Johns Hopkins University Press, 1997.

Carter, Sarah, *Capturing Women: the Manipulation of Cultural Imagery in Canada's Prairie West*. Montreal: McGill-Queen's University Press, 1997.

Chaat Smith, Paul and Robert Allen, *Warrior, Like a Hurricane: The Indian Movement from Alcatraz to Wounded Knee*. New York: New Press, 1996.

Churchill, Ward, *Indians Are Us: Culture and Genocide in Native North America*. Toronto: Between the Lines, 1994.

Churchill, Ward, *Struggle for the Land: Indigenous Resistance to Genocide, Ecocide and Expropriation in Contemporary America*. Toronto: Between the Lines, 1992.

Cipriani, Lidio, *The Andaman Islanders*. New York: Praeger, 1966.

Coates, Ken and Robin Fisher, eds., *Out of the Background: Readings on Canadian Native History*. Toronto: Copp Clark Pitman, 1988.

Coates, Ken and John Taylor, *Indigenous Peoples in Remote Regions*. Thunder Bay: Centre for Northern Studies, 1995.

Cocker, Mark, *Rivers of Blood, Rivers of Gold: Europe's Conquest of Indigenous Peoples*. New York: Grove, 1998.

Colchester, Marcus, and Christian Erni, eds., *Indigenous Peoples and Protected Areas in South and Southeast Asia*. Copenhagen: IWGIA, 1999.

Comaroff, John and Jean Comaroff, *Ethnography and the Historical Imagination*. Boulder: Westview, 1992.

Cook, Noble, David, *Born to Die: Disease and New World Conquest, 1492–1650*. Cambridge: Cambridge University Press, 1998.

Cove, John, *What the Bones Say: Tasmanian Aborigines, Science and Domination*. Ottawa: Carleton University Press, 1995.

Crosby, Alfred, *The Columbian Exchange: Biological and Cultural Consequences of 1492*. Westport: Greenwood, 1972.

Davis, S., *Victims of the Miracle: Development and the Indians of Brazil*. Cambridge: Cambridge University Press, 1977.

Diamond, Jared, *Guns, Germs and Steel: the Fates of Human Societies*. New York: W.W. Norton, 1999.

Dickason, Olive, *The Myth of the Savage and the Beginnings of French Colonialism in the Americas*. Edmonton: University of Alberta Press, 1984.

Engstrand, Iris W. ed., *Noticias De Nutka: an Account Of Nootka Sound In 1792 / by José Mariano Moziño*. Seattle: University of Washington Press; Vancouver: Douglas & McIntyre, 1991.

Etter, Carl, *Ainu Folklore: Traditions and Culture of the Vanishing Aborigines of Japan* Toronto: Wilcox and Follett, 1949.

Early, John, and John Peters, *The Xilixana Yanomami of the Amazon*. Gainsville: University Press of Florida, 2000.

Fagan, Brian, *The Great Journey: the Peopling of Ancient America*. London: Thames and Hudson, 1987.

Ferguson, Brian, *Yanomami Warfare: a Political History*. Santa Fe: School of American Research Press, 1995.

Fernández-Armesto, Felipe, *The Americas: a Hemispheric History*. New York: Modern Library, 2003.

Fladmark, Knud, "Routes: Alternative Migration Corridors for Early Man in North America," *American Antiquity*, vol. 44, no. 1 (1979), 55–69.

Flannery, Tim, *The Eternal Frontier: an Ecological History of North America and Its Peoples*. New York: Atlantic Monthly Press, 2001.

Flannery, Tim, *The Future Eaters: an Ecological History of the Australasian Lands and People*. Chatswood: Reed, 1994.

Forsyth, James, *A History of the Peoples of Siberia: Russia's North Asian Colony, 1581–1990*. Cambridge: Cambridge University Press, 1994.

Goehring, Brian, *Indigenous Peoples of the World: an Introduction to Their Past, Present and Future*. Saskatoon: Purich, 1993.

Golovnev, Andrei and Gail Osherenko, *Siberian Survival: the Nenets and Their Story*. Ithaca, NY: Cornell University Press, 1999.

Goodall, Heather, *Invasion Embassy: Land in Aboriginal Politics in New South Wales, 1770–1972*. Sydney: Allen & Unwin, 1996.

Hall, Anthony, *The American Empire and the Fourth World*. Montreal: McGill-Queen's University Press, 2003.

Harvey, Graham, ed., *Indigenous Religions: a Companion*. London: Cassell, 2000.

Hemming, John, *Red Gold: the Conquest of the Brazilian Indians*. Cambridge, MA: Harvard University Press, 1978.

Hochschild, Adam, *King Leopold's Ghost: a Story of Greed, Terror, and Heroism in Colonial Africa*. Boston: Houghton Mifflin, 1998.

Howe, Kerry R., *The Quest for Origins: Who First Discovered and Settled New Zealand and the Pacific Islands*. Auckland: Penguin, 2003.

Howe, Kerry, *Where the Waves Fall*. Honolulu: University of Hawai'i Press, 1984.

Hughes, Robert, *The Fatal Shore: a History of the Transportation of Convicts to Australia, 1787–1868*. London: Collins Harvill, 1987.

Iverson, Peter, *"We Are Still Here": American Indians in the Twentieth Century*. Wheeling: Harlan Davidson, 1999.

Japan's Minorities: Burakumin, Koreans, Aino Okinawans. London: Minority Rights Group, 1983.

Jennings, Francis, *The Founders of America: From the Earliest Migrations to the Present*. New York: W.W. Norton, 1994.

Jennings, Francis, *The Invasion of America: Indians, Colonialism and the Cant of Conquest*. New York: W.W. Norton, 1976.

Jull, Peter, *The Politics of Northern Frontiers: In Australia, Canada and Other First World Countries*. Darwin: North Australia Research Unit, 1991.

July, Robert, *A History of the African People*. Prospect Heights: Waveland, 1998.

Kame'eleihiwa, Lilikalā, *Native Land and Foreign Desires*. Honolulu: Bishop Museum Press, 1992.

Kaul, H.K., *Travellers' India: an Anthology*. Delhi: Oxford University Press, 1979.

Kay, Charles, and Randy Simmons, eds., *Wilderness and Political Ecology: Aboriginal Influences and the Original State of Nature*. Salt Lake City: University of Utah Press, 2002.

Kehoe, Alice Beck, *The Ghost Dance: Ethnohistory and Revitalization*. New York: Holt, Rinehart & Winston, 1989.

Las Casas, Bartolomé de, *The Devastation of the Indies: a Brief Account / Bartolomé De Las Casas*, trans. Herma Briffault. Baltimore: Johns Hopkins University Press, 1992.

Lee, Richard, and Richard Daly, eds., *The Cambridge Encyclopedia of Hunters and Gatherers*. New York: Cambridge University Press, 1999.

Leonard, Iriving, *Colonial Travelers in Latin America*. New York: Knopf, 1972.

Lewis, Norman, *The Missionaries: God Against the Indians*. London: Arrow Books, 1998.

McFarlane, Peter, *Brotherhood to Nationhood: George Manuel and the Making of the Modern Indian Movement*. Toronto: Between the Lines, 1993.

McNeill, W.H., *Plagues and Peoples*. Garden City: Anchor Books, 1976.

Miller, J.R., *Skyscrapers Hide the Heavens: A History of Indian–White Relations in Canada*. Toronto: University of Toronto Press, 2000.

Monbiot, George, *Poisoned Arrows: an Investigation in the Last Place in the Tropics*. Suffolk: Abacus, 1989.

Moody, R. ed., *The Indigenous Voices*, 2 vols. London: Zed Books, 1988.

Neill, Stephen, *A History of Christian Missions*. London: Penguin, 1986.

Nettle, Daniel, and Suzanne Romaine, *Vanishing Voices: the Extinction of the World's Languages*. Oxford: Oxford University Press, 2000.

Pape, John, "Black and White: the 'Perils of Sex' in Colonial Zimbabwe," *Journal of Southern Africa Studies*, vol. 16, no. 4 (December 1990).

Parry, John and Robert Keith, eds., *New Iberian World*. London: Times Books, 1984 .

Perry, Richard, *From Time Immemorial: Indigenous Peoples and State Systems*. Austin: University of Texas Press, 1996.

Poston, Larry, *Islamic Da'wah in the West: Muslim Missionary Activity and the Dynamics of Conversion to Islam*. New York: Oxford University Press, 1992.

Reynolds, Henry, *Aboriginal Sovereignty: Three Nations, One Australia*. Sydney: Allen & Unwin, 1996.

Reynolds, Henry, *The Other Side of the Frontier*. Harmondsworth: Penguin, 1982.

Sahlins, Marshall, *How "Natives" Think: About Captain Cook, For Example*. Chicago: University of Chicago Press, 1995.

Sale, Kirkpatrick, *The Conquest of Paradise: Christopher Columbus and the Columbian Legacy*. New York: Penguin, 1990.

Salmond, Anne, *Between Worlds: Early Exchanges Between Maori and Europeans, 1773–1815*. Honolulu: University of Hawai'i Press, 1997.

Salmond, Anne, *Two Worlds: First Meetings Between Maori and Europeans, 1642–1772*. Honolulu: University of Hawai'i Press, 1991.

Samson, Jane, *Imperial Benevolence: Making British Authority in the Pacific Islands* Honolulu: University of Hawai'i Press, 1998.

Sandall, Roger, *The Culture Cult: Designer Tribalism and Other Essays*. Boulder: Westview, 2001.

Sashagún, Bernardino de, *Conquest of New Spain* (1585 Revision), trans. Howard Cline (Salt Lake City: University of Utah Press, 1989.

Sayer, John William, *Ghost Dancing the Law: the Wounded Knee Trials*. London: Harvard University Press, 1997.

Shinichiro, T. "The Ainu of Northern Japan: a Study in Conquest and Acculturation," *Transactions of the American Philosophical Society*, New Series, vol. 50, part 4 (1960).

Smith, Paul C. and Robert Allen, *Warrior, Like a Hurricane: the Indian Movement from Alcatraz to Wounded Knee*. New York: New Press, 1996.

Sponsel, Leslie, *Endangered Peoples of Southeast and East Asia: Struggles to Survive*: Westport: Greenwood, 2000.

Thornberry, Patrick, *Indigenous Peoples and Human Rights*. Manchester: Manchester University Press, 2002.

Thornton, Russell, *American Indian Holocaust and Survival: a Population History Since 1492*. Norman: University of Oklahoma Press.

Tickner, Robert, *Taking a Stand: Land Rights to Reconciliation*. Sydney: Allen & Unwin, 2001.

Tierney, Patrick, *Darkness in El Dorado: How Scientists and Journalists Devastated the Amazon*. New York: W.W. North, 2001.

Todorov, Tzvetan, *The Conquest of America*. New York: Harper & Row, 1982.

Tuhiwai, Linda, *Decolonizing Methodologies: Research and Indigenous Peoples*. London: Zed Books, 1999.

Valkeapää, Nils-Aslak, *Greetings from Lappland: the Sami – Europe's Forgotten People*. London: Zed Books, 1978.

Weatherford, Jack, *Indian Givers: How the Indians of the Americas Transformed the World*. New York: Crown, 1988.

Wilson, James, *The Earth Shall Weep: a History of Native America*. New York: Atlantic Monthly Press, 1998.

Windschuttle, Keith, *The Fabrication of Aboriginal History*. Sydney: Macleay, 2002.

Wolf, Eric, *Europe and the People Without History*. Berkeley: University of California Press, 1997.

Wright, Ronald, *Stolen Continents: the "New World" Through Indian Eyes Since 1492*. Toronto: Viking, 1991.

INDEX